BIKE FEVER

This book is for Pamela, whose love makes me free . . .

Manufactured in the United States of America

First Printing

Library of Congress Catalog Card Number: 72-94778

ISBN: 0-695-80380-8

Contents

Solitary, singing in the west, I strike up for a new world.
Walt Whitman

Days and nights:
from Pittsburgh— south

Air leaked into my rainsuit and inflated me. The rainsuit collar flapped fast in the wind, plastic against plastic, sounding like the propeller of a small airplane. After a while, the rainsuit ripped from the force of the wind, and water soaked the jacket under it. The weight of the wet jacket was heavy on my shoulders. The wetness stuck to my warm skin and I shivered as I rode. Periodically, I wiped water from my face shield, drenching my gloves. The water rolling from the gauntlets of my gloves swept under the shield and soaked my face. My cheeks started to itch and I scratched them with my wet gloves. The rain, blown by the wind, pricked my chin and rolled down my neck. Cold water puddled on the seat, shriveling my crotch. Trucks coming in the opposite direction punched me with mud, while my tires skidded over the pavement on water mixed with oil leaked from hot engines. The brake linings got wet and grabbed dangerously. The water, rolling off the seat, drained down my leg, filling my boot.

Burt and I were riding our motorcycles on Skyline Drive near Staunton, Virginia, and it had been raining for eight straight days.

Three hours out of Pittsburgh, the rain had started. We detoured south into Cumberland, Maryland, then into West Virginia, but the rain kept up. We went northeast back into Pennsylvania, then south into West Virginia and Virginia, but the water dogged us. We stopped at taverns and diners along the way for television weather reports, then headed toward the warm fronts, looking

1

for a dry pocket in which to rest. During the day, rain soaked our gear. We couldn't cook at night. We bought plastic garbage bags to cover everything, but when the wind was strong, it ripped the plastic. Every morning we first found a town with a laundromat, and for twenty-five cents, bought some man-made sun.

On the eighth day, the fog came up in the Shenandoah Mountains. We traveled the whole day through fog that stuck in our eyes and wafted over the road. We followed the road by watching the shapes of the trees that lined the edge of the pavement. I could see the wheels of my motorcycle as we crept through the mountains, but not where they touched the ground. I could see the glowing eyes of cars coming in the opposite direction, but never the exact shape of the cars or the people inside. Sometimes I could see Burt's red taillight in front of me and sometimes I couldn't. It was the thickest fog I have ever seen. Creeping through it the whole day, we could make only fifty miles.

I have never been skydiving, but driving through that fog is how I would imagine it. We floated through the clouds, guided by the way the wheels sounded against the road; we could tell when we neared the edge of the road, because some of the pebbles spilling from the shoulder, swept up by the tires, would clink against our exhaust pipes.

And we relied on our memories of riding in the past. If you think back hard enough to a special day, when the sun was warm and you cruised a long mountain road, if you can remember how it was and can concentrate, then you can duplicate that ride even though you cannot see. Taking the turns just as you have so many times before, leaning just enough, straightening slowly, feeling for the right balance, rolling that way. You don't always need eyes to ride a motorcycle, as long as you have a good memory and the ability to recreate what you know you should see.

The persistence of the rain dulls your perceptions, but the fog reactivates them. You can taste the rain in the fog. And since you cannot see trees, grass, and wildflowers, you smell them. There are actually lines in the fog; it is not just a milky haze; streams of fog of different shades come together to make a screen. It feels strangely warm against your face, slightly wet. You push away the fog with your hand and, like water, more flows in to take its place. Floating through the fog seems both prehistoric and futuristic; it is in that gap where earth loses contact with the heavens.

In Jonesville, Virginia, townspeople gathered around our motor-cycles, fingering our helmets and the heavy plastic that pro-tected our gear from the rain and wind. A little kid mashed his face up against the window of the Jonesville Diner, watching us. Even the waitress was outside looking at our bikes, but she came into the diner behind us, a young girl with thick legs and a flat face, smiling through spaced-apart teeth.

We washed sugar donuts down with black coffee, licked our fingers, and lighted cigarettes. She smiled and gave us a free donut. The man we assumed was her husband was much older than she and he sat on a stool in the back of the diner, staring out the window, his gaze cocked far away.

"This is good coffee," I told her, motioning for another cup.

"It should be," she said.

"It's good," I said again.

She nodded and studied the coffee urn and the brown stains splattered on the spout. "Well," she blurted, "it's Maxwell House!"

We smiled and there was a long silence while she stared at us. Again, we lighted cigarettes.

"Where ye goin'?" she asked. Her voice echoed the high-pitched whine of the Appalachian back country.

"Don't know," Burt answered. "Out West."

"What fer?"

"Just a ride."

"Ye lookin' fer jobs?"

"No."

"Well what ye goin' to do when ye git there?" she wanted to know.

"Come back," we told her.

"Don't nobody ever work in the North?" she asked.

We laughed and walked outside. That's when the truck pulled in behind us, the driver honking his horn. He stuck his head out the window, a white man's head, burned red in the sun, and sprayed the door of the truck and running board with tobacco juice. "Ain't you gonna move?" he asked.

Burt was occupied with his cameras. He wanted to take a picture of the diner and the townspeople gathered outside. "Let's go, Burt," I said.

"In a minute." He selected his camera and walked slowly toward the curb on the other side of the street. He studied his light meter, then looked at the scene through the camera's eye.

The man got out of the truck, a heavy man whose paunch failed to conceal the power in his arms and chest. His chin and cheeks were bristled gray, stained tobacco-brown in places. In Appalachia, they shave once a week. "I got to git in there," he said, pointing at where our bikes were parked.

"C'mon Burt," I said.

"In a minute," he answered.

I turned to the man. "Can't you park somewhere else?"

"Ye mean ye ain't gonna move?" In exasperation, he rested his hands on his hips.

"We were here first," I said, glancing at Burt through the corner of my eye as he clicked shots of the scene. I could imagine how it must have looked were it being captured on film with sound and movement, a lone cyclist with moderately long hair and Pennsylvania plates, surrounded by a couple dozen rednecks. It was Pulitzer Prize material, although I wasn't happy being the object of it.

"Can't you park somewhere else?" I said, making a pretense of getting ready to move by starting my machine.

"Ye lookin' for trouble?" somebody said from the crowd in front of the diner.

"No," I said, "I just can't understand why he can't park somewhere else."

"I always park there," the man answered, pointing at our places.

"He always parks there," said the voice in the crowd.

Burt walked slowly back across the street, wrapped his camera in a slab of foam rubber, dropped it in the saddlebag, locked the bag and climbed on his bike. It all seemed to take a very long time, although it was probably no more than a few seconds. We pulled on our helmets and Burt kicked his machine to life. Noboby said anything as we rode away from the curb and rolled out of the town, but I could feel their eyes stabbing our backs.

It was near the end of June in Jonesville, Virginia, and it had just rained for eight days. But the rain was gone and there was no more fog.

In Tennessee, there was a mountain road, newly surfaced asphalt, black as a jewel, neither car nor man in sight. We swirled down the mountain like knots at the end of an unraveling cord. We cruised back to the top, rolled down again, grabbing at leaves hanging over the road, dancing ahead, falling behind, gliding to the bottom like landing airplanes, climbing to the top once more. We played like children, then slept in the sun.

We seesawed up and down that good black road for most of the morning. And we sat in the meadow at the bottom of the hill, drinking canteen wine, smoking, and watching the golden blue line of the sky jag around a nearby mountain. Near the end of the afternoon, an old man from Memphis stopped to talk. He wanted Burt to take his picture.

"Ye gonna do it?" he said.

"Sure." Burt held up his camera, pointed at the old man hanging out of the window of his car, and clicked the camera once.

He wanted Burt to develop his picture and deliver it to relatives in Pittsburgh. "I got people in Pittsburgh, but they never seen me," he said.

The old man was drunk and his breath soured the car, although he never got out of it. Every time we moved in front of the car, the old man started up his engine. We could get him to start his engine just by walking in front of his car, and we could get him to turn it off again just by walking away from it. After the old drunk man left, we mounted up and rode the rest of the way down the hill and into the green valley.

In Harriman, Tennessee, there's somebody with a BMW motorcycle in town. I ride a BMW 600 (about 50 horsepower) and it is not a very common bike, but wherever you stop there always seems to be somebody who knows somebody who has one. Burt rides a Honda 350, but not many people want to talk about his machine. Lots of people use the words "Honda" and "motorcycle" interchangeably. A Honda is a motorcycle, a motorcycle is a Honda; a BMW or a Harley or a Triumph is something special. They are big, expensive machines. Especially in the back country, there aren't that many people willing or able to invest $2,000 to $3,000 on a motorcycle. So it was a topic of conversation and curiosity for those interested in two wheels.

Our asses hurt in Harriman and we stopped at a diner for coffee. Our wrists ached from manipulating the throttle, and our feet cooked in the heavy boots that rest on pegs over the hot, baking road. You don't particularly notice the discomfort while traveling, until you pour into a hot, lazy town. It was good to rest, and we lingered long in the cool diner, sipping coffee, smoking cigarettes, listening to the voices of the waitresses and their patrons, yet not hearing the words that were said.

Later, there were two kids playing on the road near the diner. "Whatch ye gonna give us?" they asked.

"What do you mean 'what are we going to give you?'" said Burt.

"You're from the North, ain'tchye?" said one kid with a mustache of dirt under his nose. They were both about seven and wore cowboy boots without socks and shorts that looked like underwear.

"We're from Pennsylvania."

"Then whatch ye gonna give us?"

"Why do we have to give you anything?"

"Cause ye're from the North."

"So what's that mean?"

"Ye're rich, ain'tchye?"

We turned over a ballpoint pen that didn't work. Then we wound further down into the valley. It was very hot in Tennessee that day, and the air hung like the fog, except invisibly, although we could feel it.

The boy with no teeth at the gas station outside of McMinnville told us he had gone to Florida on his motorcycle last year. He was on a toll road, coming into Tallahassee without money to pay, and near the end of the road, he swerved around a pay booth and took off over a swamp.

"There was a canal that some basti'd hid behind a row of bushes. I din't see it, 'cause it was right behind them bushes, so I rode through and plopped—cycle and all—three fit into the damn mud. It cost $25 to hire a fella with a truck to pull me out.

I had to wire Mama back here for the money. I slept in the swamp for two days to guard the motorcycle before that basti'd would pull me out. And ye know what? Ye know what?" he repeated, pulling a wooden match from between pink gums. "Them basti'ds made me pay the toll anyway."

It started to rain at the gas station where the boy worked, but it was only a summer shower. The water on our hot faces and arms felt good for a while. The rain got harder, but we knew it would stop. Trucks threw mud against our legs and the wind blew branches from the trees, but at any time it was bound to stop. We were already soaked when we decided to put our rainsuits on. We unbuckled our saddlebags, pulled out our rain gear and put it on. We had bought new rubberized canvas rainsuits in Kentucky, but while we pulled them on, the linings got wet. We buckled up our saddlebags and rolled back on the road. Over the next hill, the rain stopped and the sun came out. It was nice the rest of the day.

In Fayetteville, Tennessee, near the Alabama border, where eggs, biscuits, grits, bacon, and coffee are served cheerfully for fifty-nine cents, and all the chicken you can eat costs a dollar, a kid invited us to his Pony League baseball game.

"Nobody ever comes here to talk to," he told us, " 'cept some relatives I got from California. After the game, we could go down by the river and talk. I got some beer to drink."

The clerk in the motel offered his car so we could tour his city, but we said we were tired and could see it just as well on our bikes. In the motel we took our first shower in three days, washed and wrung out our mud-sopped clothes, packed away after the rain, and went to bed early, with our sun-scorched faces aching vigorously, the way men's faces once always ached on quiet nights after hard, good days.

And cross-country cycling is very much a ticket to those pleasant discomforts of the past. It is not something that could or should be swallowed in annual and ever-increasing chunks. But as a sabbatical from civilization and the responsibilities of it, cross-country cycling is impeccable.

Most people think the wind, noise, and vibration is the source of the cyclists' exhilaration. But after thirty minutes of wind, you feel no wind, after an hour of noise, you hear no noise. The vibration is numbing. The wind, noise, and vibration seem to cancel each other. And in that vacuum between himself and what is going on around him, the cyclist hangs in limbo, seeing only what he wants to see, feeling what he wants to feel, cushioned by concentration and the transformation of time.

For those who have walked the earth, it is impossible to understand and identify with those who have roamed the moon. How can those who, for decades, have climbed only stairs, understand the joy of the few who have conquered Everest? The motorcycle is much more exhilarating in fact than in articulation. So it is difficult for disciples of four wheels to identify with those who ride only two.

Of course, there are words: Tranquility. Solitude. No, it is not just a question of going blank, but more a time for quiet meditation, a way of being put in a position to see things with more perspective, with the clarity of lengthy consideration. There is nothing to do on a motorcycle but think. It is a release from all the responsibilities of living in a contemporary society and working your way up to an ulcer.

On a motorcycle all feeling of time, speed, and distance dissolves. Fifty miles become an hour, 250 an afternoon. Time is drunk down like a cold beer on a warm day. You mount your bike in the morning, suddenly it is night. You are never dry of memories or predictions while riding, or burdened with them when you dismount.

Yes, you can daydream in an automobile, but your thoughts are guided and interrupted and fragmented by sounds from the radio, a stereophonic tape deck, the conversation in the back seat, the whir of the heater fan. Cross-country cycling provides instant isolation. And with isolation, there can be rare communication, between man and himself.

So you ride and ride. Not to any special destination, just in one particular direction, just to keep moving until the sun goes out and you find a place to stay. You are exhausted, physically, from holding up yourself and a 500-pound machine, and emotionally, from the thoughts that have just gone through you. A bed in a cheap motel; a $2 campsite; a free meadow below a pine-covered hill. Food goes down, sleep comes quickly—a laborer's sleep, deep and dreamless. A dog barks, bars of neon glow in the distance; chains of stars hang from the night.

Burt and I hardly talk except at meals. Most of the time when we're not riding, we're listening to the country and to the lingering echoes of our motorcycles, wailing their jazz in our ears.

When we do talk, it is about the kind of motorcycle to buy for the next trip and where the next trip will take us. We haven't been on the road for too long, but we are mesmerized by the nomadic feeling of it. I am convinced I can go on forever, and I am already saddened to think that I eventually must plan to return. In our discussions, Burt and I pledge to travel all of North Africa, the Soviet Union, and many Soviet satellite countries; we are certain of taking the run from Alaska to Argentina.

And everywhere we go—Lexington, Virginia, to Fayetteville, Tennessee—is where, in our discussions, we say we will someday settle. We are always saying that we will settle wherever we just were that we thought was nice. All the while, we know we are dreaming, yet without the dreams our trip would not seem real. The dreams at home are always hollow. But new dreams, although actually quite bizarre, seem somehow brilliant and plausible, while we are fulfilling the old ones.

The most significant aspect of cross-country cycling is the internal satisfaction. I am continually amazed that I have come this far on a motorcycle. Sometimes I literally pinch myself with glee, look at my machine and laugh. I think a lot about the people at home who might envy me. They don't envy me, I know, because they don't know what they're missing. They will live in the darkness of ignorance, virgins in adventure, frustrated by the limitations of respectability. Freedom to roam. And time. Time is what a man needs to find himself, to regain respect for himself, and if nothing else, the motorcycle makes the time for that. I have a book to write and, theoretically, that is why I am here. But I am almost sure—not absolutely, but almost—that I would have made this trip anyway.

Burt needs the time more than I. He is unhappily married. In Pittsburgh, Burt sells draperies, but wants to become a sculptor. He sculpts in metal and welds with precision. He wants to know what I think he should do. I cannot tell him. He knows if he sculpts, he cannot keep his wife, who is used to a more traditional way of life, or make enough money to support his children. Yet, he has taken the classic pose of the *artiste*. At thirty-seven, his art is still young, but material things are no longer important—only the way he swirls the brass and copper and knits them with a red-hot flame. Burt has a lot to think about and, without his saying it, I know he doesn't want to be bothered thinking about me.

I remain silent mostly and let him talk. He hardly ever mentions his wife, but says a lot about his father, who is dead. His father and mother died two months apart and Burt no longer had a family. His wife filled the void. They married early and loved each other very much. But now it is over and he wants to leave, but can't. He wants to be a sculptor, but he can't be one with his wife, he says. I think he wants his wife to leave him—it would be easier that way. Although still it would be painful, he would not feel as responsible. On the motorcycle, Burt is caught up in his memories. At night, his thoughts close around him, his eyes look over the fire at me, but his gaze is carried far away as he searches for a compromise, some sort of internal peace.

We have a nylon tent that perspires inside with dew at night so that in the morning our sleeping bags are soaked and it is hard to climb out without getting wet. We chain our motorcycles together and then chain both to a tree before sleeping. Often at night, I peek through the mosquito netting to look at our machines through sleep-caked eyes. When the night is clear, our gas tanks reflect the sky.

If you think hard enough, there's little you cannot remember on these good nights. I am twenty-nine years old, yet could name all of the girls in my classes through high school. Then I would figure out what they were doing today and whom they married. Fifteen years later, they all looked fat, except for the ones I liked a lot. I made up movies in my mind of how my life might have turned out if I had married one of those girls I liked. In every case, I was happier with the wife I had. If my wife would have attended high school with me, I wouldn't have married her, though. The only people in high school I think I would have married were the teachers. I wondered how it would be marrying a woman twenty years older than me. I listened to the crickets chirping and the animals rustling the leaves in the woods, wondering if the teachers I remembered were actually as pretty as I thought then. They probably weren't, but I couldn't bring myself to accept that idea. Sometimes, when I felt too excited, too content, too happy to sleep, I would think that way through the whole night, and not be tired in the morning. Maybe I slept, but I can't remember. It was so nice to have time to make my own dreams.

THE MEN

One

First, there are the gypsies. They roll from town to town, from place to place, like marbles shot into a maze. Like the machines they ride, gypsies are usually older and bigger than the diverse culture, more stubborn with enemies, more reliable with friends. Gypsies do not look too good. They are faceless men, heads hooded by helmets or old-time, beat-up leather hats and goggles. Their wardrobes are never coordinated. They may wear workman's overalls with a white shirt and a bow tie. The tie protects their necks from the wind. Or you might see them dressed in gabardine pants and suspenders and a denim jacket over a gray T-shirt. The T-shirt is gray because of countless washings in streams along the road or in bathtubs with hand soap in cheap motels. But you recognize a gypsy and judge him primarily by his hands: heavy, big and dry, cracked and black—almost like tree bark. A gypsy's hands have been scraped along gravel and concrete and macadam many times from falls, torn by stubborn bolts and faulty tools, lubricated with new oil, blackened by old grease; they have been broken and broken and put back together in slightly different variations every time. A gypsy's hands, mangled and calloused, will scratch a woman's arm.

Sometimes a friendly gasoline attendant will offer a gypsy coffee and donuts, or ask him if he has "mosquitoes in his teeth" or if he belongs to an outlaw gang. Other times a gypsy will be refused both friendliness and simple consideration. Occasionally he might find an inexpensive boarding house with clean sheets and towels and home-cooked meals. More frequently, especially when it's very late, or raining and cold, there will be nowhere at all to eat or sleep.

A gypsy has worked at a hundred different jobs to support himself and his machine—as a shipyard worker, a carpenter's helper, a driver for a beer distributor—but he hasn't worked at any of them for long. Now that motorcycles are fashionable, there is always work available, sometimes selling, but mostly fixing two-wheeled machines. He prefers the latter because it requires neither a suit nor fancy clothes.

Most gypsies have no real destination, but a motorcycle gypsy has far too many places to go. Real gypsies characteristically know only the nomadic life; they have been wandering and migrating, supporting their families as they can, in Europe since the fifteenth century and since the nineteenth century in the United States. But a motorcycle gypsy isn't born to the clan. He may have started from a stockbroker's home, a plush estate, or a politician's suburban split-level. He may have had a house of his own once, and the children, credit cards, and cars that go with it. A motorcycle gypsy has not been granted a lifestyle, he has chosen it: what he does or will ever do revolves around the motorcycle. And that's why he'll always have friends, places to head for and people to see.

In March he will appear at Daytona for Speed Week; in June you'll see him at Laconia for hillclimbing, speed tests, or dirt racing. The next month he might go to Birmingham or Amarillo or Tulsa for scrambles or motocross races, or to Ohio for endurance events. He has participated in them all at one time or another, including ice-racing and cycle polo. He has done everything on a motorcycle that can be done. Like the legendary French lover, he has tried every position and variation, every trick and trail.

He will always reserve some time for touring. There are new places to see and many old ones to visit again. His memories might bring him back to the Great Smoky Mountains, to the Mammoth Caves in Kentucky, or the Everglades. He might roll down into Mexico or climb for Canada, traveling as far north as Alaska, dipping as far south as the Argentine. He is not haltered by responsibilities, except for those pledged to himself and his machine. Many people will question a man's total dedication to a machine, but a gypsy and his motorcycle are like a cowboy and his horse. A gypsy cannot conceive of life without his machine, so he works hard to preserve what is, in truth, his only link to stability and security.

Some men become gypsies later in life. Like Henry Gill, a sixty-nine-year-old retired carpenter who, while on his way to visit friends, made a wrong turn at a traffic light one summer and decided it was easier to keep going than to turn around.

Or like Julius Kegel, a retired businessman who turned eighty in 1970, probably the oldest active cyclist in the world. He hitched his first ride on a motorcycle back in 1911. Next day, he bought one for himself. He's been sitting on or sprawled under one ever since, first as a dirt track racer, next in 1917 as a driver in a sidecar outfit for a brigade adjutant in World War I. Kegel's been back to Europe thirteen times since, logging hundreds of thousands of miles, officially accounted for in plaques, in honor of his voyages, presented by the BMW motorcycle factory in Germany. And he has no plans to hang up his helmet.

"I intend to keep up just the way I am," says Kegel, "as long as the good Lord keeps my system in repair."

Some men become gypsies quite early. Red Madison is one. After his freshman year in college in 1937, Madison hooked up with Jess Tunney, and they took off on their motorcycles for the summer. They haven't gone back to school or found a permanent home since.

Some men, like sixty-four-year-old Stanley George, a Presbyterian minister, become gypsies for a purpose. The Reverend George thunders, in a cloud of commandments, out of La Puente, California, and covers 12,000 or 15,000 miles each year, seeking out and talking to America's younger generation, delivering his psychedelically-decorated epistle on the love chapter of the Bible. A black leather jacket and motorcycle boots are his vestments, but his message is love. And he says his rewards have been peace and a feeling of optimism about our country and a greater respect for young people.

There aren't too many motorcycle gypsies left. There were thousands at one time, when cars and gasoline were expensive and jobs were scarce, when men were much freer and not pressured into leading socially acceptable lives. There were once thousands of gypsies, when riding a motorcycle meant ri ing a big motorcycle, a machine most enjoyable and designed to go fast on a long, straight road. Now, at best, there are probably only a few hundred gypsies remaining.

But the gypsies were important, just as important as Barney Oldfield, or the Wright Brothers, or maybe Henry Ford, because they were the pioneers. And they're still important because they are the ones who have remained free. Back at the beginning, when gypsies bought a motorcycle they had their choice of two or three, at most, all of which were of relatively the same size, weight, and capabilities. They cruised on roads dogged with dust clouds, tripping on ruts, their way often blocked by boulders or fallen trees. They were their own mechanics, repairing machines with cuttings from empty soup cans, bent coat hangers, pieces of fishing line, or string.

Today, if you consider all the brand names and different models, there are more than 500 bikes from which to choose. Today motorcycling is easy. Bikes with year-long warranties, shops for service, fancy tools, and electronic gadgets to tune your machine are available almost anywhere. There are laws to protect the cyclist and statewide safety standards. Many things have been made easy for the modern motorcyclist, partially because of men like Kegel or Gill or Madison, men like Lawrence of Arabia, King George VI, Charles Lindbergh, and George Bernard Shaw, all of whom rode motorcycles when horses were cheaper and cars more practical. These men, plus a few thousand others, rode through war and peace and depression, holding onto the machine, preserving its life, until the machine could hold its own. These men were the fathers not only of a multi-million dollar industry and popular sport, but of what can today be called America's national pastime.

Noted the *New York Times* on August 22, 1965:

In Detroit, a grandmother hops on her Harley Davidson and rides to Florida to visit her grandchildren.

In New York's suburban Westchester county, an Episcopalian minister makes his pastoral rounds on a Lambretta scooter.

In Sanford, Florida, a pair of middle-aged men start off on a 12,000-mile motorcycle trip just for the fun of it.

In Hartford, Connecticut, a state representative on his motorcycle is a common sight at the state capitol when the

General Assembly is in session.

In New York, Mrs. Chet Huntley, wife of the television newscaster, cruises across 69th Street on her lightweight motorcycle on a trip to the supermarket. On her way, she passes film producer Ted Devlet, heading for the studio on his heavyweight cycle.

In Beverly Hills, California, singer Dean Martin and his wife beat traffic jams on their motorcycle, making the trip in 15 minutes.

Baseball is no longer our national pastime. Neither is basketball nor football nor hockey. We hardly ever *play* baseball anymore; in this world of specialization we spend our time watching others play for us. There are three million tennis players, seven million bowlers, and twelve million golfers in the United States. But there are many more motorcyclists, many more people actually participating in the motorcycle experience. Altogether, there are close to twenty million motorcyclists—enough to make motorcycling, far and away, our national pastime.

Motorcycles, of course, are popular in other lands—first in France, England, and Germany, the countries that developed the first motorcycles and the many recreational and practical ways to use them. A motorcycle culture has emerged in the Soviet Union, and Russian-made bikes will soon be offered on the American market. A person wanting to buy a motorcycle in India must wait nine years after registering for one before he receives delivery. In Udaipur, in September 1971, prospective cyclists smashed through police lines to register for their bikes. There were four people injured that day—and ten people killed.

But the largest and most lucrative motorcycle market exists in the United States. You can find a motorcyclist on practically every residential street in the nation. There is probably a cyclist in every subway car, in every delicatessen, in every office building in New York City. Every Lions Club, American Legion post, synagogue, hospital, college, department store, lumber camp, factory, museum, law library, police department, plumbing union, movie studio, or talk show audience contains at least one. Anywhere you look, there'll be a motorcyclist, a former motorcyclist, or a future motorcyclist. You can recognize one by looking in the mirror.

There are not only more Americans participating in the motorcycle experience, but more different kinds of people. You will see motorcycles jamming the parking lots of downtown Philadelphia, lining the curbs in Harlem or Watts, stationed around Columbus Circle or Rockefeller Plaza in New York. In the mornings, men in suits and ties, or in coveralls and steel-toed boots, commute to work on motorcycles. They call on clients, chug to lunch, head to the health spa, a local bar, or a gym. In the afternoons, housewives go to beauty salons or bridge club meetings on motorcycles. Their children travel back and forth to school or deliver papers on two-wheeled machines. Motorcycles are used in Vietnam to speed pilots to waiting bombers, used by doctors speeding to hospitals to deliver a baby or to cut out an appendix. On the average, there is one motorcyclist in every four American families, and twice as many as there are college students, doctors, and attorneys combined. Everybody rides motorcycles. Steve McQueen, Paul Newman, Polly Bergen, Hugh Downs, Keenan Wynn, Michael Ansara, and the Smothers brothers. Even General Dwight David Eisenhower rode a motorcycle before visions of the Presidency danced in his head.

People even get married on motorcycles. As it happened in June 1971 on the edge of the reservoir in Pittsburgh's Highland Park when Walt Rogowski, sitting on his chromed, customized chopper, and Shirley Piper, standing beside, exchanged vows. Shirley wore maroon, crushed-velvet hot pants, with a white and blue garter, a leather vest, and a see-through blouse. Walt had on black leather bell bottoms, and a red, white, and blue jersey and, naturally, a sleeveless denim jacket.

Little children have been bitten by the motorcycle bug. More than two million mini-bikes have been sold in the United States since 1967. Mini-bikes are shrunken replicas of the big machines, with power mower engines and fancy designs that can rip and snort around a backyard at forty miles per hour or faster. The super-charged variety can be purchased at cycle shops for as much as $700, or as little as $99 for the assemble-yourself, discount store variety.

Mini-bikes are not big or powerful enough to be made street legal. But they are used in the woods or on miniature race-tracks around the country. Kids from four to twelve years old race mini-bikes under the guidance of the American Motorcycle

Association. The mini-bike competition, according to industry prophets, is the beginning of a minor league system for the professional cycle racing circuit. Now, with mini-bikes, cyclists need not wait until they're sixteen to sophisticate their skills racing two-wheeled machines.

Older kids like to customize their mini-bikes, adding long front forks, lower saddles, and icing them with chrome. Some of the least experienced kids have training wheels on their mini-bikes. And a few of the most confident refuse to honor the restrictions their parents and the law have imposed. In December 1971, a boy from Illinois was arrested and charged with, among other things, driving his mini-bike at fifty miles per hour in a twenty-five mile per hour zone. He was seven years old.

But generally speaking, most motorcyclists are much older and more mature than the average four-wheeling American might expect.

Early in 1971, Charles Clayton, publisher of the weekly *Cycle News*, circulation 50,000, reported that the average motorcyclist is between the ages of twenty-one and thirty-five. "He is," said Clayton, "a highly skilled blue collar worker or an executive working his way up. He owns his own house, has a wife, more than one child, and at least one car. His income reaches more than $13,000 annually."

And *Cycle Magazine*, the largest monthly cycle publication (circulation 279,000), in its bi-annual reader survey for 1971, stated that the median age of subscribers owning a bike was 25.7 years old. The median yearly income of all subscriber households was $11,078.

"Approximately 55% of you," said editor Cook Nielson in a recent editorial, "are businessmen, 3% of you are in the professions, and 9% are in civil service. And out of the whole of businessmen, 41% are executives, managers and professionals."

In a 1970 survey of 506 motorcyclists conducted for *Cycle News*, Barbara Adams Dahms reported an average of 1.5 bikes per person. Of the families, 37% had two riders, 15% had three, 14% had four, 7% had five, and 4% had six riders or more. The largest mentioned was ten riders per family.

The men of the Imperial Council of the Ancient Arabic Order of the Nobles of the Mystic Shrine ride motorcycles. Shriner motorcycle units, operating in 300 towns and cities across the

United States, might be as large as a drill team of fifty riders or as small as a ten-man patrol. For nationwide activities, Shriners can muster 5,000 vehicles, ranging from small mini-bikes to mammoth Harleys, at a total vehicle valuation of close to $2 million. In any area, a Shriner motorcycle unit might work with the city police or county sheriff's office as escorts for dignitaries or on civil defense alerts. Like any top-flight marching band or drill team, Shriner motorcycle units have left-obliqued, right-flanked, to-the-rear marched and Virginia-reeled in football stadiums, town squares, hospital parking lots, prison courtyards, and on parade grounds across the country.

Besides the Shriners, there are more than 2,000 motorcycle clubs and organizations officially sanctioned by the American Motorcycle Association (AMA). Of the non-sanctioned variety, the most prominent are the outlaw gangs—like the Hell's Angels, the Animals, the Axemen, the Pagans, the Vultures, and the Wheels of Soul. These groups, according to the AMA and a number of newspapers and national magazines, are composed of unwashed punks, hoodlums, sadists, crooks, drug users, drug pushers, rapists, and others practicing their own particular perversions. There are only about 3,000 men and women of such ilk in all, yet they have descended from a strong heritage of petty crime, beginning with what they could take from their two-wheeled brothers, thirty years ago.

Originally, outlaws would steal motorcycles and disguise them for re-sale by stripping the machine of all accessories and chopping the top part of the frame to make the seat, and the whole machine, look more low-slung. Today, such motorcycles are called choppers, and artists and customizers are doing amazing things to sophisticate and elaborate on the primitive designs.

They begin by replacing the standard front forks with long springers. Some are so long that they run almost parallel to the road. Then they adjust the neck of the bike—the section of the frame to which the original forks were once attached—to accommodate the new design. They call this process raking, although to the outlaws who originated it, modification meant straight customizing.

Today, outlaws bedeck their bikes with short mufflers called shorties, sissy bars (somewhat of a chromed backrest for riders or passengers), teardrop-shaped tanks, and very high or very low handlebars. Footpegs are mounted high, saddles slung low, so that the rider looks like he's cruising in a cockpit.

Good looks, rather than riding practicability or safety, are the objectives of the chopper artists. Every part that can be chromed is chromed. Eight to one hundred coats of metal flake paint, sometimes even more, are burned into the body of the machine. Some chopper riders in California are now even commissioning artists to paint murals on their gas tanks. The newest chopper gas tanks are shaped like coffins and on them artists are painting panoramic views of western scenery or more intimate pictures of the rider's nude wife or girl friend. Or there are cartoons, zodiac signs, astrological happenings, and other examples of acid art. It is a far cry from the original attempt at motorcycle halloweening, but that is one of the many trends outlaws established more than a quarter of a century ago.

It's difficult to tell just how many members other non-sanctioned groups contain. They are loosely structured, made up of people not willing or able to commit themselves, just groups of cyclists who meet at a special diner, or at a bar, or in vacant lots on Saturday mornings or Sunday afternoons. One such group in Denver gathers at Shelby's Cycle Shop; another in New Jersey gets together at Dilner's Diner; members of a third in southwestern Pennsylvania find each other on Sunday mornings at an abandoned strip mine, near Ohiopyle Reservoir.

The more structured groups, legitimized by the AMA, run the gamut in type and purpose from the Klondike Kids, for cyclists under sixteen interested in safe riding, or the Smelts MC for cyclists under twelve who want to race, to the Early Wheels— active cyclists over sixty who join together once a year at Daytona, during Speed Week, to reminisce. You'll find many gypsies in this bunch. If you're over sixteen and not yet sixty, but still past forty, you could join the Retreads, an organization started in the United States a few years ago that boasts of thousands of members and chapters in twenty countries, including South Africa and Australia. If you believe that the family who plays together stays together, the AMA has something for you too: the Over-the-Hill Gang is made up of families, each member riding a two-wheeled machine. If you believe that real estate and motorcycles mix, buy a share of the Sunset Riders' farm in Chicora, Pennsylvania. If you think that money and motorcycles go together, join

the Morgan Cycle Association, a group of business and professional men who buy broken down and dilapidated bikes and
fix and sell them, pocketing the profits when they have any.

There are even consumer organizations for bikers frustrated
with faulty equipment, uncooperative manufacturers and dealers.
One such group, the Four Owners Club, is composed completely
of owners of four-cylindered Honda machines. Their objective
is to exert pressure until it pays off. Pressure on the manufacturers to redesign faulty parts and correct existing manufacturing
defects, whether or not the machines are still under warranty;
pressure on the dealers to live up to existing warranty commit-
ments and expand and improve facilities and expertise. The
Four Owners Club may lack the force of persuasion of the Hell's
Angels, but their power is more far-reaching, and will someday
be absolute.

There are organizations for people enamored of a certain brand
or special-sized machine, clubs for conservationists and those
concerned with pollution. There are clubs for road riders and
desert racers, woods riders, for women, for advertising men, for
Black Americans. And there is one called the Mystery Motorcycle Club, open only to those who dislike motorcycle clubs.

It may be difficult to recognize members of the respectable
motorcycle clubs, but the AMA knows who they are. The average
AMA member, according to R. L. Polk and Company of Chicago, is fit, active, industrious, and responsible, is probably
married and has at least a high school or trade school education.
He is neat, with average hair length, friendly, out-going, and is
either muscular, average, or thin of build. And, according to the
report, he is rarely hostile or overweight.

Many motorcycle clubs field special events to bring together
cyclists with similar interests from all parts of the world. The
Black Hills Cycle Association, for example, welcomes more than
10,000 riders each year to an organized, 300-mile run through
the Badlands, past the wild burros and roaming buffalo of western
South Dakota, the granite images of four presidents carved into
Mt. Rushmore, and on through the Little Big Horn country, where
Custer last stood.

For their Midnight Road Run, the Crotona Motorcycle Club
gathers at Nathan's, a popular Yonkers, New York delicatessen in
the middle of January. The riders wear three or four layers of

pants, and as many as a half dozen sweaters and socks. Their motorcycles come dressed up too, in windbreakers of fiberglass or windbreakers crafted for the run in plywood and thick corrugated board. And then, when everybody is there, lined up and ready—usually seventy-five or ninety bikes in all—somebody shoots a snowman, or toots a trumpet, or a waiter from Nathan's claps a couple of frozen bagels together, and they're off—sliding over the blue ice, crashing through snow, falling and almost falling, and always pushing forward doggedly, for six or eight or ten hours, and one-hundred frozen miles.

John and Thelma Boone, on their sidecar outfit, finished first in the 1971 Crotona Run. It was twenty-two degrees below zero that night in Yonkers, and the Boones were one of the few entries to finish at all. Leslie Pink, the only woman to complete the race, took second.

There are thousands of women who ride motorcycles, incidentally, although they make up only one percent of all cyclists, according to the Cycle reader survey. Women ride for approximately the same reasons as men do: they commute back and forth to work or school or to go shopping, just to have fun, or visit friends. Women race, like Kitty O'Neal, a former AAU platform diving champion, and Kerry Kleid, who, in court, proved the AMA's ban against women racing as professional nonsense; or like Sammy Dunn of Los Angeles, the first woman to follow Kleid into the professional racing circuit. And women cruise their cycles cross-country, as Mayra Scarborough did a few summers ago.

Mrs. Scarborough, a member of the Mayflower Descendents, is chief librarian for the marketing division of Hoffman-La Roche, Inc. in Nutley, New Jersey. She had a paper to present at a librarians' conference in San Francisco the summer she turned fifty-five and she traveled from New Jersey across the northern part of the United States on her high-powered Honda to the west coast. Afterward, she chugged down through Nevada, New Mexico, and Texas, and went deep into Florida to visit friends. In six weeks on the road, Mrs. Scarborough logged 11,000 miles.

"I spent every day on my motorcycle," she says, "and every night in my sleeping bag, along the highways, in the forests and campgrounds. And I found what I was looking for—the joy of solitude, which is so fragile."

There are many women's motorcycle clubs, such as the End Does, chartered in southern California, District 37, of the AMA. Originally, the End Does were formed by wives of the Rams MC to participate with their husbands in desert racing. Their activities have since diversified, and members include one high school music teacher and two topless dancers.

Some cycle clubs have special uniforms. The Shriners often wear black pants with red braid, red and white helmets, and bolero jackets with a red and yellow Shriners shield sewed on the back. The Motor Maids, Inc., the largest and oldest U.S. women's cycling organization, with more than 600 members in the United States, are very explicit about how their compatriots must dress:

"The official Motor Maid uniform," according to by-law number seven of the Motor Maids' constitution, "shall consist of gray slacks, royal blue cotton shirt with white silk square folded three cornered and tied in a knot under the collar of the shirt, one inch wide belt and white boots. Also white gloves for parades. Unofficial items include the blue and gray Motor Maid sweater and the blue cotton shirtwaist dress. Children may wear blue shirts, which have been lettered, 'My Mother is a Motor Maid' on the back."

As with many other respectable and sanctioned motorcycle clubs, the Motor Maids are very careful about the conduct of their associates:

"A secret membership board composed of six (6) members," it is written in Article Five, Section Twelve of the Motor Maids' constitution, "shall be appointed to investigate new members and vote on them if necessary, and to send warning letters to members whose conduct reflects on the club unfavorably or for any other reason. Prospective members shall be required to go through a three (3) month probation period. No member on probation shall be eligible to wear the club uniform or emblem."

Most clubs and organizations are concerned about their image because of the tenuous position motorcyclists have held over the years. To many people, the motorcyclist is America's bogeyman, the villain of the highway, causing accidents and clubbing cops, the violator of virginity, the filth of America's roads. This has never been true, but the truth, no matter how many times it is repeated, and in how many different ways, will often not dispel man's images of evil.

Motorcyclists are still feared and punished essentially for what happened in a little town in southern California a quarter-century ago.

Two

It is July 4, 1947, and we are in Hollister, California, population 4,800, the city that produces 74 percent of all the garlic consumed in the United States.

Every Independence Day, city fathers sponsor speed tests and hillclimbs for those townfolk and area farmers who ride motorcycles. But this year, many more people than expected are here. Estimates range from 2,000 to 4,000, including some unwanted guests. A gang called the Booze Fighters had rolled into town that morning on their big, black Harley Davidsons and converged on the open taverns like camels stocking up for a trek through the Mohave.

By dusk, downtown Hollister is littered with broken beer bottles and drunken people smeared with grease and vomit. Cyclists are ripping up front yards and porches and drag racing up and down the normally quiet Hollister streets. Then the police, gathering volunteer deputies and aided by vigilante bands of outraged citizens, counterattack. Fist fights, broken windows, and looting follow, and after the glass and the dust and the rage has settled, fifty are treated for injuries in a nearby hospital.

A *Life* magazine photographer is in Hollister that day, and he has taken a picture of one Booze Fighter, sprawled on a Harley, showing off his inflated stomach, chugging a bottle of beer.

It is sometime in 1949 and Frank Rooney, a not-too-prominent writer, has just finished one of his best short stories, entitled "Cyclists Raid." Near his typewriter is an issue of *Life* magazine, opened to page 31, which shows a picture of a young motorcyclist, sprawled on a Harley, showing off his inflated stomach, chugging a bottle of beer. Rooney's story will be published in 1951 in *Harper's* magazine, and anthologized in a number of volumes of short stories. An obscure Hollywood producer, Stanley Kramer, will read it.

It is sometime late in 1953 and we are anywhere in the country. It is evening, the movie has just ended, and we are all walking away from the credits and coming attractions, filing into the lobby and out onto the streets. Most everybody is quiet, lighting cigarettes or watching the sky, helping ladies on with their coats or searching jacket pockets for keys. We are all breathing a little easier now, but still too quickly to want to talk logically, still too shaken by what we have seen portrayed on the screen. We can clearly hear our hearts thumping against our chests, and when a motorcycle rides by, we look at each other self-consciously, and then turn and glare at the cycle's tail light as it merges with the city's neon. We have our coffee, or smoke a cigarette, take the baby sitter home, and the next morning or the following week, open a newspaper or magazine, and read about what we have so recently seen:

"A little bit of the surface of contemporary American life is scratched in Stanley Kramer's 'The Wild One' which came to the Palace yesterday, and underneath is opened an ugly, debauched and frightening view of a small, but particularly significant and menacing element of modern youth. Although the reality of it goes soft and then collapses at the end, it is a tough and engrossing motion picture, weird and cruel, while it stays on the beam.

"The subject of its examination is a swarm of youthful motorcyclists who ride through the country in wolf-pack fashion and terrorize the people of one small town. Given to the jive of bebop lingo and the grotesque costumes and attitudes of the 'crazy' cognoscenti, these 'wild ones' resent discipline and show an aggressive contempt for common decency and the police. Reckless and vandalistic, they live for sensations, nothing more—save perhaps the supreme sensation of defying the normal world."—Bosley Crowther, December 31, 1953, *The New York Times*

"Audiences who like their facts dished up with realism, no matter how painful, might pay attention to 'The Wild One'—a picture that is factual in that John Paxton's provocative script is based on a story by Frank Rooney which in turn is based on an actual incident that happened in California. It displays a group of hoodlums, motorcyclists who ride around the country with a contempt for the law and a fondness for annoying people, who take over a small town.

"I'm not sure what Stanley Kramer had in mind in producing the picture, but if he wanted to show us a slice of contemporary Americana at its worse, he has succeeded."—Phillip T. Hartung, February 5, 1954, *Commonweal*

There is something about the motorcycle that disturbs, often infuriates, a lot of people. A cyclist's appearance indeed has something to do with this.

Motorcyclists frequently are dirty. The outlaw image is soaked in grease and oil, layered by weeks of grime and crud. The average Hell's Angel may very well have a bathing problem, but the typical cyclist, whose flesh will touch water every day or so, often resembles that grease-soaked portrait. Pollution in the air leaves its mark in the lines of a cyclist's face. On the highway, he is machine-gunned with mud, bombarded with bird droppings; his cheeks, like a car's windshield, are splattered with blotches of crushed insects.

Probably, it's the machine that angers people. Motorcycles are loud, though tractor trailer trucks are louder. But trucks are big and carry heavy cargo; they make America move. But motorcyclists seem loud just to afford their riders the joy of sounding off. In the woods, motorcyclists scare animals. In suburbia, they wake up babies and tired businessmen by bellowing up and down quiet residential streets.

Perhaps it's what the machine might symbolize that irritates some people. We live in a four-wheeled culture. Every vehicle we know to be efficient and proper moves over highways on four wheels, except for trucks, which often have more. But the task of riding two wheels asks a little bit more of a man; his balance and stability is not so well guaranteed. Every society treasures the values and ideas that have been passed through generations. Two wheels are a repudiation of the four-wheeled culture and many people have traditionally been unable to accept it.

But still . . .

None of this really explains the sheer hostility and fear Americans have harbored for motorcyclists over the past quarter-century. Although a motorcyclist's physical appearance may perpetuate a poor image, there is little correlation between how he looks or how he gets where he is going, and the origins of that image. There must be something more.

Motorcyclists—especially of the black-leather-jacket ilk—are deviants. They were so in the 1920s and 1930s when the gypsies in large numbers rolled over the American plain and through the depression on two wheels. The depression may have made some men into gypsies, but it did not affect the lifestyles of those who had roamed before them. The gypsies spurned the good times of economic boom after World War I, relinquishing their opportunity to make money and settle down. Their nomadic lifestyle continued during the years of economic bust, when all of those upstanding, hard-working businessmen and craftsmen were fighting to keep their families under roofs and in food. The gypsy's self-imposed isolation galled many people. Their reluctance to join the society around which they rode planted unconscious seeds of doubt within it that eventually turned to conscious feelings of fear. Many resentments were formed. People who had boomed and busted with the economy resented the ambivalence of the gypsies, resented their presence at soup kitchens and Salvation Army dinners because, after all, these men were gaining without, like the rest of them, suffering any major loss. Not all motorcyclists, nor even the majority of them were gypsies. But we tend to mold our stereotypes on the most bizarre of what we have seen. We don't notice the Jews, with short hair and derby hats—only those with skull caps and scraggly beards. We don't see, or at least we do not retain the image of black Americans driving Fords—only those driving Lincolns and Cadillacs. And in the 1920s and 1930s we forgot, or we ignored, those neighbors who rode motorcycles—the doctor who treated our children, the lawyer who defended our names in court. But we remembered that lone figure, shadowed in black, who bellowed down main street, dogged by clouds of oil smoke, as he rolled unshackled and untroubled in the world of trouble, from town to town.

The war changed everything, however. Japan and Germany did for America what America could not do for itself. A new prosperity came with bombs, bullets, battleships, and planes. When it ended, we were not only rich, but in the best possible position as victors at peace. Yet, not counting the dead and wounded, there were casualties of which we could not conceive.

After the war, there were thousands of young men returning to this country who had lived through five years or more of vile excitement, whose lifestyles had been raped and who had forgotten the discipline required and boredom resulting from living in a society of sanity and order. Most returning ex-soldiers settled down. They went back to college, or found jobs and clean-cut American women to marry. A few, however, were still caught up in the withdrawal from a real-life drug, temporarily tempered by peace.

Not all, or even the majority, of these men turned to the motorcycle, but it was a natural alternative. For years, these ex-soldiers had a nucleus around which their lives could function: the enemy, the war, their weapons, their friends. All of that was gone. Even the people with whom they had lived and fought for five years had separated, returning to their own part of the country. College wouldn't replace it, nor could family or the job at a local hardware store. But the motorcycle could come close. It gave reason to gather, provided a common exhilaration, one that might suffice until another war came along.

On the motorcycle, a smoking, fire-eating, 74-cubic-inch iron lung, there was the noise, that thundering, ear-splitting bellow of bombs and machines. And you could feel the noise like you could feel the shells bursting. There was the wind, a blowing release and freedom, and that ever-pressing awareness of danger, the knowledge that at any moment, if luck was lost, you could be reduced to a bag of bones and blood, shattered and scraped against macadam and cement.

These weren't the only people affected by the war, nor the only reasons they turned to the motorcycle. Some of the men who readily adopted the motorcycle gang style were so jaded because they never had the opportunity to fight in the war. In a country where literally hundreds of thousands of heroes were returning, those men who were physically or mentally unfit for the army, and those who had joined the army but had never been called on to fight, were sure to feel inferior. America was peopled with patriots, smothered with the feeling of self-righteous conquerors who had saved the world from certain destruction and dictatorship.

There were others who had not qualified for the war—the youngest sons whose cousins and brothers had fought and died and fought and lived in the name of peace and right. Those boys who had been too young to hold a rifle or drive a tank were now old enough to buy and ride a motorcycle. They, too, discovered that they could prove themselves on two wheels.

The motorcycle was a single-man's machine, and it took a particular kind of skill to ride it well. Although we had won the war by group effort, Americans still fancied their best men as rugged individualists, who could do almost anything, succeed where all others had failed. For these over-affected youths the motorcycle symbolized what they thought they were supposed to be—a modern version of the mythical American cowboy. Tom Mix, Wild Bill Hickok, Roy Rogers and Trigger, Gene Autry and Champion, the Lone Ranger and Tonto, the kind of people we have traditionally admired most—peaceful, but powerful and brave, riding alone across a range of evil, bringing freedom and courage to jelly-livered townspeople and defenseless old men.

Finally, there were other casualties of the war, the poor whites and the even poorer blacks. The ones who hadn't had much of a job or very many prospects for a better life before the war. Now they had nothing but memories. In the five or seven years since they had been home, machines had, in many cases, taken over or would soon be taking over the only jobs their unskilled hands could do. Some of these men stayed in the armed forces, for they liked the security of three meals, a cot, a locker, and regular pay. It was more than their fathers had ever had, and far more than many could expect now on the outside. Their people, from Appalachia, the Ozarks, Harlem, and San Antonio, had been destitute for a long time, and they would be destitute for a long time to come. They had fought—and some had died—for peace like everybody else, but instead of spoils, they got medals, instead of credit they got congratulations. They had returned older, wiser, but no more educated or eligible than before. They had fought somebody else's war and except for physical survival, benefited not at all from the peace. It was a sad end.

So they turned to the motorcycle—not all of them, or even a majority of them, but equal representations of all of these lost and bitter groups. They turned to what seemed to be their only option for acting out their very personal and hackneyed vision of the American dream. Riding a motorcycle was not as satisfying as fighting a war, however, because this lifestyle lacked a common enemy. So bitterness was often vented, mostly on an individual basis, on the establishment, on those who had benefited from their labors, on those who seemed most civilized and secure. Like the people who celebrated Independence Day in 1947 in Hollister, California.

In Hollister, as in all parts of the country, there were long-time resentments and fear of motorcyclists, some conscious and some deep-rooted, from the days of the gypsies and the depression before the war. Many of these fears surfaced during the war. The German army was very often portrayed with men on motorcycles, wrapped in leather, pictured in newspapers across every allied country as running down babies, violating defenseless women, machine-gunning our courageous young men.

In 1947 there was a definite correlation, in the minds of many people, between motorcycle gangs, no matter what their intent, and Facism. The gangs were made up of former soldiers and led by former soldiers. Most gang members wore identical costumes similar to military uniforms and rode at all times in a disciplined, military-like formation. There were platoons within the gangs, supervised by self-appointed petty officers who could, up to a point, keep their men in line—or unleash them. And, in 1947, the country was still on edge, unused to peace, with millions of Americans floating in a sea of promises of prosperity.

That riot in Hollister upset America's reverie. And the media, which during the war had been breast-fed with the greatest and most spectacular feast of news in all world history, were well prepared to report it to the hilt.

In a full-page story two weeks later, *Life* magazine said that 4,000 members of a motorcycle club had roared into the town on a three-day convention. *Life* went on to say that police arrested many for drunkenness and indecent exposure, but they could not restore order. Other magazines carried similar stories, but *Life*, with a circulation of nearly five million, was the largest weekly and its comments the most damaging to the motor-cyclist's already tenuous image.

There can be no doubt that *Life*, hungry for news, had gorged itself on a feast of exaggeration. Actual Hollister police reports which, according to the AMA were grossly inflated, estimated that 4,000 people in all took part in the riot. This included townspeople, motorcycle outlaws, and thousands of respectable motorcyclists as well. At full strength the Booze Fighters could probably mus-ter no more than fifty soldiers. Even in 1970, with more than ten times the motorcycles registered in this country, no motor-cycle club could claim 4,000 members. Furthermore, the Booze Fighters were not at a convention. Hollister had been sponsoring a motorcycle hill climb on the Fourth of July for many years, and the club had merely come to participate in the action and the fun that usually goes with this sort of thing. A few thousand people might very well have participated in the riot. But fifty outlaws, no matter how tough, could not have precipitated it. *Life* obviously played on sensationalism after reading a press service wire story filed from Hollister and issued July 6.

Instead of "4,000 members of a motorcycle club," the wire story said "hundreds." Instead of "many arrests" as reported by *Life*, there were, out of 4,000 participants, only 38, none of which, according to the wire service, had to do with indecent exposure. There were 32 special officers called in to aid the seven-man police force and in 36 hours the disturbance was quelled.

Hollister was the first of what has commonly come to be known as a "motorcycle riot" and also the last for the next fifteen years. Compared to post World War I vintage anti-Com-munist crusades, or the peace demonstrations of the 1960s, it probably should not be termed a riot at all. Perhaps, in truth, the Booze Fighters did come to Hollister to make trouble. But the ramifications of the trouble they received in return were far in excess of what they deserved. We don't punish petty criminals by hanging their wives or throwing their brothers in jail. Yet many Americans have indicted and convicted all motor-cyclists for that disturbance in Hollister 25 years ago.

After Hollister, many of the motorcycle gangs—including the Booze Fighters—disbanded and the entire motorcycle scene was sort of outside the world for a while, as though it were under siege. There were probably anywhere from 200,000 to 300,000 motorcyclists then who, as always, continued their ac-tivities, racing and riding under the auspices of the AMA. But the image sketched out by *Life* lingered on, until Stanley Kramer could paint a picture in even more detail.

In late 1953, and early 1954, when "The Wild One" was released, the country again was recovering from a war, but this war we hadn't won, a war with no real enemy or common purpose. We had been told we were the strongest nation in the world, powerful enough to demand everlasting peace. And yet, as many people saw it, we voluntarily stalemated in a war with second-class powers, countries we could have systematically crushed.

At the time, we were locked in a name-calling cold war with the Soviet Union. Day and night, Americans could turn on the television and watch the enemy insult and threaten the United States from the United Nations Building, from our country. From New York! In the Senate, a man named McCarthy was Commie-hunting, digging up traitors and Communist conspirators like a gardener pulling up weeds. That sea of prosperity and security had suddenly been drained. We were isolated in a canyon of confusion, electing scapegoats, Communists, neo-Nazis, motor-cyclists, anyone on whom we could blame our national ills.

People in the early fifties were especially receptive to visions of villainy, but even in the best of times, Kramer's production, long accepted as a cinematic masterpiece, would have had its effects. Orson Welles' "War of the Worlds," a radio play pre-sented in the late 1930s, which realistically documented the invasion of Earth by men from Mars, caused unbelievable panic across this nation to those who had tuned in after the fictional origins of the program had been announced. And Kramer's film was based on a wholly more realistic idea than an invasion from another planet.

Today we have put men on the moon and have lost through assassination one President of the United States. Today many young people fight not for a war, but against it. And members of our own armed forces have shot down in cold blood young Americans in the streets. But in the early 1950s we were a society, in the very traditional sense, of law and order. Police had the power, elders had the power, Cadillacs had the power. The mere idea of roving, looting bands of wild-eyed motorcyclists was terrifying to the point where many men were pledging to fight at all costs to put the tyranny down.

And Kramer's film was based on an actual incident. The truth about what happened in Hollister, which was never fully communicated, was suddenly clouded in a maze of dramatic, spine-tingled fiction. Most people were unaware of what actually had happened at Hollister. And many thought Stanley Kramer had finally told the tale.

For those who did not see the movie, the reviewers were equally misleading. Crowther blatantly told the readers of The New York Times that what they would see in "The Wild One" was an accurate portrait of contemporary American life. He was supported by Phillip Hartung in Commonweal who called the film "a slice of contemporary Americana at its worse." Newsweek inadvertently added to the myth by relating the motorcyclist to "hipsters" and including some butchered historical documentation, no doubt cribbed from the 1947 Life, repeating that "4,000 members of a motorcycle club held a riotous convention in Hollister, California."

It didn't take too long. America's long-lingering suspicions of the evil and wickedness of the motorcyclist, were forever confirmed.

Three

"Early in the morning of June 2, 1962," California Attorney General Thomas C. Lynch disclosed, "it was reported that three Hell's Angels had seized a 19-year-old woman in a small bar in the northern part of Sacramento and while two of them held her down on the barroom floor, the third removed her outer clothing. The victim was menstruating at the time; her sanitary napkin was removed and the third individual committed cunnilingus upon her . . . .

"Early in the morning of October 25, 1964, nine Hell's Angels and two of their female companions were arrested by Gardena police and sheriff's officers after a riot call had been received from a Gardena bar. Police reported that the group 'started ripping up the whole place' after someone had splashed a mug of beer over one of the group. The bar was left in shambles, and pool tables covered with beer and urine."

And so, from under the tables and out of the bushes, emerging from seedy bars, grimy garages, and hidden dark corners, crawling out of jail cells, moth-eaten mattresses, mental hospitals, and haunted houses, the Hell's Angels have arrived.

They are, according to some people, part of the international Communist conspiracy. Others see them as an especially sadistic bunch of homosexuals, and still others consider them Fascists. But anyone who has ever had a fetish for Hell's Angels fantasy agrees with the Florida police official who said in 1966:

"These punks with their cycles and their Nazi trappings have it in for the world—and for everyone in it. They're a menace, a damned serious menace, that's growing bigger every year."

It is Labor Day, 1963, a day of rest and relaxation for most people, a long weekend for picnicing or playing with the kids or mowing the grass, then sipping beer, lying in the hammock out in the sun.

But we are not resting. We are rolling south down Highway 101 on our motorcycles, and the Angels are rolling with us. Magoo and Terry the Tramp, Tiny the Enforcer, Mouldy Marvin, Mother Miles, and God knows how many other dudes, are all following Sonny Barger, the president of the Hell's Angels Oakland chapter, the Maximum Leader, heading the pack. It is a beautiful day. The sun has coated the trees and the grass and our cycles with a translucent yellow sheen, and we are all mesmerized by how we feel together: like a gigantic, roving thunderclap, leaning into the road, making the whole world tilt, eating up the macadam and concrete that snakes out in front of us.

The annual Labor Day Run for the Hell's Angels and most other outlaw gangs is similar to New Year's Eve for normal people, except better. It's the biggest drunk, the highest trip, the greatest free-for-all of the year, and everybody attends. All the women and lots of children, all the members from different parts of the state, and the drop-outs who have become too old, or maybe too respectable to ride with us regularly, but who can still fit into their leathers and hoist themselves up onto greasy machines. There is no telling how many are here, but it is a very big run. A truce has been called throughout the state with the other clubs and some have joined us. We see the colors worn by members of the Gypsy Jokers, Satans Slaves, the Coffin Cheaters, Galloping Gooses, all leaning back against their women and resting brown beer bottles on the seat between their crotches. We stop at Porterville. According to *Newsweek* magazine, this is what happened:

"A roaring swarm of 200 black-jacketed motorcyclists converged on the small, sleepy, southern California town of Porterville. They rampaged through local bars, shouting obscenities. They halted cars, opening their doors, trying to paw female passengers. Some of their booted girl friends lay down in the middle of the streets and undulated suggestively. In one bar, half a dozen of them brutally beat a 65-year-old man and tried to abduct the barmaid. Only after 71 policemen from neighboring cities and the Highway Patrol, police dogs and water hoses were brought into action did the cyclists jump on their Harley Davidsons and roar out of town."*

The run, highlighted by an alleged rape of a town girl involving Terry the Tramp and Mouldy Marvin, set Attorney General Thomas C. Lynch to work. The bulk of a fifteen-page report on crime, issued by Lynch a few months later, was devoted to developing and depreciating an extraordinary phenomenon in that state: organized motorcycle-riding villainy, estimated in strength of more than 1,000 members.

The 1963 Porterville rape and run made headlines for a couple of days and then, when Terry the Tramp and Mouldy Marvin were cleared of the rape charge, California journalists, by now bored with Hell's Angels sensationalism, dropped the matter. It was virtually ignored by the national press until the Lynch report was issued in 1964. *The New York Times'* Los Angeles correspondent picked it up first and rehashed the report in a story headlined: "California Takes Steps to Curb Terrorism of Ruffian Cyclists."

"The Hell's Angels members," the story read in part, "have criminal records totalling 874 felony arrests, 300 felony convictions, 1,682 misdemeanor arrests and 1,023 misdemeanor convictions. Of the 151 members involved in the 300 felony convictions, only 85 have served time in state prisons or reform schools.

"Chapters of the organization are reported to exist in Phoenix, Ariz. and Portland, Ore., and even in New Zealand."

Ten days later *Time* magazine expanded and expounded on the phenomenon:

"No act is too degrading for the pack. Their initiation rite, for example, demands that any new member bring a woman or girl (called a 'sheep') who is willing to submit to sexual intercourse with each member of the club. But their favorite activity seems to be terrorizing whole towns . . . .

"When they are not thus engaged, the Angels—sometimes

accompanied by the young children of a member and by the unmarried females who hang out with the club—often rent a dilapidated house on the edge of a town where they swap girls, drugs and stolen motorcycle parts with equal abandon. In between drug-induced stupors, the Angels go on motorcycle-stealing forays, even have a panel truck with a special ramp for loading the machines. Afterward, they ride off again to seek some new nadir in sordid behavior."

"Who is a Hell's Angel?" asked *Newsweek,* also responding to the Lynch disclosures. "You can tell him by his back and his odor,' says the report. 'The common sign of membership is the embroidered patch scraggly-haired members wear on the back of their jackets: a smiling skull in a helmet. 'But,' the report continues, 'probably the most universal common denominator . . is their generally filthy condition.'

"They don't want baths. 'When you walk into a place where people can see you,' one member recently explained, 'you want to look as repulsive and repugnant as possible. We are complete social outcasts—outsiders against society. And that's the way we want to be. Anything good, we laugh at. We're bastards to the world and they're bastards to us.' "

There can be no doubt that prior to the Lynch Report, the Hell's Angels were little more than a bunch of local hoods, a mini-Mafia on motorcycles. California has not cornered the market on crime in this country, but it is a state that seems to attract the most bizarre perpetrators of crime, ranging from mass religious murders to desert dune buggy raiders. The Hell's Angels were merely one of many such sated groups of punks in 1964, until the media (*Time, Newsweek* and *The New York Times* with a combined circulation of more than six million) turned them into a national catastrophe.

At the peak of their fame, the Hell's Angels allowed a young journalist, Hunter S. Thompson, to spend some time with them. He had been with the Angels briefly before, as early as 1963, on his own motorcycle or tagging along behind in his car, shuttling busted jaws and squashed noses back and forth to hospitals, or banking and dispensing beer to the roving rene-gades as needed. Thompson was at work on a book, published in 1966, called *Hell's Angels: The Strange and Terrible Saga of the Outlaw Motorcycle Gangs.* Although it is now out of print, the book has done well, and periodically it is re-issued in paperback, updated with a new cover.

Thompson generally admits that the Angels were the kind of people the media said they were, and he presents a number of quotes from interviews and conversations to illustrate that point. Said Birney Jarvis, a charter member of the Hell's Angels who later became a *San Francisco Chronicle* police reporter:

" 'Some of them are pure animals. They'd be animals in any society. These guys are outlaw types who should have been born a hundred years ago—then they would have been gun-fighters.'

" 'We're one percenters, man—the one percent that don't fit and don't care,' " Thompson quoted from another Hell's Angel. " 'So don't talk to me about your doctor bills and your traffic warrants—I mean you get your woman and your bike and your banjo and I mean you're on your way. We've punched our way out of a hundred rumbles, stayed alive with our boots and our fists. We're royalty among motorcycle outlaws, baby.'

" 'People will just have to learn to stay out of our way,' " one Angel reminded a policeman. " 'We'll bust up everyone who gets in our way.' "

It's not a pretty picture, and yet Thompson maintains that before the Lynch report and the subsequent outbursts of national publicity, there was not much of a picture at all. The Angels were merely a group of hoods and have-nots whose lives revolved around the motorcycle. Some criminals are seduced by drugs or booze or witchcraft or gambling, but two wheels turned the Hell's Angels on. But it was the media that gave the Angels prominence and power. Before *Time* and *Newsweek* the outlaws were a dying breed:

"The significant thing about *Time's* view of the Angels," writes Thompson, "was not its crabwise approach to reality, but its impact. At the beginning of March, 1965, the Hell's Angels were virtually nonexistent. The club's own head count listed roughly eighty-five, all in California. Routine police harassment had made it impossible for the outlaws to even wear their colors in any city except Oakland. Membership in the San Francisco chapter was reduced to a handful of diehards determined to go down with the ship. In Sacramento, a two-man vendetta in the form of Sheriff John Miserly and a patrolman named Leonard Chatoian had made life so difficult that the Angels were all planning the big move to Oakland . . . and even there the heat was on for real. 'Shit, we never knew when they was gonna bust into the El Adobe (the tavern hang-out of the Angels) and line us up against the bar with shotguns,' Sonny Barger recalls. 'We even started drinking at the Sinners Club because it had a back door and a window we could get out of. I mean the heat was *on*, man. We were hurtin.' "

The Lynch report identifies 463 active Hell's Angels, but Thompson reports there have been no more than 200 members since 1960 and "easily a third of these are Hell's Angels in name only . . . old grads gone over the hump to marriage and middle age, but donning their colors once or twice a year." Another discrepancy had to do with chapters that purportedly existed in other states and countries. Thompson claims that an Angels' charter has never been granted out of California.

This disagreement is not too unusual. Numbers are easily inflated and deflated for seemingly legitimate reasons or simply on the whim of the tabulator. To the police, there were 463 Angels, and to the Angels, who looked at their men rather differently, there were only 200. And the Angels probably didn't grant charters to people in New Zealand, Oregon, or Arizona. But what prevents another motorcycle group, hungry for similar publicity, or even an old ladies' canasta club, from christening themselves Hell's Angels? Motorcyclists were not the first to own the Hell's Angels label. Long before Porterville, or even Hollister, the Hell's Angels were a crack fighter squadron for the United States Army Air Force.

Exaggeration of the facts has happened a thousand times before. It has happened to police departments accused of excessive brutality, to the Black Panther Party, and to the SDS. Objectivity is impossible, subjectivity is human. Few journalists and writers have not, at one time or another, been guilty of succumbing to sensationalism.

There is probably some median point between what the Hell's Angels were in the middle sixties and what they were reported to be. Whatever that point may be, the publicity they received was probably more than they deserved. And both the journalists who reported the news and the Angels who made it, will long feed on those stories, like babies sucking on their mothers' breasts.

It is June, 1965, and there are 15,000 of us, vrooming on our motorcycles, or beer-packing into Laconia, New Hampshire, Weirs Beach. The air is purple with exhaust fumes and our engines bellow at each other like wild animals. We are all yelling obscenities, some of us are bombarding bikers and police from a building's second story windows. Those of us on the second floor work our way slowly downstairs and out onto the street, past tattoos ironed on beer bellies, grimy leather jackets, and smelly denim pants, past men wearing earrings and women with rings in their noses. A pick-up truck on the street has already been turned over and some of the bikers, chains wrapped around their fists, are chasing after the fleeing police. We work our way to a car and start to rock it. There are kids inside, a bald old man, and a shrieking fat lady, but we don't care. Somehow, the people get out safely as we push the car over. Gas spills from the tank and somebody tosses a lighted cigarette. We retreat, smelling the fumes, watching it explode.

The Laconia, New Hampshire—Weirs Beach debacle was probably the biggest motorcycle riot of all. There were many hoodlums with and without motorcycles who probably precipitated the fun, but there were a lot of respectable bikers participating, too. Often, even the nicest people are as susceptible to savagery as anyone else. Caught midst bedlam, the average person would prefer turning crazy, rather than be the only one remaining sane. And so, Weirs Beach was destroyed. And so too, was any good will gained by respectable motorcyclists over the past decade of relative quiet and calm.

And yet, blame was heaped on a group that had, almost overnight, been made legendary: The Hell's Angels. "We know they [the Angels] were around," said police chief Harold Knowlton of Laconia, "and that they had taken over a town out west, but they weren't going to do it here."

Laconia Mayor Peter R. Lessard, said *Newsweek*, also blamed the riot on the Californians [the Angels] whose activities, he said, "seemed to be anti-democratic."

Lessard further stated, two days after the melee, that the Angels had planned the riot in advance, and "trained for it in Mexico."

The Angels were further indicted by *The San Francisco Examiner* in a story headlined: "Hell's Angels Terror at N.H. Cycle Race. Cops, Guard, Slug Rioters." The number of rioters was also bandied about, ranging from 5,000 in the *New York Post* to 25,000 in the *National Observer*.

Hunter Thompson claims that all of the Angels were in California at the time of the riot, but even if a contingent of ten or twelve had come East (no more could have sneaked across the country without being noticed, nor was it the Angel's way to ride singly or in pairs), it would be difficult to believe that even their charismatic charm could motivate 15,000 people to madness. But the statements of Lessard and Knowlton, plainly ridiculous in context, imply something else. Both men had seemingly become carriers of a contemporary sociological disease called scapegoating. Politically speaking, it could be defined as that art of blaming all of the nation's (or a group's) ills on something despicable, blatantly recognizable, easy to despise.

Hitler did it with the Jews in Germany, Joseph R. McCarthy tried scapegoating in the United States, and Attorney General Thomas C. Lynch attempted the same ruse in California. There was a sharp increase in crime in California—22 percent during the two years prior to the Lynch report, 37 percent for 1960 to 1964—and the word crime, to those who are not victims, is not precise nor does it describe a criminal. How do you recognize a criminal from a rabbi or a prison warden? But to recognize a Hell's Angel, you need only to look at his back, or grab a whiff of the air. It is the kind of message a politician likes to communicate to his electorate. Quoted *Time:*

"They will no longer be allowed to threaten the lives, peace and security of honest citizens of our state, said he [Attorney General Lynch]. To that, thousands of Californians shuddered a grateful amen."

And, according to *Newsweek:*

" 'Publication of this report,' he [Lynch] said, 'serves notice on Hell's Angels that law enforcement will not tolerate their hoodlum activities in California.' 'The signal was clear,' said one law man: 'Go get those punks.' "

The Angels perhaps deserved to be destroyed; nothing seems wrong with Lynch's objectives. But again, it is a question of emphasis. Based on figures supplied by the FBI's Annual Report on crime in the United States, the Angels were responsible for approximately six hundredths of one percent (.06 percent) of all serious crime committed in California in 1964. Yet they had been baited and branded with more fervor than had the Mafia. "It was sex, violence, crime, craziness and filth," says Hunter Thompson, "all in one package."

Lessard and Knowlton committed the same kind of ruse. The vast majority of the people vrooming and zooming around Laconia were citizens or tourists who come regularly to spend money each year. How could officials afford to knock anybody else but the Hell's Angels?

When asked about the "home grown bikies" participating in the riot, one city official put it this way: "Some of the finest people in the world ride motorcycles."

And unless the AMA put the rap on the Hell's Angels, the organization had a lot to lose: "We condemn them," said one AMA director, "they'd be condemned if they rode horses, mules, surfboards, bicycles or skateboards. Regretfully, they picked motorcycles."

"One percenters," said another AMA official, "weirdos who spoil it for everyone else."

One percenters. A phrase coined jointly by the Angels and the AMA, designed to refer to cyclists riding with outlaw packs. And although it seems to have caught on, even that figure is grossly inflated. There were probably no more than 3,000 to 4,000 outlaws in all in the United States in 1965, a number that seems to remain relatively constant, a mere fraction of the purported one percent.

Today, the Hell's Angels are still headquartered in California. Sonny Barger remains the president, Tiny the Enforcer, Magoo and Terry the Tramp and most of the others are probably still around. The creed is still the same as well: Angels live communally, giving and sharing, one for all. But the Angels are generally younger now. There are hardly any over thirty, except for the old stand-bys in California, and many are under twenty-one.

You hear of them periodically. They are hired for movie or cycle-stunting roles, take jobs keeping order at rock concerts, and you see them sometimes on television, having a news conference or wearing their expensive, flashy leathers, roaring on their cycles down sunny California streets. Recently, the Angels have granted charters across the country. They are not as big as the Lions, Kiwanis, or Shriners, but they might get there someday. By inflating images and egos, while tempering the Angels' thunder, the media and the police have inadvertently siphoned much of the menace out of the Hell's Angels myth. All is well.

Which doesn't necessarily mean that the Angels are prime prospects for being husbands to our daughters or Presidents of the United States. With their Philistinian philosophy, their blind loyalty to one another and their colors, and their lifestyles revolving around a grease-soaked god, it will never be possible for them to live in total peace and harmony in this or any other society. There are no islands in America, no independence except that which all Americans share. One cannot live outside the system. He must capitulate to it, compromise within it, or fight against it. There are no other options remaining.

"We don't have much bread," said Sandy, New York City Hell's Angels president in 1971. "But do you know something, we're very rich. What we have is love and a family. And brothers we can trust completely. We don't like violence, we just want to do our thing. But we're proud. Very proud. We just want to teach people what we've learned. And we want to be left alone. But if somebody starts something, they can't get away with it. We're a brotherhood."

"One on all," goes the chorus to the Angels fighting song, "and all on one."

Four

On their machines, motorcyclists are children reborn. The world is their playground. Those narrow country lanes that swing from this side of the sky and back are their seesaws. The wilderness is a sandbox where castles of mud are clawed by wheels operated by men who suddenly forget their stations and their goals in life. Motorcyclists are children reborn. They frolic with mechanized dogs and stay out long past their bedtime. They come home grimy and exhausted, hanging their helmets sheepishly, little boys ashamed. Mounted on two wheels, they ride backwards over the bridge of time.

Like children, motorcyclists often hunt eggs on Easter Sunday. Colored hard-boiled eggs are hidden in fields, under sagebrush and rocks and on top of steep hills. Each color has a different point value and each rider, working independently or for the common good of his team, is awarded points for eggs collected within a prescribed time.

Motorcyclists also play mysterious games. They follow splotches of lime through obstacle courses, the winner being the cyclist who makes it through the course in a time nearest to the official's pre-set secret time. On a map run, cyclists are given route sheets and started at one-minute intervals. As with the lime run, not speed, but precision, is important. The road run is similar to a sports car rally, with check points and officials measuring the rider's ability to maintain a schedule. Map and lime and road runs are difficult, but not dangerous, and motorcyclists who like to test their courage will often schedule these events in the snow.

Since it is usually held at night, many people get lost in a snow run. They carry flares and gasoline heaters and chains to wrap around their wheels for hauling and pulling. Many lost motorcyclists have been saved from frost bite by warming their gloved hands on hot exhaust pipes. A few motorcyclists sometimes signal their position by igniting gas syphoned from their tanks. Not too long ago, one cyclist left a trail of spilled gasoline from his bike to the site of his fire. When he struck his match the fire exploded his machine.

At certain points in a run, participants are often fed clues leading to hidden treasure, or hidden junk. Like any scavenger, they will often search for pictures of Rutherford B. Hayes, bottle caps, hockey sticks, and other cumbersome loot.

Motorcyclists also play grown-up games. On poker runs, they are given a card at each check point. The cyclist with a combination of the highest hand and the most accurate time will win.

Field meets are rodeos on wheels—backward races, potato races—anything goes as long as it goes on two wheels. Economy runs discover how long a rider can go on a tea cup of gas. Marathons decide how long a rider can last.

Motorcyclists play many games with their clubs and friends and machines. But, according to some people, the most popular game is the one they will play alone.

"The motorcycle is obviously a sexual symbol," says Dr. Bernard Diamond, University of California Criminologist, in 1965. "It's what's called a phallic locomotor symbol. It's an extension of one's body, a power between one's legs."

Said an editor for a New York publishing firm: "I was riding with a girl in New Jersey and we met a pack of about twenty other cyclists. This was in 1959, and these guys were riding big 'hogs' and 'thumpers' and they asked us if we wanted to ride along. I never experienced anything like it before. There we were riding and the noise from all those bikes was booming into the trees and I could feel my girl's crotch pressing into me. And all of a sudden I had an erection. Can you believe it? I had a damn erection!"

Writing in the *American Journal of Psychiatry*, psychiatrist

Armand Nicholi II, of Harvard Medical School, outlined the basic symptoms he detected in college-student-cyclists suffering from "The Motorcycle Syndrome."

It begins with a day and night preoccupation with the machine. "When the patient is not actually riding a motorcycle," Dr. Nicholi explains, "he tends to daydream continuously of doing so. The mere sound of a distant motorcycle stimulates vivid fantasies."

Unlike the healthy cyclist, a person with "The Motorcycle Syndrome" embraces his machine. Without it he is empty, haunted by a sense of "something missing and an acute awareness of inadequacy."

"If I got rid of that bike," said one patient, "there would be nothing but me, and that's not enough. . . ."

A Harvard graduate student expressed it this way: "Driving is a very personal, almost sexual feeling. You accelerate fast and there is nothing between you and nature. The wind blowing in your face is a marvelous sensation. It has tremendous appeal. My new machine has a huge motor. With this under me, I can do anything I want to."

The speaker had just purchased his third motorcycle despite having been seriously injured in two cycle accidents during the previous six months. All of Dr. Nicholi's patients, in fact, were accident prone. Most had been "wiped out" at least once, yet none could detach themselves from their machines.

Dr. Nicholi reports that his patients were mostly impotent, obsessed with worry over discovering they were homosexuals, and haunted with fears of mutilation and death:

"They openly discuss fear of castration," he reports. "As with most fantasies, this one has some basis of reality: The loss of a testicle in a cycle accident is not unknown. . . .

"They rationalize impotence away on the basis of fatigue, alcohol and drugs. They often attempt to alleviate anxiety resulting from failure to perform sexually by riding the motorcycle."

Each student considered his motorcycles extensions of his masculine self. "The noise is all you hear," said one. "It's masculine and makes me feel strong. I approach a girl on a cycle and I feel confident."

"In their associations and dreams," Dr. Nicholi goes on to say, "they reveal deep-seated, often unconscious feelings of being ugly, unintelligent, fat, weak, feminine and defective, and frequently express a sense of having something missing. They choose to be passive to avoid competition, lest they fail and confirm their negative self-image. The motorcycle serves to compensate for this defective picture of themselves."

Without their bikes, Dr. Nicholi's patients lacked confidence, both socially and academically. They were apathetic and inactive, spending most of their non-cycling hours sleeping, talking aimlessly, drinking beer, escaping reality in television and drugs. Overwhelmed with anxiety, loneliness or fear, even in the middle of the night, they mounted their motorcycles, comforted by the thought of "doing something and going somewhere."

Such symptoms are explained by the patient's tenuous masculine identification, often caused by difficult childhood relationships with demanding, critical, and successful fathers, according to Dr. Nicholi. The sons felt it hopeless to try to be like their fathers, and used their motorcycles to compensate for feelings of effeminacy and weakness.

Most motorcyclists, especially those gentlemen cyclists who acquired the cycling urge during the recent two-wheel boom, adamantly oppose theories about motorcycling that dig deeper than the clichéd picture of wind-ripped hair and roads twisting around mountains. Riding a motorcycle is like wearing a uniform or carrying a flag. And there can be no doubt about the symbolism: virility, masculinity, both fine and respectable attributes of American manhood. One wonders how many cyclists would be riding if such symbolism were not attached.

"Look man," a cross-country rider from San Francisco once remarked, "no matter who you are, the motorcycle makes you something special."

"I live in a suburban neighborhood," says a used car salesman from Pennsylvania. "Every Sunday my friends and I go riding. You should see how the women in that neighborhood stare when we get our bikes all revved up and ready to pull out. They're happily married women, most of them, but I'll bet I could have any one, if I'd take them for a ride. You better believe it."

"I really admire you," said a waitress to a cross-country cyclist in a Connecticut diner, "riding a motorcycle all over the country is almost legendary. It's the most exciting thing I can imagine."

Of course there are many reasons why people buy and ride motorcycles, reasons that are honest and obvious and sensible. Motorcycles pollute the air less, and move through and around traffic more smoothly than cars do. They are reliable, sell for a relatively low price and, depending on the size of the bike, can provide a ride of up to 150 miles for each gallon of gas. Motorcycles are easier and more economical to park, and even the largest bike will cost less to operate, on a day-to-day basis, than the smallest compact car on the road.

But motorcycles are generally considered a more dangerous means of travel. And Americans have never been the kind of people to risk their lives to save a few dollars, and those who truly worry about air pollution will pump a bicycle or walk. If motorcycles had only practical values to offer, they would have long ago died without distinction, following the course of the Edsel. Yet motorcycling becomes more popular every year. And more than anything else, more than Dr. Nicholi's Motor-cycle Syndrome, more than its sexual symbolism, this popularity has been triggered by an American absurdity, a classic example of a negative stimuli working positively.

The black leather jacket image. The sensational publicity wrought by the Hell's Angels in 1965. The belief that motorcycles are dangerous. That motorcycle riders are disrespectful, disruptive, dirty. The absolute contradiction of two-wheels operating within a four-wheeled society. Here is the frame to wrap around the picture of the motorcycle, the reason to hang the portrait of two wheels in place in the gallery of our culture.

Most Americans were initially offended by the Beatles in the early sixties—white young men wearing women's hair—yet those males seeking individuality, wanting to repudiate the sameness of looking respectably American, suddenly started to let their hair curl around their ears or hang limp to their shoulders. Women in pants, men with purses, the twist and the frug, were originally all expressions of a minority of people, usually the trend-setting young. The hotrodders of the forties, disgusting characters, were primarily responsible for the engines produced in Detroit in the fifties. The custom car artists of the fifties, equally disgusting, indirectly designed the automobile of the early sixties. From Elvis Presley, the Maximum Greaser, we got sideburns.

Each decade, we look for some other way of establishing our individuality—usually in a way counter to the culture. We covet and coddle such excesses until they become parts of our vastly expanding American lifestyle. Then we move onto something new. Yesterday it was the automobile, tomorrow it may be helicopters. And today, because of the movies and the super movie stars who ride them, because of the continual condemnation and criticism by the establishment—the motorcycle has become the key to and the symbol of contemporary self-expression.

Motorcycle Syndrome aside, it seems as though people, especially the older, more established people, thunder around on two-wheeled machines because it inflates their self image. A man on a motorcycle, shooting to the barber shop or zipping to the hardware store and back, is some kind of a middle-aged, middle-class hero, if not to anyone else, then at least to himself. As he sits high on his machine, gliding in the wind, visions of "Easy Rider" or the "Wild One" dance like leather-covered sugar plums in his head. He is daring, young in spirit, if not in years, Steve McQueen smiling haughtily, Marlon Brando mumbling inaudibly, flaunting danger, rejecting the values of his parents, his associates, his contemporaries—the classic example of the modern American individual.

Although Dr. Nicholi isolated the Motorcycle Syndrome in a small group of graduate students, Hunter Thompson has also found paralleling symptoms in the relationship of the motorcycle to the Hell's Angels:

"The whole—man and machine together—is more than the sum of its parts. His motorcycle is the one thing in life he has absolutely mastered. It is his only valid status symbol, his equalizer, and he pampers it the same way a busty Hollywood starlet pampers her body. Without it, he is no better than a punk on a street corner. And he knows it. The Angels are not articulate about many things, but they bring a lover's inspiration to the subject of bikes. Sonny Barger, a man not given to sentimental rambling, once defined the word 'love' as 'The feelin' you get when you like something as much as your motorcycle. Yeah, I guess you could say that was love.' "

Says a Los Angeles policeman about the Hell's Angels, quoted by Thompson: " 'They worship their motorcycles. They take them inside their homes at night. They sleep on grease-caked beds, but their bikes are spotless.' "

But neither Dr. Nicholi's study nor Hunter Thompson's observations are so all-encompassing nor so conclusive as to apply to a majority of motorcyclists.

"This syndrome," explains Dr. Nicholi, "involved a group of patients whose illnesses found expression in riding a motorcycle. Their conflicts were closely intertwined with the machine. Although the response I received from the publication of this article indicates that the syndrome is worldwide, it does not at all mean that it applies to everyone who rides a motorcycle."

Most cyclists are probably as emotionally stable and yet can be as idiosyncratic as anyone else. And a good psychiatrist could probably isolate similar mental failures and self-destructive tendencies in professional football players, boxers, or long distance runners. But the motorcycle, because it is an artificial extension of human potential, can and does affect man in more pronounced and provocative ways.

Five

There are always daredevils. They come part and parcel with automobiles, airplanes and sailing ships, underwater experiments, outer space expeditions and wars. The daredevils debate death with candor and deny the impossible with confidence. They bring new dimensions to spectators' tired lifestyles, give color to drab worlds, plug cords of excitement into sockets of hope and promise. The daredevils believe in Captain Marvel and Superman. They search for Aladdin's magic lamp and Rapunzel's golden hair. They believe they can dive or sail or crawl or burrow or tumble or jet, claw, leap or cannonade, over or under the earth or sea, toward riches and fame, happiness and love. They believe, with Theodore Roosevelt, that courage leads them toward the finest and most honorable of destinies.

"Far better it is," Roosevelt once said, "to take a chance to win glorious victory and triumph even though checkered by failure, than to take rank with those poor spirits who know no victory or defeat because they live in the grey twilight and have tried neither."

Many men dare death with motorcycles. They wear steel-toed shoes and ski behind their machines on asphalt. Or do hand stands on the handlebars at 100 miles an hour, crash through walls of fire, dive into burning swimming pools, get shot out of a cannon, or climb hills on one wheel while sitting backwards.

Some will dare death on behalf of other men. They work for movie studios and torpedo over cliffs and fall into rivers as doubles for Sean Connery, James Garner, or John Wayne. Others display their bravado as test riders for motorcycle manufacturers, spark plug companies, or petroleum refineries, experimenting with new products at 150 miles per hour, on snow or gravel or under 100 degree heat.

The lesser-known cycle daredevils might participate in the Cycle Circus at Saddleback Park in California's Orange County. There are jousting events, modified from the time of King Arthur, in which a man races to lance a ring hanging from a wire instead of trying to dump another man. There are mud hill climbs, contests to see how skillfully and accurately a man can ride on one wheel, and a motorcycle limbo event—somewhat of a high jump in reverse—testing how low a man can lean his bike under a pole at 25 or 30 miles per hour, without spilling or touching the ground. Motorcycle limbo is difficult and dangerous most of the time, but when the pole is lowered eighteen inches below the handlebars, it becomes near impossible. Yet men try.

Some cyclists are daring and successful enough to perform at amusement parks, during intermissions at rock concerts, or as the main event at speedways on an evening of stock car races and demolition derbies. But they must be very ingenious. And skillful enough at their craft to succeed, or fail with blood and gusto, almost everytime they try. Like Lee (Iron Man) Irons, who performs more than fifty times each year.

First Irons buckles a coal shovel blade to his rear. He will ease his Yamaha around the track until it is going at eighty or ninety miles an hour before setting the throttle steady. Then he slides off the back of the machine. And riderless, it pulls him, midst a tornado of flying sparks and fiery geysers, round and round the track for a couple of miles. Later Irons boils a barrel of water with his hot rump before he can take the shovel blade off.

Some cyclists like Agostino 'o Pazza, the Mad Motorcyclist of Napoli, dare authority as well as death. "Agostino the Madman" performed more than a dozen times in Italy in 1969 for crowds of up to 25,000 hero-worshipping Neopolitans, and sometimes as many as 2,000 pursuing police.

His act would usually end at the Piazza Trieste e Trento, right where the water shooting from the fountain in the center of the Piazza rains into the silvery granite pool below. Agostino, dressed in black, would barrel down the boulevard on his motorcycle, leap the curb and smash into the Via Roma Cafe, knocking over tables, chasing the suave continental diners, shooting saucers and wine glasses into the street. Back on the boulevard, he would charge cars going in the opposite direction, and then thunder into the Piazza to circle the fountain ahead of the pursuing police.

Sometimes Agostino would reverse his direction and turn his wailing machine on his pursuers. Riding with one hand, contemptuously flashing the middle finger of the other, he made them scamper behind trees and jump into the fountain like blue-suited bullfrogs.

Then, as a finale, the Madman performed what came to be known as "the Flight of the Angels." He stood on his motorcycle with one foot, spread out his other foot and both arms like a one-legged swan diver and, in that manner, thundered off into the night.

Agostino's real name is Antonio Mellino. He was caught by the police one evening while walking lazily through the Piazza. The police claimed he was working with a band of robbers who burglarized houses and held up businesses while the Madman diverted the law to the Piazza on the other side of the city. Agostino never confesssed, but was tried, convicted, and sent to jail.

Sooner or later, no matter how good the gimmick or how popular the performer, the serious "cycle psycho" will try to jump. For that seems to be the only satisfactory measure of just how good he really is. Like the Sergeant Major in the British Royal Artillery who, in 1970, claimed a world's record after hurtling on his motorcycle over the prone bodies of 41 of his widest, bravest men.

Or Steve Droste, who has jumped a dozen cars without the benefit of a landing ramp to smooth or soften his descent. Or Gary Davis and Rex Blackwell who have perfected what is called the double jump. They approach each other in opposite directions in mid-air, traveling at sixty or seventy miles an hour, and hanging two or three stories above the floor of the stadium. The object is to see how close they can pass without colliding, and often they have missed by less than three feet.

Then comes Gary Wells, who tours with his father in a $40,000 mobile home, performing all over the United States, Canada, Mexico, Germany, and Great Britain. The first time Wells went before a live audience he jumped a dozen cars and, to prove it was not a fluke, he pulled himself out of the dust and did it again. One time in Phoenix, Wells jumped fifteen cars and overshot the landing ramp by twenty feet. When he regained consciousness in the hospital he discovered he had gone 155 feet 10 inches through the air, a distance longer than half the length of a football field, longer by five feet than the previous world's record.

Some cycle psychos were fine athletes before turning to daredeviling. Steve Droste was a championship water skier, and Wells, in 1967, was winning steadily in small bike competitions and in motorcycle steeplechases.

In 1971 Iron Man Irons was twenty-one, Mellino was nineteen, and Steve Droste only eighteen. And at the time of his world record, Gary Wells was too young to qualify for his drivers license: he was only thirteen years old.

Daredevils don't often die natural deaths, unless being sandwiched between asphalt and molten machines, sliced by chains or shredded by violent contact with concrete are natural ways of dying for this particular and peculiar way of life. Many will be killed. Some, like the stunting Hell's Angels in California, are so committed to their machines that they are buried with them. Or their relatives and friends offer what is left of the man's motorcycle to the gods at a blazing midnight sacrifice in the desert.

Those that live can make a lot of money. Gary Wells demands $25,000 each time he agrees to jump. Droste receives $5,000, and Irons' going rate, probably because his act is not as spectacular or potentially as gory, is a little under $3,000.

Some daredevils don't make much money, but like all men living so tenuous a life, they dream. They dream amazing dreams of mountains of jewels and riches and fame and gold, and of the way to earn that mystical treasure with the supreme stunt, the unbeatable, unsurpassable triumph. To a daredevil, there is nothing cheaper than an old stunt. They are always searching for something never before conceived or completed. Like riding across Niagra Falls on a tightrope, or parachuting from an F-111 fighter bomber. Or maybe being launched into moon orbit, or chugging across the Atlantic, or crashing head-on into a barreling tractor trailer truck. They must keep their imaginations as alert as their defenses against death and reflexes from accidents. They must keep dreaming and hoping and praying for a brainstorm, a vision that will help them overtake The Man.

In every sport there is only one super-champ, one who is smarter and sometimes richer than all the rest combined. In baseball it is Willie Mays or Hank Aaron; in football, Joe Namath or Bart Starr, and in basketball perhaps it is Wilt the Stilt. And in motorcycling it is Evel Knievel, the stunter supreme—the greatest death-darer and devil-duster of them all.

Whatever Droste or Wells or Irons have accomplished, their deeds cannot even be measured on the same scale as the fantastic feats of Robert Craig Knievel, more commonly known as Evel Knievel (rhyme it—Evil Kaneevel).

There is hardly a way to describe him. Daredevil seems somehow an inadequate word. Cycle psycho, motorcycle maniac, the high-jumping, super-stunting, two-wheeling fool. He has been called almost everything, and nothing quite fits.

Evel Knievel has been hit in the groin by a motorcycle going 100 miles an hour. He has sailed, clutching a parasol, behind a motorcycle going even faster, crashed through thirty successive walls of fire in one afternoon, traveled five miles at 75 miles per hour on one wheel, jumped thirteen Cadillacs in a single bound. In one gigantic leap, he hurtled 21 cars parked side by side, two mountain lions, two pick-up trucks, and a crate of rattlesnakes. In Missoula, Montana, he shattered his left arm and all his ribs, and had such serious head injuries that the doctors had to wait two weeks before they considered it safe to operate. In Graham, Washington, he tried sixteen cars, made fifteen, and earned a brain concussion. Back in Graham less than a month later, he broke four ribs, cracked his left wrist, and smashed his right knee. In Seattle, a few months later, he broke his lower spine. And after rocketing over the ornamental fountains in front of Caesar's Palace in Las Vegas, the largest privately-owned fountains in the world, Knievel fell, drove his hipbone through his pelvis, and barreled, via back, belly, and crown, 165 feet across an asphalt parking lot. Weeks later, at Southern Nevada Memorial Hospital, they said he'd never walk again. But five months after, aided by crutches, a steel plate, and a plentitude of pins connecting hip and pelvis, Knievel hobbled onto a drag strip, mounted his motorcycle—and jumped thirteen cars.

"I'm the only guy in the world doing what I'm doing. I'm a jumping son-of-a-bitch. I'll jump anything. This summer [1970] I'm going to jump at Circus Circus, a new casino they're building at Vegas. They want me to jump the scoreboard at Soldier Field. I can jump Candlestick Park. I'm probably one of the most brilliant guys in the country as far as trajectory is concerned. Man, I can leap with a single bound."

Although Knievel has tried virtually everything possible with a motorcycle, his activities and accomplishments have not been limited to those performed on two wheels. He was a championship pole vaulter (once clearing 14 feet six inches), a paratrooper (he made thirty jumps during a four-year hitch), an amateur rodeo rider, and the Northern Rocky Mountain Ski Association Class A ski jumping champion. Knievel was general manager, coach, and superstar of the Butte Bombers semi-pro hockey club, and played one season for the Charlotte Clippers in the Eastern Hockey League. In one year, he was simultaneously a private detective, safe-cracker, card cheat, and swindler.

"If I had $20 for every safe I've peeled, I'd have a new Cadillac—and some of them didn't have any money in them. I can blow them, peel them, beat them. Floor safe, round door, square door, vault. I can crack a safe with one hand tied behind my back."

His confidence is continually reinforced by his apparent immunity to death and an unbelievable series of wild, but successful schemes and stunts. He walked from Montana to Washington, D.C. in 1961 carrying a set of antlers for President Kennedy in protest of the proposed slaughter of the rangeless elk roaming Yellowstone National Park. Two days later, the Department of the Interior agreed to have the elk trapped and transported to another home.

In Warm Springs, Montana, as a salesman for the Combined Insurance Company of America, he sold 110 three-dollar policies to the staff of the state mental institution—in one day. He sold 271 policies in that week.

As a Honda dealer in Moses, Washington, he advertised $100 off the price of a motorcycle to anyone able to beat him at arm wrestling. Not even when he offered a free motorcycle could anybody succeed.

Unlike those of most daredevils, many of Knievel's dreams and ambitions have come true. He jumped doors and buckets on his two-wheel bicycle behind his grandfather's garage when he was ten. Now he jumps cars. When the father of the girl he loved refused to allow him to see her, he kidnapped the girl. Now she is his wife. He dreamed of driving big, beautiful cars. Now he owns a cream-colored stationwagon, a mobile head-quarters with air-conditioning, padded bar, draft beer dispenser, and zebra-striped carpeting, and a purple Rolls Royce ("I've always wanted a purple Rolls Royce. Everyone should have a purple Rolls Royce.") with a telephone and a bar inside. He makes more than $100,000 a year from jumping alone, has had a successful movie based on his life and two songs written about him (one performed by a midget band). He has been the subject of hundreds of magazine articles, a frequent guest on national television programs and, on a recent visit to New York, he purchased 65 pairs of pants to go with the 100 shirts he carries wherever he travels.

And yet, at 32, Evel Knievel also dreams of the stunt supreme. He once wanted to jump the Grand Canyon, but the Department of the Interior refused him permission. So he leased his own canyon for $25,000 on the Snake River, near Twin Falls, Idaho, a chasm with a mouth 1,300 feet deep and lips three quarters of a mile apart.

On the site, a quarter mile approach road leads to a ramp, 67 feet high and 440 feet long, made from 100,000 tons of salt from the Bonneville Salt Flats. Knievel will mount his Harley-Davidson-equipped Olympia X-2 Sky Cycle. Wearing a snow-white skin-tight leather suit with red and blue trim and stars on his helmet, he will be screaming at 200 miles an hour when he reaches the base of the ramp. He will hit 250 miles an hour before his wheels disconnect from the salt and the earth. And 1,500 feet of clean mountain air later, he should be soaring at the rate of a little more than seven miles per second.

At that point, his tracking team will buzz him by radio, and if he has the right trajectory he will complete the mission. To scrub, he will use a parachute landing system. If go, the parachute will be used to safely drop him on the other edge of the canyon, handlebars up for a picture-perfect one-wheeled landing—a finale certainly befitting the Evel Knievel tradition.

The tradition: super thrills for super money. He says he is selling the television rights for more than $1 million. It will be a real festival, three days of motorcycling prior to the jump, with Knievel owning the concessions, selling Evel Knievel buttons and pennants and shirts and magazines. Even before the scalpers go to work, canyon-side seats will be on the market for $100 or more.

And in the Sky Cycle, the machine that will generate 1,400 pounds of pressure at 240 degrees, there is a secret weapon: Tumwater. Tumwater is one of the fine ingredients that makes Olympia Beer so good, Evel will tell you. He will also tell you that the Olympia Brewing Company of Tumwater, Washington is one of his major sponsors.

The Evel Knievel super tradition for super suicide:

"One," says Knievel, "the machine could come apart and tumble and kill me. Two, when I hit the bottom of the ramp and throw the jets on, one might not fire, and I'd go cartwheeling off the ramp at such an incredible speed I don't think a man could keep his equilibrium. Three, if the motorcycle's not basically stable and starts to tumble or spin at 300 miles an hour, I'd better be in damn good shape. Four, when it comes time to get off, I hope I have my senses so I *can* get off. I'd also like to come off on top, so that when my parachute opens the motorcycle doesn't come through me. . . . There is a chance of a head-on collision with the opposite rim of the canyon." Splat.

Nor does the great Evel know whether his parachuting system will work, or if the net 1,300 feet below the canyon rim will hold him. He is staking his life on the speculation of engineers and on his own uncanny ability to survive.

"I don't care if they say 'Look kid, you're going to drive that thing off the edge of the canyon and die.' I'm going to do it. I want to be the first. If they let me go to the moon, I'd crawl all the way to Cape Kennedy just to do it. I'd like

to go to the moon, but I don't want to be the second man
to go there."

Before each jump, he waits until the parking lot is full,
the grandstand bulging, and the hotdog and souvenir vendors
have doubled their daily sales. He waits near the lockers inside
the stadium, or hidden in a hotel room, sipping Wild Turkey
bourbon, while outside in the bleachers and private boxes
people begin to doubt whether the great Evel Knievel will
do his death trick that day. He waits while fans demand refunds,
get dizzy from too much beer under the too hot sun, and
cannonade the empty cans down on the empty track. He waits
while they shriek through saliva-foamed lips for him to "show-
up or throw-up" and still Evel waits.

Then suddenly, when faith has almost been abdicated to
the heat, he walks out toward the skeletal microphone on the
platform near the ramp, in the red and blue silver leathers
with the stars and stripes and neat little American designs
sparkling patriotically from his chest and back, and he says,
"Where you people been? I been waitin' for ya!"

And that is when everybody goes crazy. Because they know
he is there. They know he is going to jump. They know he
might break himself. They know he might die.

Maybe 5,000 people wait for Evel Knievel on those afternoons
when he plays his games. But today, he has manipulated a
much larger audience. From London to Borneo, half the world
is waiting for him now.

There was really never any hope of Knievel getting permission
to jump the Grand Canyon on his motorcycle in 1968, according
to Department of the Interior spokesmen, yet he steadfastly
held to his commitment until very near the fatal date. Then
he opted for Devil's Canyon, that three-quarter mile gap over
the Snake River in Idaho, near Twin Falls. He leased the
canyon for three years for $25,000 and set a proposed target
jumping date of sometime in 1970. Which became sometime
in 1971. Which was cancelled on behalf of Labor Day 1972.
Which has now been pushed back to Memorial Day 1973.

Contrary to many people's beliefs, Evel's Sky Cycle is ready
to roll and to leap, and its proficiency, at least on the ground,
has been satisfactorily tested. The details of the jump have

been sophisticated and mathematically confirmed by engineers who have worked for the National Aeronautics and Space Administration on the moon shot. And the approach ramp is ready for launching time—whenever that may be. Even Evel, although hobbled by a few minor injuries, was in better condition in May 1972, when he announced the most recent postponement, than at any time in the past years. Nobody really seems to know what is going on, except for the man himself, who is not saying. But many are guessing.

One explanation comes from a publisher of a prominent motorcycle magazine who claims that Evel is fighting for his life. Or more specifically, he is fighting for more time to live and more money for his family to live on once he is gone. "I think Evel is convinced jumping the Snake River is impossible," says the publisher. "I don't think it's a death wish, it's realistic. I think he's milking the idea now, demanding more money for his smaller jumps, preparing an autobiography to be published in conjunction with the jump, and a sequel to the first financially-successful movie based on his life."

Even Lloyds of London won't insure Evel Knievel's life for this jump, so he will continue to postpone until his lease on Devil's Canyon runs out. Or so the theory goes. And if he can get an extension on the lease, he will postpone the jump a few more times until both pride and public pressure confront him with the final choice of jumping or forever sitting down.

No one has yet publically admitted the possibility that Evel will not jump. But that could very well be the best bet of all.

This is the age of the hoax. *Life* magazine serialized the late Nikita S. Khrushchev's memoirs in 1970, which Khrushchev denied writing. Yet, the million or so dollars stockpiled for his payment in a Swiss bank has mysteriously disappeared. And Clifford Irving, the pseudo-biographer of Howard Hughes, became more prominent and eventually, after a brief term in jail, will probably be wealthier dealing in deception than his skills could have ever earned him dealing with the truth.

Evel Knievel could do worse. He could jump tomorrow or the day after and splatter himself across the bottom of the 1,300-foot deep canyon. In the name of glory. Or he could keep fiddling with the frustrations of an America hungry for an honest-to-goodness super-hero while his assets continue to inflate.

And he could get away with it, far more easily than Clifford Irving, without relinquishing his honor or his freedom. No one would ever accuse Evel Knievel of cowardice because of what he has accomplished in the past. For Knievel is, and probably will always remain, the genuine, All-American, 100 percent God of Thrills. And he need not do any more, he need not hurtle as much as a kiddie car, to permanently bask in the glory of this reputation.

"The people I want to hear about are the people who take risks," Robert Frost has written. The poet could have also written that the risk mustn't necessarily threaten death or destruction. For the craftiest men often live in luxury long after the bravest men have died in vain.

Six

Theresa Wallach is not a daredevil, but she is among the most courageous and hearty cyclists of all. She owns a motorcycle shop at 2612 E. 75th Street in Chicago, but she is more interested in giving motorcycle riding lessons than in selling two-wheeled machines. It takes courage as well as an adventuresome spirit to ride alongside novices and instruct them on the finer points of cycling. There is nothing wilder than a runaway cycle with an inexperienced and usually petrified cowboy aboard. But that is not where Theresa Wallach first showed her bravery and persistence, nor why she is today called "the first lady of motorcycling."

Born in Wembley, England half a century ago, Miss Wallach baffled her conservative parents who had piano playing and raising children in mind for their daughter, by becoming the first woman engineering student at the University of London. And she baffled her classmates by disappearing between classes, instead of walking from building to building, talking about boys and dances and books.

"I'd go down to the boilerhouse, around and out the other side, past where the boys parked their motorcycles," she has said. Like in the movies, the pretty girl met the handsome man, Stephen Turner, and although they never got married to complete the scenario, he did teach her how to ride his BSA motorcycle, and helped her buy one of her own. She was living on the family farm and commuting to college by train, and for the first couple of weeks, so that her parents wouldn't find out, she would ride the bike the fifty miles from Wembley to London and back, hide the motorcycle, and walk into the family farm at train time. She left home soon after her father discovered her two-wheeled machine.

In 1932, she tuned her BSA, raised the compression ratio, changed the tires, and won her first trophy race. In the subsequent four years, working by day as an electrical tester and racing on weekends and at night, Miss Wallach won additional trophies for trial competitions, hillclimbs and 24-hour endurance runs. All of that experience only stimulated her appetite for more cycling and in 1936, along with a friend, Florence "Blenky" Blenkiron, she rode south from Algiers, through the Sahara south to the Cape and South Africa.

It is 1,600 miles of blowing sand and blistering sun across the Sahara. There were six oases, some as many as 500 miles apart, and the going was slow, since the cycles were loaded with equipment and supplies. The gritty sand sucked into the cycle's lubrication system, forcing them to replace a crankshaft. But they still kept going.

"Sometimes a good day was twelve miles," says Theresa Wallach, "and much of it was walking. You could recognize the hard patches of ground by their darker color, so we'd go prospecting, then unload everything, carry it to the next hard patch, and push the machines. We sometimes wondered if it wasn't a walking tour."

Theresa Wallach saw something similar to the Sahara a few years ago, when the United States televised man's first landing on the moon: "The moon has the same sort of mountains and soft dust. The only difference between the moon and the Sahara is that we had air." It took almost a year to move from Algiers south on their motorcycles, down and around the old red road to the Cape, where they were personally greeted in Pretoria, South Africa by Premier Jan Smuts.

In subsequent years, Theresa Wallach became the first and only woman to exceed 100 miles per hour on a motorcycle at England's famous Brooklands track. In World War II, as a sergeant in the British army, she became the first woman motorcycle dispatch rider. But neither blazing speed nor blazing among the bombs could make Theresa Wallach forget the joy and the freedom of a motorcycle on an open road. In 1947, she set her motorcycle down for the first time on the soil of the United States.

She rode first to Niagara Falls to compare it with South Africa's Victoria Falls. She thought it would be an easy short ride because it was only two inches on the map from New York City. ("The maps are half an inch to the mile in England," she explains.) But it took her two days.

Theresa Wallach went through Canada, and down into Michigan, Indiana, and Illinois. She headed west, sleeping in her tent, looking at one interesting place and then another, working when she needed money, wandering when she got it. Working and wandering, for more than a year, became the rhythm of her life. She met Black Horse, the famous Sioux Chief, and posed for a picture with him sitting on her motorcycle; she dabbed her toe in the Pacific, remained in Santa Monica for a while before heading east, singing "Deep in the heart of Texas" over and over again as she rode along across the hot Texas plain. It was an odyssey many men and women don't even permit themselves to dream about, a fantasy almost too pure to be real. Theresa Wallach never could forget it. Nor could she forget the land she crossed, and in 1951 she moved her belongings and her life from England, settling permanently in Chicago, the heart of the middle of the United States.

To Theresa Wallach and to others, riding a motorcycle is like riding a dream. And for many, the impeccable dream is the one that takes you over and across the country—one that permanently molds your soul to the machine.

More than 40 percent of all motorcyclists are touring bikers. Touring means country riding, highway running, heavy traveling. It means long, winding roads, wild winds, and machines wailing like turbines, strung out over macadam and concrete. Touring could mean as much as a three-year parole from the rigors and clichés of the metropolis. It could mean as little as an afternoon's sabbatical from civilization. Although the majority of touring bikers are conservative travelers, exploring tiny pockets of rural America in their home city's backyards on weekend afternoons, some of the more adventurous will go almost anywhere.

Starting in New York, some touring cyclists have climbed into Canada and roped their way across the provinces. Guided by faint green lines on oil company maps, they have looped down through Saskatchewan into Montana, Wyoming, Colorado. Or, from Vancouver, they have slipped across the border and rolled over the coastal highway to Los Angeles.

One group of touring bikers rides the coastal highway regularly and has been for twenty years or more. The club has no name, but everyone meets at a certain cycle shop, where free donuts and coffee are served, for what is called simply, "The Sunday Morning Ride." The bikers, maybe twenty in all, swallow the coffee while the steam burns the Saturday night fog from their eyes and throats. The first engine comes to life at about 8:14 and in another minute everyone else is ready and rolling in pairs and in threes down the road that leads to the coastal highway cut-off.

The houses stop, the trees begin. There are straightaways, and there are roads that curve around and up and down the rolling hills. The moist air coming in from the ocean casts droplets of water over the goggles and shields of the riders. The morning air is cold, and shoulders hunch over to cut off the wind. The road twists and turns, from ridge to valley, inland then toward the sea. The riders float under the redwood and eucalyptus trees, the whole forest seems to be hanging over them, and upon emerging, they can see the blue sea. Sometimes they can see boats from the San Francisco fishing fleets cutting white lines over the blue, but most riders are too busy flinging their machines back and forth along the twisting roadway to look. But it is there. It is sometimes just as important merely to know what is around you as it is to see it. The men ride on Sunday mornings along the coastal highway near the Tamalpais Valley in California not just because of the scenery. It is something more private, something having to do with the emotions, hardened by a tough week, that are released by the force of the wind; the feeling of freedom of two roaming wheels, that lessen the frustration of city life and the problems bred by it.

Departing California, other bikers with more time pull up in Tucumcari, Mexico. They roll into Yucatan; they start in Alaska, bisect the United States, cruise the Pan American Highway, confronting the winding mountain roads, the boulders and washouts, the spartan conditions of the Central American countryside, to camp in the Argentine.

From Florida, some bikers connect Nova Scotia. From Paris, they roll toward the Suez. Because motorcycles are not inhibited by delicate steering mechanisms and useless pounds of foam rubber and chrome, they will go almost anywhere. Touring bikers have spliced deserts to mountains, blizzards to palm trees, rivers to arid plains. They can squeeze through narrow gullies, ride over covered footbridges, climb up and out of dead-end ravines. Depending on local law and the health and personality of his machine, a cyclist could travel across the country almost as the crow flies.

Most touring bikers remain in the United States. But others creep into connecting countries and some even ship their machines across oceans to ride the roads and tilt the earth from a different, a faraway perspective. Many college-age people do this to save money on transportation and conserve the time it would take to hitchhike. And since motorcycles are less expensive in Europe, a cyclist can buy his machine from a cycle shop or through the mail while he is in the United States, pay Continental prices, and have his cycle waiting for him in any of a dozen European countries.

Malcolm F. Goodwin of Gunnison, Colorado, tried this in September 1970 and claims to have received a one-month European vacation and a brand new BMW 75/5 motorcycle for a total of $171.28 more than the machine, minus the vacation, would have cost him in the United States.

His expenses, as outlined in the January 1972 issue of *Cycle World,* included:

$ 331.70	for transportation from Gunnison to Stuttgart and return
299.31	for European transportation, food and lodging
218.27	for motorcycle license, insurance, terminal service, and import duties
1220.00	factory price of motorcycle at Munich
$2069.28	total cost of month's trip plus motorcycle

From this figure, Goodwin then subtracted the price of the same motorcycle if purchased in Denver, $1898.00. And concluded with a net cost and 4,000 miles in Europe, of $171.28.

"The net cost could have been reduced," he writes, "well below the $171.28 by taking a stand-by fare from Denver to Chicago, a savings of $20, and by taking the shorter bus route from Denver to Gunnison, saving $4, not to mention European lodging in youth hostels, an indeterminate savings. It must also be assumed that staying at home for a month would cost something, which was not taken into consideration, and would be saved while in Europe. More leisurely travel, covering fewer miles, would also reduce expenses."

Jeffrey Crane, a cyclist from Salt Lake City, was even more economical. He financed his European-purchased motorcycle in the United States, paid student air fares to London and then cycled and camped across the continent. When he returned he sold his motorcycle for $400 more than it cost him in Europe.

"I paid back my loan, he explained, and when I figured all my expenses, I came up with a $26 cost for a European vacation."

There are also "Mo Tours," co-sponsored by travel agent Edison Dye and KLM Royal Dutch Airlines for cyclists too lazy to plan their own itinerary or too insecure to travel alone.

For a few hundred dollars more than the price of a certain brand of motorcycle in the United States, a touring biker will receive the same motorcycle in Europe, a monogrammed jacket and helmet, meals, accommodations, and a choice of ten organized motorcycle tours of Europe or the Mediterranean. A cyclist could ride to Monte Carlo, to the Olympics, or to the LeMans. From May through September, he could rally in Scandinavia, Alpinia, or the Isle of Man. Each year, many cyclists on organized tours, run, like helmeted Hemingways, from the bulls in Pamplona. A competent mechanic, a practicing physician, and three beautiful female guides are included with the price of some tours.

Some touring cyclists plan very exotic expeditions. In 1969, Frank Fanger, Russ Rehm, and Dick Ewing crossed the Sahara on Harley Davidson Rapidos. In 1970 John Warren, a veteran of the Vietnam War, started in Singapore. Skirting water buffaloes and rice paddies, he toured Malaysia, Thailand, and Cambodia, before returning to Singapore, traveling 3,000 slow, oriental miles in three short months.

And then there are the two men from Pittsburgh, Dick Beck, a physical education instructor, and James Joseph, an accountant, modern Ferdinand Magellans, who spanned Europe, Africa, and Australia on motorcycles—a distance of more than 13,000 miles. Although traveling cross-country on any vehicle, especially motorcycles, is inherently dangerous, Beck and Joseph while in Africa came across native terrorists, hostile border guards, and poisonous flies. Their closest call, however, was a collision with the deadly African green mamba snake.

It was nearing evening, the fading sun mixing with the clouds of dust on the bumpy road leading to Blantyre, Malawi. Jim Joseph was leading and his cycle hit an object that looked like a long stick. Suddenly, the object coiled. It was a snake, but Beck, behind Joseph, running at about forty miles per hour, had no other choice but to keep going. The reptile coiled again on impact, struck the back tire of Beck's motorcycle, missing his bare leg by inches. Later, the natives in Blantyre told Beck that to be bitten by a poisonous mamba was to be dead in twenty minutes.

Most touring bikes are heavy, powerful machines, costing anywhere from $1,500 to $3,000. Built for fast speeds, and long, smooth roads, they are awkward to handle in the city, difficult to manuever in tight traffic situations, too heavy to lean around a curve comfortably at under 25 miles per hour. Touring machines might weigh up to 1,000 pounds, fully equipped, and be charged with more than 100 horses.

Although some people will tour on lighter weight machines, the intelligent biker will select a cycle durable enough to hold the road against bumps, potholes, strong winds, and rain. Bikes with thick tires and power to quickly run away from dangerous situations. Bikes that are strong enough to pull in high altitudes when the thinness of the air chokes and suffocates the carburetors of weaker, less sophisticated machines. Bikes with soft seats on which a man or two men can comfortably sit out a day, which can carry fiberglass saddlebags, 100 pounds of clothing, camping equipment, souvenirs, and cameras.

In 1971, 49-year-old Perry R. Gilbert and his friend Bob Myers, a motorcycle dealer from Bladensburg, Maryland, carried themselves and their wives on motorcycles from June 24 to July 12 across the British Isles. John Warren reports that people touring in Malaysia carry whole families across country on motorcycles —in addition to baskets of fruit and coops stuffed with chickens.

And John Miller, a well-known touring biker from California, carries his goggled, 55-pound Chow/German Shepherd known as "Baron Von Red Dog" on his back, riding from place to place on their 1,000 cc Vincent Black Shadow.

Other tourists carry things that aren't so tangible. Emulating Pony Express riders, they bring spiritual mail or political messages from one end of America to the other. They find that people will listen to their messages more attentively and regard them with greater awe when the speakers have traveled on two-wheeled machines. Like the Reverend Stanley George, who carries the words and love of Christ to young people across the United States and Canada. Or Specialist Fourth Class Douglas Reitmeyer and Michael Speegle of the United States Army, who cruised the country in 1971 to tell American boys how a strong professional army can prevent war and stop killing.

Touring cycles have also gone to war. Submachine gun-equipped motorcycle scouts were an integral part of the Army armored divisions during World War II. And one of the first Yanks to enter Germany in 1918 was on a Harley Davidson with a sidecar.

Touring bikers represent a more mature wing of cycling society. You need plenty of money to buy a good touring bike. And money for such luxuries is mostly lodged in the pockets of those with the experience to earn it and the time to accumulate it. Touring bikers are older today because when they started with motorcycles, a decade or more ago, there were only big machines to ride. There were few smaller bikes before Honda invaded America in 1961 and veterans have not been able to get used to the new "pop cycles," preferring rather to sharpen their talents and have their fun on the machines they know best.

Since touring is a more gentlemanly, less-physical activity, tourists stay on the highway or hard road, rather than stumble through the woods. Woods riding means falling and bruises and dirt and mud. Many consider it brutal, savage, and styleless. Road riding is a cleaner exhilaration. A road rider will siphon his pleasure from the country, the smoothness of winding roads, body rhythm, and great speed.

It is the establishment's way of motorcycling, although tourists do not possess the power and influence of the motorcycle establishment. A touring biker is usually a part-time-do-it-when-I-get-a-chance kind of biker. He can save a week or two weeks time to ride, but at irregular intervals, and he is usually too busy with other things to ride with any consistency. He lacks the time and patience to devote his energies to motorcycling because of his position in the community and the responsibilities of his job. So the power base of the motorcycle industry lies with the fanatics who sell motorcycles, or race for a living in regular professional amateur competitions. Of the many AMA member-managed executive committees, only one relates primarily to people who ride the open road.

And yet, more and more touring bikes are sold and more and more cyclists become tourists every year. That's partially because Americans have always hungered for gargantuan machines. Nothing has ever been powerful enough for Johnny and the rest of the boys who come marching home every week or two with their money. But more so, as racers and woods riders mature, find families brightened by children, guarded by fuzzy little dogs, they become increasingly concerned with their own well-being. At the same time, they grow more affluent. So they buy heavier, more expensive, more comfortable, cleaner, safer machines, and join their contemporaries on the road.

Though touring bikers have traveled almost everywhere, the vast majority are too burdened with the responsibilities of day-to-day living to zip back and forth across the continent of the United States.

Yet for those who try, nothing will ever replace the joy of it. For cross-country cycling is the only remaining adventure truly accessible to modern, middle-class man.

Seven

The first recorded motorcycle race took place in 1897, as reported by the *Horseless Vehicle Journal*, when W. J. Stocks ran second in a two-vehicle competition, losing by 300 yards to a gentleman pedaling a bicycle.

At the turn of the century, both Britain and France were leading the world in motorcycle development and possessing the finest machines, and fastest riders became a question of national honor. Britain defeated France at the first international meet in 1903 and took the £1,000 prize. In the same year, Harry Martin rode a 2¾-horsepower Excelsior a full mile, from a standing start, in one minute, 24 seconds. In 1904, France, Britain, Austria, Germany, and Denmark competed in the first international cup race, sponsored by the Federation Internationale des Clubs Motocyclistes.

The elimination trials to select a team to represent England in the Internationale were held at the Isle of Man. The Man government imposed no speed limits on roads and had nothing against closing off highways for a competition that would bring people and money to its island. In 1907, the Isle of Man became the location for the first and most spectacular act in what was soon to become known as the Continental Circus.

Sixty-five years after the first Tourist Trophy (TT) road race, with dozens of races now run at diferent sites on the Continent each year as part of motorcycling's Grand Prix Circuit, competition on the Isle of Man is still the most popular, prestigious, and arduous of all.

For the committed cyclist, the Man competition is a night-mare of great purity. There are 219 distinct bends for each 37¾ mile lap, and seven laps to live through. Two hundred sixty-four miles of backcountry bumps, bordered by behemoth stone walls, masonry rails, and pockets of fenceless thousand-foot drops.

Beginning at Douglas, the course grades down a series of plateaus where side streets cross, leading to a hairpin just past Bradden Bridge. Past Ballagarey, Crosby, past Greeba, the riders rocket at 150 miles per hour down hills, slamming into S-curves at 110. They fly past Greeba Castle and Ballig Bridge and Cronky Voddee, boring into wet winds slapping their faces and shoulders, flat out and full throttle, generating friction and energy that literally lofts them up over the hard, old roadway.

Past Mountain Mile they see the clouds and almost immediately are swallowed by them. The roadway is fogged with a kind of celestial white mist, and the riders are vague features that sway and bend and mingle with the fog and trees. Often there is sleet. Or rain and 100 mile per hour wind. Sometimes there is a blowout, and a glowing hot engine will tornado over the side, leaving a fading tail of yellow hanging above the mountain long after the machine has exploded below.

Down the mountain, the rest of the riders needle the final hairpin past Governor's Bridge. And flat out at 130 miles per hour or more, they press bullet-like against the gas tank, pushing for inches more headway on the first lap flag—all the while knowing there are six more laps to go.

In 1964, there were 64 racers at the first lap, with 45, including members of a dozen factory-sponsored teams, abdicating for various reasons before the last was completed. Eleven more were disqualified for not participating up to the quality required for Isle of Man competition. Among the eight men and machines finishing, Jim Redmon broke a course record by averaging 97.45 miles per hour for all seven laps. Redmon received the silver winner's trophy that year, but seven bronze replicas were awarded to those who finished for having run an excellent contest on the toughest road racing track in the world.

It is hard to tell how the Continental Circus started, slipped between two world wars and hundreds of border and trade disputes. In 1914, a number of riders from many different countries registered for the French TT, but it was cancelled because of the outbreak of war. It finally ran in 1920, followed in the next five years by similar events in Belgium, Ireland, Italy, Holland, and Germany.

Except perhaps for the Isle of Man, which is as pure and hellish as any course devised, the tracks are equally difficult, but in different ways. At the Assen circuit in Holland, the road wriggles through 4¾ miles of private and public road. In some places the roadway is no wider than a bicycle path, with deep ditches on both sides, cut sharply into the edge of the asphalt and concrete.

The course is longer and straighter at Francorchamps, near Span in Belgium, and tests more the swiftness of machines than the skill of their riders. The West German Grand Prix is moved occasionally, but it is most challenging when held at Nurburgring. There are 170 bends and corners, snaking riders over fourteen miles of gradients, bridges, varying camber and road surfaces. Situated in a park, Monza in Italy is the most beautiful of the Continental courses, with sweeping curves and few tight corners, allowing the rider to burn rubber with little worry. But in France, Clermont Ferrand allows no straightaway longer than 650 yards.

Sachsenring in East Germany, Fisco in Japan, Dunrod in Ireland, Brands Hatch in England. There are links to the Continental Circus in Czechoslovakia, Sweden, Finland and Spain. In the United Staates, you visit Daytona Beach, Florida, for the 200-mile classic.

Daytona is the most important race in the world. It was motorcycling's first super-speedway and has always been its fastest track. Because Daytona is the first race to be held every year, it marks the only time in the season when the best riders are sure to be healthy and factory teams and equipment at full strength. In 1971 Daytona generated more interest in the foreign press than any single link in cycledom's Grand Prix, including the Isle of Man.

It is a smooth bowl of speed, 3.8 miles long, and banked 310 feet on the far edge to increase traction and ease in cornering. Tough for the rider, the course is torturous for the machine. Because of the banking, the bikes are burned wide open for a good part of the course, which often means a steady 170 miles per hour for almost an hour, through the whole race and the consequences in engine temperatures, frame vibration, and brake fade.

In 1964, the same year Jim Redmon averaged 97.45 miles per hour on the Man track, Mike Hailwood broke the world's one hour cycle speed record at Daytona by averaging 145.2 miles per hour per lap. Now men are tickling 175 miles per hour and more.

Although auto drivers at Indianapolis or Watkins Glen have recorded even higher speeds per lap, there can be no comparison. The cars are fifty times more powerful than motorcycles, their drivers tucked in foam bucket seats, belted away from the wind and the dust. In motorcycle racing the rider is not a supplement to the machine, but an equal part of the racing process. No wheels turn into narrow hairpins, the man's body must lean into the speed. The weight and agility of the man, and the rhythm generated by man working in unison with machine, is the measure of success or failure, life or death.

Every large motorcycle manufacturer in the world either supports his own team or is indirectly subsidizing an independent crew. The factories, sometimes representing countries, seem to take turns being supreme. One will work hard and invest money to gather in the glory. With the glory comes publicity. With publicity come sales and profits. With profits assured, there is often complacency, and another company assumes the advantage.

Frenchmen were originally responsible for the development and sophistication of the early motorcycle, and the French, in the beginning, naturally dominated the racing circuit. The British, soon after snaring the finest TT at the Isle of Man, overtook the French both in mechanical and riding ability. Englishmen on their Triumphs and Nortons won regularly in virtually every racing circuit for nearly three decades. Then the Germans, spurred by the Bavarian Motor Works—BMW—shattered British motorcycling prestige. BMW, a manufacturer of aircraft engines, hadn't made a motorcycle until 1923. But the company developed a twin-cylindered machine that has yet to be equalled or radically altered in the subsequent 45 years. In the last senior TT, before competition was interrupted by the Second World War, a German cyclist on a supercharged BMW finished two minutes and twenty seconds ahead of his nearest challenger. The Italian Guizis and Gileras dominated from 1950 to 1957. Guizi, most especially, added a new dimension to the science of motorcycle design by constructing a wind tunnel to test wind resistance and develop a more efficient body shape.

Today, it is the Japanese. In 1962, Honda established sixteen new world racing records in the 25 races the company entered. In 1970, less than a year after its introduction, the Honda four-cylindered 750 cc won the Daytona classic. Now Suzuki, Yamaha, and Kawasaki are burning into the racing circuit, and it seems to be only a matter of time before they will win the prestige.

There are events in the Continental Circus for motorcycles as small as 50 cc. Although larger machines are faster, smaller cycles are more difficult to control. The wider tires of a big motorcycle can more easily handle bumps and rocks. The stronger frame can bang into other bikes, scrape against walls and possibly stay upright, hold fast in heavy rain and wind, and stay glued to the sharpest corners. But lighter bikes are merely wisps in the wind, especially at seventy or eighty mile-per-hour racing speeds. On a track a rider must avoid minor obstructions; he must work much harder because there is much less machine with which to share the burden. And he must realize that at those speeds he is riding a machine that is as vulnerable and fragile as a long-stemmed crystal glass.

Motorcycle sidecar competition is an entirely different proposition of riding and staying alive. From the air, it looks like a trotting horse pulling a sulky with rider sideways. The racing sidecars, called chairs, have very little resemblance to the ice cream man's freezer compartment or the traveler's passenger seat. Sidecars are reduced to mere platforms, and the fall guy, the passenger, to a leathern monkey. All three wheels are equipped with brakes, but the rear wheel is the source of power. The pilot on the cycle has the rather elementary job of operating the controls and keeping up the speed, but the second man makes up for the agility and grace the rig characteristically lacks. On a corner, he will extend his body over the road, often low enough to scrape his leathers on the speeding concrete. In

1964, at the Isle of Man, one crew member was killed on a practice run. Hours later, a second sidecar pilot was lopped off his platform when one rig tried to pass another on a bridge.

Sidecar competition is dominated by Continental riders. Americans see it as an awkward and unfulfilling aspect of motorcycle competition, lacking the streamlined qualities, the smoothness in rhythm of a man alone with his machine.

Motorcycle sprinting, a race of acceleration over a measured distance, usually no more than a quarter mile, is very popular in Great Britain. The bikes, at a standing start, build up engine revolutions with clutches out. When the machine is heated and roaring, the rider slams the clutch in and the bike literally blasts off, leaving a black line of smelling, smouldering rubber down the track.

The English sprint (called dragging in America) on abandoned airstrips and stretches of deserted beach, mostly on the island's eastern shore. But generally, in such a small and densely populated country, there are few unused lines of smooth, hard road long and straight enough to provide the starting and stopping room that would allow Englishmen to seriously consider attempting to break the world's record for what is known as "the flying mile."

That is one of the reasons Americans dominate in motorcycle speed accomplishments. For in Utah, 120 miles west of Salt Lake City, lies the lonely white crystaline speedway known as the Bonneville Salt Flats.

Except for wagon tracks—tracks made by pioneers who crept across the salt a century ago racing evaporating water supplies—Bonneville is barren, incapable of supporting anything but man's insatiable desire to defeat time. It is said that a bird wandering aimlessly into this brilliant mirror of sun and salt is doomed to perish, lost forever without water or food, or the capacity to fly up high enough to see a way out. And yet men come.

At Bonneville, where 100 miles is like stopping at a red light, men on both two- and four-wheeled land rockets have been going against the clock for decades. At Bonneville, no matter how hot or uncomfortable, men from all over the world come for the pure joy of going as fast as they please and chipping, like delicate sculptors, a few seconds off the clock of speed.

They are men like Germany's William Herz who, in 1956, first brought the official world's two-wheeled speed record to the United States soil by barreling 189 miles an hour down the two-mile track. Two months later, on a different bike, Herz increased his record by 21 miles per hour. Also, men like Cal Rayborn who, in 1970 on a Harley Davidson, shattered all previous two-wheel speed records, by achieving 265.492 miles per hour. And cyclenaut Bob Leppan, a former bicycle racer, who has reportedly designed a two-wheeled machine, the Gyronaut X-1, is aiming at hitting more than 300 miles per hour and breaking the 1971 record held by the Honda Hawk. Powered by two turbo-charged 750 cc Honda four cylindered engines, the Hawk beat Rayborn and Harley's short-lived accomplishment by barreling over the hot sand and salt at 286.7 miles per hour. Purportedly, it eventually will exceed 311 miles per hour.

The men look like astronauts and the machines are silver cigars. Riders climb into cockpits, rest their heads on padded cushions while their assistants and helpers and friends close the hatch that seals in the heat. Then there are two miles of fire and hell, within which each man attempts to clutch the tail at the edge of time.

Eight

Louisville Downs, Ascot Park, or Roosevelt Raceway. Or DeQuoin or Hammond or Nazareth or any of the hundreds of tracks that string together an American motorcycle racer's year. None of the glamor and tinsel of the Continental Circus, none of the flavor of foreign lands and fanatically dedicated people gathering around the circuit 24 hours in advance to get a good seat. This is America, where everything happens fast and new things begin before old things have ended. America, where the cycle racer is fed from a menu of eastern vinegar, southern hospitality and western funk. None of the grace of swirling country lanes or the loveliness of green, park-like settings. Nor little towns and narrow bridges, suspenseful hairpins or ballets of curves. American racing usually means speedway racing, flat track racing, man and machine boring deeper on each revolution into a coughing, choking bowl of speed. Where-as, through skill and cunning, the Continental racer outfoxes death, the American motorcycle racer wins over the danger and potential destruction by sheer intimidation, by a galling and unfathomable disregard for mortality and common sense.

If it is Ascot or Roosevelt we are visiting, the turf is soft, burnished, and newly rutted by the wheels of frantically clawing machines. If it is Louisville, the field crew has probably hosed it down the night before, so that the early sun would have cooked a hard smooth crust on it. If it is Nazareth, we see a long black straightaway with a banked downhill hook at the end. Oil puddles on the damp, dirt surface. The weeds in the infield sway morosely under the grey clouds of early night.

The winners of the first heat grumble up to the starting line in a cloud of purple dust. They all bunch up on the line with their handlebars flaring and their flanks twitching in anticipation. The racing machine can be the simplest two-wheeled vehicle built, except for the bicycle. It weighs around 180 pounds and the same frame is used no matter what size the engine is. A bulging gas tank, cables snaking up from the front wheel forks, an oversized racing carburetor and air cleaner, and a metal plate with a number on it, are all that separates man from what could be his undoing.

There are no fenders or lights or mufflers. Only a spindly frame, a fire-shooting engine, and a fragile, leather-wrapped man. Those machines will stretch over straightaways at 125 miles per hour, and hook into U-turn curves at 90. There are no shock absorbers; there aren't even any brakes—nothing can stop the flat racer, once started, from completing his half-mile swing, except for a corrugated metal guardrail, or another flying machine.

Flat racing is a dual of throttles. To control the machine, riders manipulate the speed between fast and faster. They turn with their bodies, and because there aren't any brakes, they slow down with their feet. The heavy "hot shoe" of annealed band saw blades they wear on one foot is often the only valve separating chaos from control.

The flag drops and the racers explode in a simultaneous breath of fire and blue smoke. Almost before coming off the line, they bunch into the first turn. There is hardly room for all of them, and certainly no room for caution; the slightest alteration of the frenetic rhythm could tangle the entire process.

On the straightaways, they stretch into an elastic chain of speed, each leather back slumped just ahead of a dogging dust cloud. Viewed from the grandstand, the leading rider's helmet seems to float along the top edge of the guardrail. We watch his action, aware all the time of the frantic fight for position among the other pursuing machines. They mesh into the far turn, but from where we are, we can only see the riders who have lost the groove of the track, fighting for traction on the highest and farthest edge. Some bikes are dropped and riders roll into the far guardrail. But most make it through.

The race is usually won in the turns. Here is where the racer gains in inches what can be stretched to yards in the near straightaway.

Coming into the turn, the racer throttles back and banks left. His front wheel slides away from the turn (because of centrifugal force), but the rear wheel holds true by building up a slight retaining wall of dirt. The rider slants the handlebars in the direction of the slide, but as a counterbalance, stands on the right footpeg, throws his body left and digs his hot shoe into the dirt. He is turning left, but the machine is sliding right. Success is contingent on how well he retains rear wheel traction and maintains forward motion.

That is both the essence of the technique and the essence of the danger of what is known as the "controlled skid." That beast blasts out one horse's power for each 3.6 pounds of machine. Though man rules on the straightaway, in the turn it is only skill and persistence that maintain that precarious balance on the far edge of disaster.

Most tracks are half-mile stretches and most races go ten laps. The groove of the track is narrow, about three out of a total of sixteen feet, and all spinning wheels must grab their share to stay in competition. Then, maybe into the seventh or eighth lap, one bike near the front may slide wide into a turn, and dump, bowling over a couple more competitors with him. A pocket, a right of way, opens up, seemingly inches from the grandstand, but enough for one, two, three bikes to pop through, before someone zippers it closed. Boldness wins the race for the three bikes that slipped past and were liberated. Mistakes lose it for the man who let them get by.

If TT racing is a solitary ballet, then flat track racing is a polished chorus line. Three bikes stretch out together down the straight at 110 miles per hour. Simultaneously, the riders throttle back to 75 for the turn. Their left boots come down, wheels slant in unison, sparks fly and dance at their feet.

Then one man comes out of the far turn ahead in the tenth lap. One man has the track's groove to himself, and the wind to himself, and he wraps his knees around the tank, tucks his chin into the bars and heads for the checkered flag. One man winds his machine over the grit like a strung-out power boat over water; in the fury of exhilaration, in the heat of emotional erection, he bears down on that flapping symbol of glory.

When the race is done, the winner carries the flag around the track, stopping at the starting line for a mere second as the grandstand salutes him. Then he moves off into the pits, his heart ceasing its frantic song only when he cuts out the beat of his machine.

Those racers frustrated by the cold, not content to feed on the memories of summer last and the hopes and expectations of the season ahead, need not hibernate their machines any longer. Although an AMA-sanctioned winter circuit has not yet developed, there are a number of indoor competitions in Madison Square Garden, Houston's Astrodome, and other dome-topped stadia, offering both purses and points for national championships.

But motordromes are not new; they are just returning after a fifty-year absence. As early as 1907, spectators willing to invest fifty cents at the Velodrome in Paterson, New Jersey, could see the finest professional riders compete on Excelsiors, Flying Merkels, Indians, and Harleys. At one time there were motordromes in most major cities in the United States, designed, owned, and constructed by Jack Prince, a New Jersey engineer. Most motorcycle races were once held indoors on wooden tracks. Later, as taxes increased and the city grew up around the cycle arenas, promoters built great open-air, banked speedways on wood planking, outside city limits. Only when the popularity of the sport was assured and costs of maintenance became prohibitive did cyclists in the United States move permanently to the loose dirt of the already constructed horse tracks.

It is like being tucked into a great pouch of thunder. Even though mufflers are required at Madison Square Garden, the bikes still bellow at 108 decibels, and the building's exhaust system strains in desperation, wrestling with the fumes of oil and gas.

But those big machines at the Velodrome, mufflerless, with

the high wheels and narrow tires rumbling across the boards, would trumpet somewhere on the far side of deafness. And 1,000 open windows wouldn't have been enough to reduce the rate of potential spectator suffocation.

And the riders were more heroic, too. With two controls, an awkward and often unworkable throttle, and a spark cut-off button to stop the engine, the riders raced at only one speed: wide open hell. These old "hogs" were fed with alcohol, which produces much more power than our pump-dispensed gasoline; they could rumble around the track twice, covering as much as two miles of wood for each minute of thunder.

The level of excitement has diminished over the years, however, as indoor racing has returned to face the restrictions of modern times.

Motordrome racing is today a sport of smaller machines, usually no more than 250 cc. And the tracks are smaller. At Madison Square Garden, it takes ten laps to make a mile. The challenge is with the rider, for the machines, limited by the flat, sharp turns and short straightaways, hardly break forty miles per hour. Once a rider takes a fairly commanding lead, because of these limitations, no matter how early in the competition, it is almost impossible to catch him, as long as he stays erect and maintains his speed.

This irks a number of veteran racers who claim that motordrome racing has become an antiseptic substitute for the real thing—a sport capitulating to gentlemen enthusiasts, who don't want to dirty their white ducks on the bleacher boards, who don't want to smell the grease or mix with the masses.

In the winter, when many of the newer cyclists are competing in safety and warmth, when it is 24 degrees below zero outside and ice lies on the turf like lumps of old concrete, members of the hard-core cycling society bend their handlebars toward Quebec.

As a writer for *Cycle World* once remarked: "The French must love the ice racer for his masochism."

The warmest of the spectators view the Championnat National des Motos Sur Glace within an unheated, but glass enclosed stadium at the Quebec half-mile racetrack. Others, layered in long underwear and warmed with wine, hunch near the edge of the track, watching the machines chop around the oval at eighty or ninety, and sometimes even one hundred miles per hour, their wheels clutching frantically at the blue, hard ice with spikes that are often up to two inches long. There are as many as 200 spikes bolted to a tire in traction-designed patterns, which take as much as fifteen hours of steady work to mount.

Ice racers fight more viciously than other cycle racers to grab and hold an early lead. For to ride behind another spike-wheeled machine is to be gunned with pellets of ice, sharp enough to penetrate a brittle cheek, large enough to smash through a shield or knock out an eye.

"In 1969," reports *Cycle World* magazine, "Geoff Salzer, a Junior Rider, dropped his machine in front of a dozen others. He received a broken leg and a nomination for the rider most resembling a garden hose—the kind that squirts little streams of water along its entire length."

"The first time you ride—particularly because you tend to go slow," explains Jim Kelly, a near middle-aged veteran, "you feel like the wheels are falling off. It just jiggles and wobbles all over the place. It's like riding railroad ties . . . once you get some speed it smooths out. When you've been riding ice for a while you start to feel a little bit like the Almighty. 'Jeez,' you say, 'I can do anything on this thing. I can't possibly fall off.' Eventually, you find out you're wrong."

"You've got fantastic traction," says former Montreal ice racing champion Don McHugh. "All you have to do is point the bike in the right direction and it goes there. You can go over so far, it scares you."

Dirt track riders lean deep into turns, keeping the bike from sliding out by dragging their left boot along the track. But the style in ice racing is to hold the bike steady by dragging a padded left knee. You move at 90 miles per hour on a 75 degree tilt. And as long as you keep moving, without having to break speed or alter direction, the racing experience is as exhilarating and pure as any rider might know.

Once you lose momentum, however, or are forced to dodge a flying rider or tumbling machine, your spikes will quit clutching and any semblance of control fades. You fly helplessly across the ice like a downhill skier at the end of a long, high slope. Ice cyclists cannot maneuver their machines quickly enough to avoid a spilled or flying rider, whose punishment for making a mistake is very often perforation.

More than anything, motorcycle racing is a duel among men. It is the kind of sport where the little guy has the immediate advantage, because of weight, quickness, and agility, over the brawny, muscle-bound athlete. But it is not a question of just size and weight alone. The little man must be a strong man. He must be able to manipulate a four or five or six hundred pound machine around swirling S-curves, help it over mountains, hold it from sliding out from under him on corners, with a firm and steady dragging boot.

Motorcycle racing is for men who can take it. Who can cling to a machine, hunched and folded, for hours under hundreds of miles of dust and grit and danger. Whose ears can swallow the noise of fifty bellowing machines, whose mind is nimble when needed, but unwavering from the objective, whose eyes can see ahead and behind and beside. Whose body can communicate with the machine, can know when it is running well, can diagnose trouble almost instantly when it is not.

Motorcycle racing is for the man able to face his last race. It is for the man brave enough to understand his own nakedness and vulnerability, mature enough to realize that failure could be worse than losing; worse than death even, it could mean anywhere from partial mutilation to total disability. To an athlete, that is much worse than dying; to a strong, brave man that is the unacceptable defeat.

At ninety miles an hour you are literally *splattered* if you hit a brick wall. With one hundred machines racing, you can be trampled ten times. A motorcycle racing accident can break every bone in your body and make mush of your face. And because of your helmet and your leathers and your luck, you can still end up alive. This is the kind of man that races a motorcycle—the kind that accepts and realizes that there can be a fate far worse than mere death.

Motorcycle racing is the last untapped source of American athletic entertainment. But it won't remain that way for long, as each year more young men commit themselves to the competition of two-wheeled machines.

And they will do so partially *because* of the risk. The absolute unpredictability of what is going to happen after the flag has waved and the machines have trumpeted off, that element of insecurity, woven into the action, the heat of the competition, the psychological intoxication brought on by the intensification of all sensations. For many, the risk is what makes it meaningful, what makes the finish secondary to the exhaltation and exhilaration provided by its pursuit.

Nine

Big time sports have plucked many adolescents off the streets, away from potentially life-long ghetto existences. That is probably the most humane aspect of our computerized corporate athletic structure today. Professional baseball, football, and basketball, for a very few in real need, have made the American dream come true.

However, there have never been athletic scholarships to major American colleges for motorcycle racers, nor big newspaper or magazine headlines stimulated by cycling achievements.

Whatever the American motorcycle racer has accomplished has been through personal perseverance. He has had little public support or assistance. Even financial sponsorship from motorcycle distributors and manufacturers is possible only after the racer has proven himself on the professional or advanced amateur circuit.

It is neither secret nor criticism, but simply a fact, that baseball, football, and basketball players do very little, at least at the beginning of their careers, for themselves. They rely first upon their naturally awarded attributes—their height, their weight, their capacity and ability to run, hit, and throw—to boost them onto the road toward the big leagues.

In the August, 1969, issue of *Harper's* magazine, freelance writer Peter Shrag pinpoints "The Forgotten American."

"There is hardly a language to describe him, or even a set of social statistics. Just names: racist-bigot-redneck-ethnic-Irish-Italian-Pole-Hunkie-Yahoo. The lower middle class. A blank. The man under whose hat lies the great American desert. Who watches the tube, plays the horses, and keeps the niggers out of his union and his neighborhood. Who might vote for Wallace (but didn't). Who cheers when the cops beat up on demonstrators. Who is free, white and twenty one, has a job, a home, a family, and is up to his eyeballs in credit. In the guise of the working class—or the American yeoman or John Smith—he was once the hero of the civics book, the man who Andrew Jackson called 'the bone and sinew of the country.' Now he is the 'forgotten man,' perhaps the most alienated person in America."

And it is into this kind of atmosphere and environment that the American motorcycle racer is born.

His parents work hard in skilled and semi-skilled professions. They make enough money to boost them over the welfare level, to adequately, but certainly not luxuriously, support a family and pay off a 30-year mortgage on a 50-year-old house. There is not enough money to send one or two children to college, but far too much to qualify for liberal scholarship aid.

Lower middle class parents are success and achievement-oriented, however, and they force their children to go to school and take it somewhat seriously. And because the schools are much better in their neighborhoods than in ghetto areas, the educational experience is not intolerable—not as valuable as it would be in upper middle class neighborhoods, but at the very least, it is moderately rewarding.

Because they are white, those children seeking after school employment can usually get it. There are many successful businesses in their neighborhoods that can afford to hire part-time help. Although this situation severely limits the time and the people available on the streets to play a team game regularly, the lower middle-class youngster is rewarded with money and the privilege of doing what he pleases with it. And that privilege usually is exercised in an old but operable four or two-wheeled machine.

While the upper middle-class youth dreams of trips to Europe, hitchhiking to freedom, and educational gratification on the Princeton campus, the lower middle-class boy thinks of wheels, engines, and camshafts and four-barreled carburetors. While the youth in Harlem or Watts plays basketball and dreams of discovery, the boy next door to the union hall or Lithuanian Club thinks of Cadillacs and Corvettes, Hondas or Harleys.

Perhaps the pattern is changing, or someday will begin to change, and certainly it doesn't apply to all. But it is true for the majority of people who race two-wheeled machines today. They are white; they have completed high school and are unable or unwilling to go any further; they are assured of a job at least as good and eventually better than their fathers and uncles. But there is no hope for the big break, no challenge, no realistic dream.

"He is a white employed male earning between $5,000 and $10,000," according to former Under Secretary of Housing and Urban Development Robert C. Wood, describing the lower middle-class man. "He works regularly, steadily, dependably, wearing a blue collar or white collar. Yet the frontiers of his career expectations have been fixed since he reached the age of thirty-five, when he found that he had too many obligations, too much family, and too few skills to match opportunities with aspirations."

There are no American business tycoons to be made anymore. Without money, connections, and education—not just one, but a combination of all three—any hope for a successful political life is lost. Maybe lower middle-class youths don't know this at the time. Maybe they never realize it. But all the same, this is their doom. The children of the lower middle become fathers of the lower middle. They go in the army, they find a wife, they settle down.

"He does all the right things," says Shrag, "obeys the law, goes to church and insists—usually—that his kids get a better education than he had. But the right things don't seem to be paying off. While he is making more than he ever made—perhaps more than he'd ever dreamed—he's still struggling while a lot of others—'them' (on welfare, in demonstrations, in the ghettos)—are getting most of the attention."

And for the boy who is not happy duplicating the life of his parents, automobile or motorcycle racing is one way out. It is a chance to do something different, an opportunity to make money, maybe not big money, but a more than generous living for those who succeed at it, a relief from the sameness and frustration of his parents' retreat. Because motorcycle racing is more an acquired than a natural skill, with practice, persistence and physical conditioning, success is possible for almost anyone. The odds are against success, but unlike basketball or football where there are physical limitations, in motorcycle racing there is hope.

While the boys in the ghettos were playing baseball, the youths of the lower middle were earning money, buying and riding automobiles and cycles, probably cycles because they are both cheaper to buy and less expensive to maintain. For perhaps as long as four or five years, they have been taking apart these machines, putting them together, supercharging engines, hanging around gasoline stations, drag strips, and cycle shops. In a way different from the ghetto youth, they too have sophisticated their skills.

They might begin by racing in AMA sanctioned amateur events and doing well enough to earn a partial sponsorship, or by helping out their brothers or cousins or friends in the pits or in garages behind neighborhood streets. Because they are white, and because they have finished high school, they can get a fairly good-paying job and earn enough money to support a weekend racing machine.

This kind of lifestyle will emerge most often from the lower middle class. The lower classes haven't the money for it and the upper middle classes haven't the stomach for it. The upper middle classes have long worshipped the beauty of Buicks and Cadillacs, but have never felt secure enough in their sociological position to do anything but drive them. They leave the mechanics to the hunkie with the dirty fingernails who lives above the garage down the street. He is among those who drink beer on Saturday afternoons at the union hall, who play the numbers and never win, who can't understand what is happening to America, and are fed up with what is happening to them.

And that is the kind of guy who will race motorcycles. It is the kind of guy who has long ago written off the possibility of intellectual, political, or financial achievement. He is the kind of guy who watches his father's toil and his family's financial struggles and fears, who has measured the style of life he can expect, and who has concluded, at least in the lower depths of his mind, that he has nothing to lose.

Nothing to lose, except possibly his life, which to many people like him is a small investment to make considering his options. Even in losing, he will win. Even in failure, success will be achieved. Losing or winning in racing, he will still have escaped through racing. He will have found new directions, new people, new goals. The motorcycle racer will probably not admit this. He is too proud and too worried to want to understand. But a two-wheeled machine extends his own potential. And the admiration and attention he gets for riding it embellishes his starved ego, which is far more than ample compensation for any potential loss.

The American Motorcycle Association governs the professional and amateur racing networks in the United States. As in most sports, the amateur competition is far more popular and steeped in more camaraderie and spirit than the professional circuit. In 1971, there were approximately 6,000 amateur events across the United States, with nearly 200,000 rider entries. Amateurs participate in virtually every kind of competitive activity, ranging from road races to flat tracking to cross-country desert runs. The only requirement is a $7 AMA membership, an inexpensive entry fee, and a safe two-wheeled machine.

Any AMA member can race professionally by passing a thorough physical examination and paying a $20 entrance fee. A professional rider is first placed in the novice class and if, during the year, he demonstrates superior racing skill and ability, he is advanced to a junior rating. The very finest riders can begin in the expert division in their third year of racing. It is similar to the minor leagues in baseball, where the shortstop or second baseman moves from Class B to AAA clubs, working his way through divisions of increasing difficulty, fighting for a slot in the big time.

Becoming an expert is a test of both skill and diversification. In other major sports the young athlete need be competent at only one position, although his value is enhanced by competency in more than one area. A good first baseman, for example, need only be superior with the bat, and acceptable in the field to play regularly in the major leagues.

But a cycle racer involved in national championship competition is faced with many different skills to master. Of the 25 national championship events run in 1970, there were four road races, nine half-mile races, two short track races, five TT races and five mile-track events. Each event calls for a different kind of riding skill, and perhaps a different kind of machine. An expert competing in the nationals might be dirt tracking a lightweight motorcycle in one race, and three days later run a 200-mile hard track marathon on a 900 cc "hog."

Professional motorcycle racing in the United States is divided into national championship events and regional competitions. After the rider has become an expert, competition in the regionals allows him to stay close to home and still gain recognition in more specialized areas. On the national circuit, points are awarded to each rider finishing high up in the standings in the important 25 national competitions. The number of points awarded depends on the difficulty of the race and the finishing position of each rider. Points accumulated from championship races are totaled throughout the year to establish an annual grand champion.

During the next season he wears a plate in front of his bike, proclaiming that he is Number One. Up until 1972, when the tradition was eliminated, all the riders finishing behind him in national standings wore a corresponding number, from two through one hundred. "What's more important than Number One?" says Gene Romero, who carried that number in 1970. "Nothing."

In 1970, Gene Romero, of San Luis Obispo, California, became the youngest man in more than a decade to win the grand national championship. He was only 22 but far from a super-rookie:

"I've put seven years of my life, one broken leg, a dozen mashed ribs, and two or three fractured fingers and toes into winning Number One."

He has been more than just lucky. For although the rewards are small in motorcycle racing, the punishments are more than man-sized. Broken legs are to a cycle racer what a blister is to a laborer. It is part of the job.

Like the veterans of Vietnam, Romero is one of the oldest "boys" in the country, visiting battlefront hospitals regularly, winning a handful of purple hearts. In 1969, at the Houston National, Romero spilled and three bikes ran over his arms and hands. At the emergency ward, the halls were stuffed with riders who had cracked up that evening at the Astrodome, and Romero stood for an hour in the corridor, waiting his turn for treatment, while the blood seeped through his leathers and dripped on the carpet.

When an orderly finally led him into the room, Romero collapsed. He was racing the next week.

Consistency is what counts on the national circuit. Although Romero won but three nationals in 1970, he was a steady money finisher, gathering seconds, thirds, or fourths in almost every race. Consistency and persistence: missing a race means not gaining any points, means loss of standings, means that the road to the number one position will be more arduous the following week. If a superstar for a major league baseball team is injured, the team can still go on and he can still be paid. But if a motorcycle racer allows his injuries to stop him from competing, defeat is imminent—by default.

Romero was suspended in 1970 for fifteen days because he forged a medical release permitting him to race a day after a crash had cost him three broken ribs. There is never time to wait for a cure. Man must heal, with spindles and bolts, wire and guts, like the machine he rides. Only the winners are paid.

The true competitor drags his cast to the starting line and unslings his arm at the drop of a flag. He must out-fox nausea with concentration, overwhelm pain with sheer grit and stamina. It is a difficult way to live, but the only way to win. Broken bones and stitched up skin will not intimidate him. To the motorcycle racer, immobility or death are the only reasons for resignation. Nothing less.

Motorcycle racing means pressure, the pressure of the duel, the pressure of the pain, the pressure of zipping from one part of the country to the other in fewer than three days—not flying like the athletes who play baseball, but hauling in the bed of a pickup truck four or five bikes for hundreds of thousands of miles every year. The pressure of keeping the machines race-ready, the pressure of the time trials and the preliminary heats. The pressure of the pressure of the pressure.

At seventeen, Romero was in his first year on the national circuit, driving from state to state all summer, driving away the night to get to the next track, sleeping in the backs of trucks in cold dirty pits, spending all of his money on gas and parts.

"I look back on those years and I still think how bad they were. Things get so bad you don't know if you want to go on racing or not. Some guys go on, others don't. Every beginner has to put up with it. The ones that go on are the ones that want to be professional motorcycle racers more than anything else—I was one of those."

Motorcycle racing is for the young man. Dick (Bugsy) Mann, *Cycle* magazine's rider of the year for 1972 is a young 37. Here is how the editors of *Cycle* describe their man's action.

"The heat is flagged off. The racers pour through the first sweeping left-hander, and then another uphill left at the top of the back straightaway, and then tuck in for the long, downhill pull, the engine noise rippling off the corrugated fence. Bugs is fourth. He's taking it easy.

"No he's not. When the racers in front of him sit up, shut off, brake and downshift, Bugs moves to the outside and leaves it on. He swoops everybody in front of him in one corner—it isn't a 'strategy' corner, or even a 'style' corner—it's a nerve corner, a big, fast, downhill banked mother that had pasted George Roeder last year.

"Bugs stretches from there, and wins the heat, and nails down the pole for the Main."

Nerve and guts are important in motorcycle racing. Determination is important. But experience is essential. You can tell the brand of the motorcycle racer by watching him in the turns In the crucial point in the skid, the novice is often unable to hold the throttle open. Shutting down the throttle, the rear wheel will bite the track, often bucking the rider off his machine. Or too much throttle, fed in the heat of excitement or fear, makes the rear wheel shoot out. But the experts, the precision pros like Bugsy Mann, who can coordinate speed and control, emerge out of the turn like invisible lightning.

Some people say that there is nobody better at this on the AMA circuit than Bugsy Mann, and most people say that he is getting better all the time. Bugsy Mann was Number One in 1963, and though he remained a close contender, he gathered little prominence in the subsequent seven years. Then in 1970, Honda gave him its 750 Four and he won with it at the Daytona Classic. And in 1971, he took four nationals, three seconds, one third, two fifths, one sixth, one eighth, one ninth. He won more road racing points than anybody, earned fourth in total half-mile points, third in total TT points and fifth in overall mile-race points to become 1971's grand national rider, Number One.

Willie Mays, Johnny Unitas. The aging men who make the money and get the publicity and who have made athletics a lifelong career. These superstars with the super salaries play the first game of a double-header or the first half of a sixty-minute game. But they never had a day as strenuous and arduous as Bugsy Mann has each day he swirls around a dirt and cindered oval track. And Bugsy Mann is getting stronger as Mays and Unitas and their ilk fade unimpressively to their respective halls of fame.

Americans seem to have lost the ability to appreciate athletics. Or to differentiate between athletes and entertainers. The gymnast is respected by other gymnasts. The average American doesn't know what a gymnast is. College NCAA wrestlers perform to empty stadiums while buffoons in professional exhibitions of wrestling gather in $50,000 or $100,000 each year. Tennis became popular and promotable when money, not trophies, became the mark of a champion. Soccer couldn't make it in America in 1967 and 1968. Frazier's fists and Ali's mouth have kept boxing alive. It is unfortunate but true.

For the past decade, athletes have been blackmailing employers into unreasonable contracts for hundreds of thousands of dollars just for the privilege of buying their skills for half a year. A quarter of a million dollars—the total of all purses paid to motorcycle professionals in its highest paying year—is sometimes not even enough to persuade one college basketball player, even without professional experience, to sign a contract to play for a team.

The motorcycle racer on the professional circuit sometimes risks his life for as little as $200 to $300 stipends in a winning cause. He is responsible for all his equipment, meaning perhaps four or five motorcycles, $200 leather outfits, $70 helmets, hundreds of replacement parts, the salary of a full-time pit man and mechanic, and traveling expenses for both himself and his crew.

The 1969 AMA Number One rider, thirty-year-old Mert Lawhill, after nine months on the road that year, brought home a little more than $20,000 for him and his family to share. Although cycle manufacturers will sponsor a rider after he has proven himself, that agreement is only for competitive equipment. The day-to-day expenses are still his to assume. The lower middle-class boy has inherited the frustrations of his fathers after all, in what has been financially, publicly, and unfairly relegated to a lower middle-class sport.

Once men played for the satisfaction of winning and of being a part of the well-balanced team. Once men played for the glory of adulation. Once they played for the pure joy of it. Now, like slot machines, they play only when money is fed into their wallets. Professional athletics in America have been taken over by agile vice presidents of pitching and executive directors of home runs. The players incorporate themselves and cash in their popularity for ready change. They bat balls with dollar signs, catch footballs of greenbacks, shoot baskets cashed for currency at an ever-increasing rate of exchange.

But with inflation, increased ticket prices, and continued financial pressure everywhere in America, public opinion is beginning to turn. People are beginning to realize that there is no purity in athletics when champions are paid in bejeweled trophies. And that is why motorcycle racing will soon become the most popular and respected sport in this country. Because its champions have always found honor and glory in what winning represents—not in what it totals on an adding machine.

The red road: from Alabama to New Mexico

From Fayetteville, we ride into Alabama. A flesh colored likeness of George Wallace welcomes us from the red and blue and white billboard.

I have always thought that the political boundaries defined by our earliest settlers and pioneers were rather arbitrarily conceived, but I have been wrong. You can tell when the states change; even without highway signs you know you have rolled into another country.

Our backs to Tennessee, the hills fade, the hot sun roasts out the greenness as we enter Alabama. God has pared away the mountains, unknotted roads, dehydrated the meadows, painted the landscape pink.

We have been warned away from Alabama and from going south by a few of the young people we've met. Their mecca is the West Coast. California. California is "where it's at," where you "get your head together." The currents of the country flow west, north, or east. Alabama, Mississippi, Arkansas, Texas, form a no-man's land, according to some people you meet on the road, where hippies are beaten up and niggers are jailed. One girl claimed to have witnessed the lynching of two black men in Texas. No one goes south, it seems, unless it is to Miami or New Orleans.

Years ago, I remember being able to distinguish between fact and fantasy, but hardly anything today seems too bizarre. So even if you don't believe the girl, you don't totally disbelieve her either. Nothing is impossible in a country where Charles Manson, James Calley, and Sirhan Sirhan live, while John Kennedy, Robert Kennedy, and Martin Luther King, Jr. have died violently.

The Civil War has ended, but the alienation caused by it has not. There is more communication and understanding between this country and Japan and Germany, than between the people of the northern and southern parts of the United States. I was told by a college student from Louisiana that he hated northerners because the Union Army had raped his great-grandfather's plantation. "I don't hate you," he said, "but I hate all the rest of those rotten bastards in the North." He hated me as well, I'm sure, but we talked casually, and I made sure not to turn my back on him when we finally walked away. Time, in the South, more than a century later, seems to have fanned the fires of resentment over a lost war for some people, rather than extinguish them.

We went south and I was afraid. I can't gauge the degree of my fear, but I shivered as I passed the George Wallace billboard and rode over the Alabama red. But at some time, I can't say exactly when, the idea of the potential danger suddenly seemed very appealing to me. I have been in danger before, but never have I approached it knowingly. Fear of danger is something usually faced after the fact. Here, I was thrusting myself into a totally avoidable situation—we could have easily bent west through Tennessee or turned north—and was stimulated by it. Everything I saw or heard seemed alien, the billboards, the voices twanging like country guitars, the bibbed dungaree coveralls worn by many of the men—they all served to fortify the wall between the cultures. Yet, the alienation excited me. My ears, my eyes—my skin—were literally electrified with the mood of adventure.

I think this feeling has a lot to do with the motorcycle and the process by which it makes you free. Isolated in a city, hunched over a typewriter, selling draperies, filling prescriptions, delivering milk, doing all of the dead and dull things of the average man making the average wage, your male identity seems pale compared to the rugged virility of America's early heroes. So you ride two weeks and a couple of thousand miles through the rain and wind, you live through the mud and fog, cold food, warm beer. You are miserable and depressed. But when it is all over, you want more. You get to thinking about how much you can do, how much punishment you can take, how well you survive under serious hardship. *Rugged Individualism* is no longer a long lost slogan. Somehow, on the road, it touches you and you are hooked by the image of it. This idea does not occupy your mind in the city, but you are obsessed with it on the road. Once you've tasted freedom and the exhilaration of beating danger, something tugs your nerves taut for more.

The threat of George Wallace—the George Wallace who at the time had not been shot down by Arthur Bremer; the George Wallace who had not yet captured the awe of the people opposed to school busing; who had not yet unwittingly helped George McGovern beat the spark out of the Muskie and Humphrey Democratic presidential primary campaigns—the threat of the bad Wallace, the old Wallace who talked of white power and of running down protesting hippies with his car, frightened us more than anything else. For there could be no justice in Alabama, no matter what happened and who was at fault. We were at the mercy of Wallace's army—the Alabama State Highway Patrol. We felt like soldiers, but it was a good feeling, not a bad one. It was the way soldiers felt in books and movies that promote the honor and glory of war. George Wallace was waiting, Alabama was waiting, and we plunged recklessly and deeply into it.

We are in Alabama and the sky is grey. The clouds hang over pink dunes of nothingness and the road stretches out into multiplying concrete slabs. That is when the car pushes us into the ditch below the shoulder of the road.

It is funny. We are the only three vehicles on the road. The whole road is empty except for the three of us. And the car swerves in. It is the car you see and the car you fear, and we swerve away, bouncing over the shoulder and into the ditch below. It is so funny that we cannot laugh, too funny to speak.

We are in Alabama and we push our bikes up the hill and back onto the shoulder of the road, straighten our gear, and start to move. We are in Alabama and the sky is still grey. The clouds hang over pink dunes of nothingness and the road stretches out in multiplying slabs. That is when the tractor trailer truck pushes us into the ditch below the shoulder of the road.

It is funny. We are the only three vehicles on the road. The whole road is empty except for the three of us. And the tractor trailer truck swerves in. It is the truck you see and the truck you fear, and we swerve away, bouncing over the shoulder and into the ditch below. It is so funny that we sink down into the dirt and breathe, as though breathing were something very new, and we have just discovered the joy of it.

It is hard to remember what next. The cars that passed as we moved along the road were all, it seemed, driven by George Wallace. And the heart of Dixie etched in black on the yellow Alabama license plates mocked our fear. At a truck stop, outside of Huntsville, we had hot cross buns and coffee, listening to Jeanne C. Riley sing, "I'll Take What's Left of You;" Mel Tillotson wail for "One More Drink;" Walon Jenkins and "Mississippi Woman;" Conway Twitty croon "My Angel Cry;" and Charlie Pride plead "Let Me Live."

The trucker feeding the jukebox smiled at us and we grinned at him. He had no idea we had just come from a battle nor that at another time he might have been our enemy. We left the front lines and rode the rest of the way across red Alabama, with the sun pricking perspiration on our faces. It was a fine ride through Alabama and most of the rest of the South after that, and we accepted our purple hearts silently.

There is nothing more to say about Alabama, except that I wish I would have stopped to talk to the trucker at the diner outside of Huntsville, who seemed like a nice guy, despite his appreciation of hillbilly music.

When we pulled up, the man closed his cash register and put on his hat, a yellow straw western hat, bent to points on three sides. He called to the other two men at the back of the store, and they walked up to the front. Through the glass of the door, we could see their lips move, but not hear their voices. The concrete block building was air conditioned and felt icy on our sweaty faces as we walked in. There were three women inside as well. The women were fat and wore flowered dresses, ripped at the armpits or shoulders. The women looked like sisters and the men looked like brothers.

We bought a cold drink and leaned on the cooler while they studied our machines through the window.

"How-far-you-comin'?" said the man at the cash register. He

talked quickly, slurring his words, leaving little space in between each for translation.

"Pennsylvania," Burt said.

"How-far-you-going?"

"Maybe California, maybe Idaho or Montana. I don't know." It was true, we didn't know, we were just riding to see the country, and we couldn't answer any better than that.

"You-wouldn't-get-me-on-one-a-them-things," said the man, motioning out the door at our machines, "less-you-bolted-two-together."

One of the women came up to the front of the store for a bag of potato chips, and I followed her back. I could only see a sample of goods on the dusty shelves as I walked through the aisles, a box of Tide, a tube of Gleem, two cans of ham. There were a lot of packaged cakes, however, and cases of soft drinks, and more cases of empty bottles, on the floor.

An infant was lying on a mattress near where the women were sitting. All three women were sitting in aluminum lawn chairs in a garden of shelves and concrete. The one with the potato chips was knitting, while the other two stared over the shelves and out the window at the road which carried few cars and baked in the sun.

Like the women, the infant without any clothes on hardly moved. His mattress too, was naked, without sheets, and lay frameless on the cold floor. If his eyes weren't open and moving I would have thought him to be dead. His skin was pale, yet not quite white or pink, and I could barely see his stomach move in rhythm with his breathing.

We were in Walnut, Mississippi, having a cold drink at a general store along the narrow highway. There was so much to ask these people, but there was nothing to say. I'm sure they wondered many things about us, but no one in that store right then had enough courage to want to try to be friends. No one quite knew how to do it, I think. That was the most disappointing part of traveling across the country. You get hungry for the country and the thrill of the ride, which leaves little time to learn about the people. Going cross-country becomes an album of first impressions, snatches of conversation, inadequate pictures of American life.

Yet, without the motorcycle, there would have been less communication. A tourist riding in a car is just one of the many tourists riding in one of the many cars. But a man on a motorcycle stimulates curiosity. There is often hostility, but always curiosity. The people in the rural South are perhaps the most curious people I have ever been in contact with. It is because of their isolation, I'm certain. Their only link to the North— even to the metropolitan South—is through television, which, during the past few years, hasn't presented an accurate nor a positive profile of the mood and lifestyle of the country. The people here ask very few questions, but they study the visitor carefully, almost hungrily, looking for a key, an answer, a tip-off to his personality or way of life. God knows what they finally decide about the visitor, but I would wager that it is usually wrong—and more than likely the worst.

On Route 7 between Water Valley and Holly Springs, Mississippi, the road burned across the hot red sod, and as far as we could see, we could see nothing.

We rode for a long time under the sun until a gas station appeared on the flat red plain bordering the blacktop. Pebbles clattered against our exhaust pipes as we coasted into the station and woke the man slouched asleep against the hi-test pump.

"You boys alone?" he said, looking past us, back up the line made by the road. We told him yes, but he watched down the blacktop for a long time, way down toward where the road bent out of sight, before pulling the hose from the pump and feeding our machines. "'Cause if you boys belong to one of them Hell's Angels gangs," he said, "I ain't gonna serve you."

We assured him of our innocence while he gritted his teeth, fed our machines, took our money, and said no more. When we pulled back onto the road, I could see him through my rearview mirror, sinking back to sleep near the pyramid of oil cans at the hi-test pump.

The South flowed by in a stream of telephone poles, corrugated metal houses, tired fences, lonely farmers, dust-stained trees. We cut a sharp "V" through the Mississippi back country, south through Bruce, Eupora, French Camp, Ackerman, Philadelphia, Carthage, into Ofahoma, Kosciusko, Vaiden, Winona, Holcomb. Once we saw a dead horse, lying bloated in the red loam on the side of the road. We saw a skeleton of a cow in a shaggy field.

But more than anything, we saw the vine. A man in a gas station said that the vine, kudzu, was planted by the state to hold the loose Mississippi soil together, but that it had grown out of control. This vine was everywhere, knitted knee high on the side of the road, choking trees and crops, layered around telephone poles, tangled with the wires that shot from the poles. We rode under bridges of kudzu vine hanging over the pavement and that was when it became eerie, the vines above us, cutting off the sun and screening the breeze that came from the water to the west. It seemed somehow too tropical. We were in Mississippi, but it looked like the Everglades.

The vines receded when the trees thinned out and the land got parched in the central part of the state. Then we climbed north into Senatobia and camped on the edge of Sardis Lake.

Early that evening, the rain came and pricked the surface of the shining lake. We were cooking dinner, but it was ruined, and we huddled inside the tent listening to the rain beat against the nylon. Burt went out when the rain didn't stop and washed his motorcycle in it. I stayed inside and took pictures of Burt's image reflecting from the clear puddles made by the water. When the rain stopped we built a fire to dry out our clothes, but we had no food.

Then a man camping nearby came and laid a ripe red half-watermelon down on the wet grass near our tent. "We et all we need," said the man, and though we tried to talk, that was all he wanted to say. We ate the watermelon, its juices dripping down and staining our chins, as our boots steamed above the fire.

In the morning, a family from Nashville, camping on the other side of the lake fed us an eggs and bacon breakfast. Nor did they want to talk; they heaped our breakfast on metal camping plates, saying there was plenty more, then moved off into their own group.

Later, Burt called home and was told Bing's father had died. Bing was Burt's best friend and Burt started to cry. The tears came down under his sunglasses as we rolled out of the campground surrounding Lake Sardis, Mississippi, and wound down the rain-cleaned road.

The Mississippi River flowing downstream was like a solid mass, brown and muddy, long as infinity and half as wide, with water breaking and swirling around the abutments where the bridge jutted out from the bank.

I was thinking of old Huck Finn, and looking for his crude raft as we rode across the bridge that connected Mississippi to Arkansas. I looked for Huck sitting in the sun along the brown banks, his clear eyes reflecting the rippling river. We stopped to take a picture and to listen to the water lapping the bank. Then we moved down toward Highway 79.

"You come from Pennsylvania on them motorcycles?" said the old black man.

"I'm looking for a way to Highway 79," I said, motioning across the field at Highway 79.

But our way was blocked. The field was protected with a high barbed wire fence, and we couldn't find a way through it. We could see the "79" sign right below a billboard on the other side of the field, and it was frustrating because we couldn't get to it. We had gotten off "79" to talk to a man fueling an old World War II trainer plane we saw landing in the distance. The man had three of these planes and some surplus engines, still crated, he had purchased in 1948. Leaving the pilot, we bounced down an old dirt road we thought would lead us back to the highway. But we got lost. We hoped this old man would help us get back on the main road.

"Where you want to go?" he said.

"Highway 79."

"Don't know it." His was an old voice, but he looked very fine and fresh in his clean panama and crisp white suit. And he wore an old, blue, clip-on bow tie. A tired flower limped from his lapel.

"That road," I pointed across the field.

"Where you going?"

"Toward Pine Bluff." We were on the edge of an old poor town near Helena, Arkansas, heading toward Hot Springs, via Pine Bluff. There weren't any windows in the houses of this town, just holes in the walls covered with plastic. And there weren't any gardens or sidewalks or paved streets.

"If you're going toward Pine Bluff," he said, pointing across the field toward Highway 79, "then take that road."

"Is there an opening in the fence or a way around it?"

"You going on them things?"

"We've come all the way from Pennsylvania."

He shook his head. "I ain't never been to Pennsylvania," said the old man, thumbing his suspenders. "I been to Pine Bluff, but never Pennsylvania."

Then he told us that if we followed a dirt road about five miles up we'd run into Highway 79. That is when the old lady who sold rags came up, dragging her high-topped tennis shoes in the dust.

"They came all the way from Pennsylvania on them motorcycles," the old man told her.

"You come all the way from Pennsylvania on them motorcycles?" she asked.

We nodded as we got up on our bikes and kicked them started.

"Then," she said, "you crazy."

While we were talking to the old people, a big black man came up and stood behind them. He stood at a distance, and I wasn't sure he could hear us, but he watched carefully, unsmiling. There are plenty of black people in the South; they haven't all been pushed North. But except for this old man and woman and the big man who stood behind them, we hadn't come in contact with any.

The towns you roll through in the rural South are white towns, although black men wash windows, clean up dishes in restaurants, toil in the fields; old black men and old black women, with faces wrinkled from work; black children with short hair and bibbed cotton work clothes. No Afro haircuts, no dashikis. On the road you see the children and the old black men, with the yellow straw hats, but you never hear them. Or we hadn't until that point. Although the faces are of two colors, the voices in the rural South are mostly white.

"What you want with that old man?" the big man asked, striding forward.

"They ain't hurtin' nothin'," said the old man, "They nice boys."

"What you want?" the big man demanded. He had on an old green T-shirt, stretched in places by the muscles of hard labor. His brown hands had white callouses on them, but there was dirt in the cracks of the callouses.

"What you want?" He walked past the old man and old lady we had talked to, he walked in front of us, blocking both our machines.

"Just directions," I said, or Burt said, or we both said. His bulk and his anger were too intimidating to allow for clear memory. "We got lost."

"You get your directions?"

"Yes," we told him.

"Then," he said, moving out of the way and motioning with his arm down the road, "go."

The farmer stood as straight as the gray fence posts sledged into the turf around the fields of his farm. Burt wanted to take his picture, and I went up to keep the man busy, but he kept looking at the camera. Wherever Burt would point, that's where the farmer would turn. I couldn't tell his age, but the creases around his face were deep highways of time.

The barn was made of wilted scrap wood, patched and roofed in corrugated rusty metal. His house was of solid concrete block, as gray and solemn as its owner.

I told him we had traveled all the way from Pennsylvania, and counted off the states we had gone through, but he kept turning toward where Burt snapped pictures. Burt went down on his knees, snapping pictures of an old horse lazing in the sun of the field.

We started in Pennsylvania, I told the man, on our motorcycles. "Ever been to Pennsylvania?" I said.

"Ain't never been nowhere," he answered.

I said to the man, as he watched Burt taking pictures, that we were riding all over America on our motorcycles. I told him how nice the people were along the many roads, and how especially we liked the South and the state of Mississippi where there is the kudzu vine.

"Ain't you got jobs?" the man asked.

"No, we're traveling for the summer," I said.

The man who was so straight and tall and gray turned then and walked past Burt and his camera. He trod along the fence around his farm, past the barn and the horse that was sunning, into his house. He closed the door and later we saw him sitting by the front window, watching us, a shotgun cradled in his lap.

We followed the lady who filled our gas tanks into the store. There were heaps of mussel shells piled all around the store, and on the road leading into Roe, Arkansas, waiting to be ground up and used for gravel.

Two men stood by the counter washing down with cold white milk cakes that come in cellophane packages. They were loggers, grimy at the face and hands, with thick five-day beards, just now returning from the wilderness with a truckload of logs. They made $180 per truckload, they said.

The young one wore an old hat on the back of his head, and he had the clearest, brightest blue eyes, like sparkling diamonds, set in deep sockets. The old one, short, with tobacco crusting in his beard, did much of the talking, mostly about the South.

"The thing is, the people here trust you. This lady," he said, motioning to the lady who filled our tanks, "she don't even know my name, but if I said I'd pay her for this cake next week, she knows I will, and I know she'd say yes. We're Southerners and there's trust between us. In the North, they don't even want to know your name unless you've got the money. Here, people are friendly. They stop and visit and we all treat each other like people."

We said that mostly the people we met in the South were friendly and generous. Which was true.

"There weren't nothin' wrong with the South," the young one said, "until those Northerners like King and Kennedy come to stir things up."

The old one had been all over the country, logging as far north as Maine and was stationed for a while in the army in Pennsylvania. His people were originally from Pennsylvania, and he still had one aunt there whose family remained when his great-grandfather headed south, many years ago.

"There's an old nigger lady from Roe, who come up to Pennsylvania some years ago. She phones my aunt periodically 'cause they both know me. It's Southern courtesy when you know somebody that might know somebody else to call them and catch them up on things."

The lady who owned the store provided the name of a friend in Humphreys (pronounced "Umphreys"), fifty miles down the road, whose family had just recently moved from Pennsylvania. "Maybe you'll know someone together," she said.

"If you're ever in Umphreys," the old man said before climbing into the cab of his truck, "look for the city dump. That's where all my people live."

We picked our way through the tourists who soaked in Hot Springs and the soldiers who looked for women at night and drank beer alone in Fort Smith, Arkansas. Then we rolled into Oklahoma.

I don't know how many Indians there are in Oklahoma, but certainly not enough to make all the Indian-made pottery you see at the gift shops along the highway, castles of pottery and statues of glass, smoked in many colors. The Indians who sell the pottery along the highway in Oklahoma are often college students from the East, working a summer job.

We met a navy ensign and his wife, riding cross-country on their Honda 750. From San Diego, they were heading to Wisconsin to visit her parents. Then they were riding to Arkansas to look for a farm to buy. We met fewer cyclists than I expected across the country, but we always stopped to talk to them. There was a high school teacher and his wife from Michigan in the Shenandoah Valley. And Larry and Bob, Ida and Susan, social workers from Chicago, on vacation in Kentucky. There was a soldier on a Triumph, riding home on leave, but hardly anybody else.

In Oklahoma, we took refuge on a concrete shelf under a new bridge and watched the rain dump down. It was the most violent downpour I have ever seen. Shells of thunder shook our shelter, arcs of lightning, two and three at a time, built fiery bridges across the black bitter sky. Everyone had pulled to the side of the road, and all we could see, huddled together like naked monkeys, were miles of wildly blowing water, diving branches and debris, and headlights gleaming like frightened animal eyes through the storm.

When the temper of the rain subsided, we rolled into Texas, where the sun steamed our wet clothes dry.

In the Panhandle, tornadoes of sand stormed across the road, stung our faces and beat our bikes. There was nothing to stop the wind, blitzing across the red, flat plains, and we took it for 100 miles, stopping periodically to bury our faces in our jackets and grab a gritty cigarette.

The wind in Texas is an invisible boxer, working his left,

showering us with solid punches. *Womp, womp, womp,* like the ghost of leather against flesh, the wind hit our faces, the impact tottering our cycles. No matter how we bobbed and dodged, skipped from lane to lane, the wind hit us harder. The wind leaks into your helmet and the helmet pulls away from your neck. *Womp, womp, womp,* the wind cracks your lips, and the welts on your cheeks from the stones blown by the wind swell red in the sun. We cannot see the wind when it hits, but can hear it coming, wheezing into the helmet. Then we lock our backs and squeeze the handlegrips until the wind attacks, *womp, womp.* We totter, recover balance, shake it off, listening for more.

If you cannot envision invisible boxers, then think of the ocean on a cold night when the tide is highest and the wind blows in from the water, and you'll know how it feels to be caught on a motorcycle behind a fast-moving truck on a Texas highway.

You are standing in the sand, watching the water, while the wind slaps hard at your cheeks. Out in the water, near the sandbar, the waves begin to well up and move into shore. As the waves get bigger, the wind dies down but you can hear it coming. Then the long cone of water claps against the beach, shatters against your body, tossing you backward.

That is how it feels, riding a motorcycle at 75 miles per hour, behind a tractor trailer truck. The wind diminishes the closer you get to the truck. There is a pocket directly behind the truck when you feel no wind, hear no sound, and the cycle sails effortlessly in the vacuum of the bigger machine. As you leave the protection of the truck to pass, the wave of wind in the distance balls up, moves forward, and somewhere between the tail of the truck and the middle, collides with you. Sometimes you are thrown into the next lane. Other times, the wind gooses you forward, then slaps you back.

Unless you choose to ride a motorcycle on a straight Texas highway at 75 miles per hour hanging in the tail of the wind, you will never experience the thrill of it. Unless you believe that danger is the ultimate joy for man, then keep your motocycle off the Texas highway, in the early summer when the sun is hot and the wind blows hard from the desert in the west.

We stopped to rest at a gas station near the New Mexico line where we met a preacher from North Carolina on a Harley

Davidson with a sign on the back that said "Grand Canyon or Burst."

Later, we talked to a dentist from New Jersey, a few miles east of Santa Fe. The year before he had traveled from Nova Scotia and back on his motorcycle. "My patients will just have to wait," he told us, "or find somebody else, but every year I have to go somewhere on my machine. My life is regulated by appointments, but traveling on a motorcycle gives me the freedom of not knowing what will happen next."

In Santa Fe, the Indians sell overpriced crafts at the public square. The rings of silver and jade were nice, but many of the handmade blankets had "Made in Oregon" tags sewn onto them. In Santa Fe, people with long hair and dirty faces sleep on the streets and panhandle on corners. Anyone who believes in the virtues of hard work hates these people who waste away their days. The merchants believe in working hard to gouge the pockets of the tourists, and they use every waking hour to do so.

We had decided long ago that Santa Fe would be our resting point, that we would spend three or four days living high and looking around. Perhaps we had looked forward to the respite for too long, made it in our fantasies seem much more idyllic than possible in fact. Or perhaps our disillusionment stemmed from our unfamiliarity with the tinsel of the tourist traps during the previous part of our journey. But more than anything, I think it was the unfriendliness of the people that made us leave. We stayed about a day and a half, then rolled onto the desert leading to Colorado.

Some of the people we met in the New Mexican back country also had long hair and were dirty and lived in tiny ranches or in tents isolated from the main road. Other people who were cleaner and more upstanding lived in houses next to their gasoline stations or apartments above general stores.

I can't tell you about the people we talked to in New Mexico because hardly anyone would talk to us. The people with the long hair wouldn't talk to us because we had money and fancy motorcycles and went across the country to write and take pictures, working for what they termed the system. The people who were cleaner and had short hair wanted nothing to do with us, either, because we looked too much like the people with long hair. We didn't like New Mexico and New Mexico didn't like us. We were happy to see the mountains of Colorado heave up in the desert. The wind died down, and herds of horses galloped riderless over the ridges of grass.

THE MACHINE

Ten

"There was a large laceration to his scalp and injury to his brain. His right lung was torn and there was a fair amount of blood in his chest. His spleen was ruptured and bleeding. There were about three quarts of blood in his abdomen. His left leg was almost amputated. His pelvis was fractured. He was not hit by an artillery shell in Vietnam, as one might think from the extent of his injuries. He was wounded while riding a motorbike . . . ."

As evidenced by this section of a report issued by the American College of Surgeons, motorcycling is more than just dangerous. There are more opportunities for death and disfigurement on motorcycles than in any other sport or means of transportation. Motorcycling is more dangerous than hockey or boxing, racing or hunting, wrestling or roller derby. Because there are no discriminatory barriers, no age, racial, or sexual qualifications for riding a two-wheeled machine, it affects everyone. Motorcycling is potentially more deadly than war.

Here are a few examples from the May 1967 issue of *Today's Health* magazine:

"Cook County, Illinois, had its fourth cycle fatality in four days when a 24-year-old man drove his motorcycle into a utility pole.

"The bodies of two teen-agers, an 18-year-old boy and his 16-year-old date, were found in a gulley along side an urban railroad track after they apparently had ridden their borrowed motorcycle down a street that came to a dead end at the track.

"In Urbana, Illinois, there were 39 accidents during a one-year period. All of the mishaps involved personal injury. 'Compound, contaminated, dirty fractures is mostly what I've seen,' succinctly commented a local doctor.

"Death from head and chest injuries came to an 18-year-old Chicago youth as a result of a crash of a motorcycle he had rented just 15 minutes before. Two young Tampa, Florida, men died in a fiery crash when the motorcycle they were riding went out of control on a curve, skidded 118 feet, smashed into a fence gate and burst into flames.

"Last June, on the morning after graduation from high school, two Jacksonville, Florida, youths were dead on arrival at a local hospital after the cycle they were riding swerved off the highway, hit a guard rail and rolled into a bridge abutment. Their bodies were found by highway patrolmen 80 feet from impact site, the motorcycle 132 feet away.

"A philosophy major who was the daughter of a prominent surgeon died just a month before graduation from a Georgia college as the result of injuries suffered in a motor-scooter accident. In California, a pair of newlyweds died instantly last summer when their lightweight cycle was struck from the rear by an automobile."

In a 1966 report presented to the Highway Research Board in Washington, D.C., Associate Professor John J. O'Mara, who teaches transportation safety for the University of Iowa's Civil Engineering Department, stated that the number of deaths and injuries caused daily by motorcycles was "equivalent to an epidemic."

The number of motorcycles had doubled in the three years prior to O'Mara's report, and the number of deaths and accidents had increased well beyond the rate of motorcycle sales. In 1962, there were 13 deaths for every 10,000 cycles on the road. Deaths increased from 882 in 1963 to 1,118 in 1964 to 1,580 in 1965. They jumped more than 200 in 1966 and again in 1967.

Nor were death and injury on motorcycles a problem only in the U.S. In 1951 in Great Britain, there were 1,175 killed and 40,000 injured on two-wheeled machines. By 1960, deaths spiraled to 1,743, injuries totaled a little less than 100,000, and approximately $134 million in damage was attributed to accidents involving two-wheeled, single-track machines. From 1951 to 1960, there was a total of 13,538 motorcycle fatalities and well over one half million injuries. And, according to the Royal Society for the Prevention of Accidents, a boy between sixteen and twenty owning a motorcycle had an eight percent probability of being seriously injured or killed.

In his report, O'Mara, supported by documentation from the National Safety Council, the Bureau of Public Roads, the National Center for Health Statistics, and other safety-related health agencies, made these points:

Only two of every 100 vehicles on the road are cycles, but at least three out of every 100 persons killed on the nation's highways are cyclists. On a per-mile-traveled basis, a cyclist's chances of being killed are about 20 times greater than those of an automobile driver.

"In Great Britain," said O'Mara, "97% of the total casualties in collisions between motorcycles and cars and trucks are motorcyclists.

"The motorcycle is the most deadly vehicle on the highway today," he concluded, "and this ghastly characteristic is inherent in the machine."

There seems to be absolutely nothing safe or secure about the motorcycle. Although it develops some inertial stability when in motion, when stationary it will not stand alone. Its brakes often lock and the more powerful machines can buck like a horse or walk on their back wheel (wheelie). Many motorcycles weigh under 200 pounds, but even the heaviest machine is not heavy or strong enough to absorb even a fraction of the energy created by itself and its motor in a collision.

"If you have your seat belt fastened and drive into a stone wall at 15 miles per hour," said Robert O'Donnell while a member of the Greater New York Safety Council, "the car will be a mess, but there won't be much damage to you. If you do that on a motorcycle, you get thrown against the wall, which is ruinous to flesh and bone...."

Other things happen too, as illustrated by Today's Health: "... You're catapulted high into the air, literally flying right over the car your cycle hit. And if you don't smash right into a lamp pole, a street sign, or another vehicle in your flight —you're going to come to a grinding, crumpling, mangling collision with concrete.

"Your skin will be abraded away in spots, loaded with sand, rubber, dust, and bits of dirty gravel in other places. If you land on your head or if, as many cyclists do, you strike your head on the hard surface, you don't have much chance for survival—and perhaps its just as well, because severe brain damage can ruin your life forever."

Automobiles are the motorcyclist's major enemy. Cycles are on a different level and comparative scale than cars. Cycles are difficult to see from the automobile driver's seat and easy to ignore. Tractor-trailer trucks are even more deadly. Motorcycles are invisible at a certain passing point, beside and from behind a truck, and cycles can be swept up and dragged by the tornadoing funnel of wind vacuuming at the rear of big tandem machines.

A motorcyclist's balance is precarious even in the best of conditions, but a heavy storm or high wind can bowl him off the road. The kickback of wind in the wake of a truck barreling in the opposite direction can knock a speeding cyclist 50 yards off his machine.

There are hidden assassins everywhere. There are potholes to trip the cyclist, grooves cut in the road for automobile traction that will grab and "trolley" his tires. Skidding is much more serious on a motorcycle. If a car skids, the vehicle might slide off the street or highway, but it will usually stay upright. A skidding cycle is most likely to overturn. When cornering, the cyclist leans into the road; he needs maximum traction. But rain greatly reduces his coefficient of friction, especially at the beginning of a shower when the new rain mixes with worn rubber and grease. Mud or clay are as slippery as ice, loose gravel acts like ball bearings. Even the paint, or the thick plastic strips used to mark divisions of lanes and center lines, are slippery and dangerous; even smooth manhole covers can cause a cycle to skid or slide.

Sudden temporary blindness is a constant and frightening threat. A heavy rain, a sudden snow, an automobile splashing mud into a cyclist's eyes or coating his goggles or shield, a speck of sand, insects, bird droppings—all can instantly cut off vision. The smallest detraction could end in injury, the slightest mistake might conclude in death.

"To turn a fourteen-year-old child loose on a motorscooter in today's traffic," said General George C. Stewart, retired Executive Vice President of the National Safety Council, "is about as sensible as giving a baby a dynamite cap for a teething ring. I would rather have a fourteen year old child of mine turned loose in traffic with a ten ton truck. . . ."

But a cyclist who is forty can die as quickly and in as grisly a manner as one who is fourteen. And it doesn't seem to matter whether he is in traffic or on the long, open road. In many states the majority of cyclists are killed on the highway. Yet in California, the state of the roaring treacherous freeways, most cyclists die at low speeds on snaking mountain roads or at intersections of Los Angeles' labyrinthine streets. And 41 percent of all cycle accidents in New York in 1967 occurred in New York City, which accounts for only 25 percent of all registered cycles in the state.

Comparison is futile. What matters is that you die, not where or when or why. Roaring over a highway or chugging down a residential street, the cyclist is equally vulnerable. The very nature of the machine offers no safety or security. There are no seat belts, shoulder harnesses, air bags, bumpers, or strips of chrome. There are no safeguards. The responsiblity for safety and survival falls completely on the shoulders of the most irresponsible and unreliable part of the entire package: Man. The slightest error, an unlucky break, can wipe out life, reduce the human form to a limp bag of blood and splinters of bone.

The driver, according to Professor O'Mara, "is a primary factor affecting the number and severity of cycle accidents."

"My 35-mile trip from Long Island to Manhattan takes no longer than the railroad," said an editor of a popular magazine in an article about motorcycles. "It takes considerably less time if you streak along illegally between lanes of traffic even when the cars are moving at or near the speed limit."

The exhilaration of the ride and the potential of the machine is sometimes too overwhelming to control. A flick of the wrist will roar us up to ninety, pull hard on the handlebars in first gear and we'll float on the back wheel. Soon, it is not enough to ride on the street. We find a highway and lean into speed. Ninety is not fast, soon neither is 120. We seek solace in the woods. We master trail riding and want to leap a creek, a small creek, three feet across and six inches deep. We leap the creek and search for a stream. On the other side of the stream there's a cliff. Below the cliff there's a canyon. The cyclist is often his own worst enemy, although sometimes, too, he is his only friend.

A cyclist must drive as if everybody is out to kill him. He must develop a paranoia about automobiles. The highways are chock-full of people out to revenge every wrong done them, bullies with four wheels who take sadistic pleasure in irritating, often devastating, his selected enemy on two wheels. A large minority of the 60,000 people dying in automobile accidents are doubtless victims of recklessness and, more often than one would expect, pure rage—troubles from the office, conflict at home— worked out on the road. A motorcycle is a far more tempting target than a two-ton automobile.

"There is an incredible disregard by the individual in the automobile for the motorcyclist," said Lawrence Ashe, a 21-year-old bank employee who has been cycling into Lower Manhattan from Queens for the last five years. "They cut you off and side-swipe you, they don't seem to care."

"An amazing number of cycles and scooters," reported *Changing Times* magazine in 1965, "are simply edged off the road or into another lane of traffic by motorists who either don't see them or who regard them as much as they do barking dogs."

There can also be no doubt that the cyclist's alienation from the four-wheeled culture in which he lives, combined with his popular image, has much to do with the man-made danger of traveling America's roads on a two-wheeled machine.

"There is something about the sight of a passing motorcyclist," said the New York *Herald Tribune* in an article about the motorcycle scene in 1965, "that tempts many automobile drivers to commit murder."

Eleven

Few politicians or soldiers believe that the only way to end the war is to obliterate Vietnam. Few doctors agree to eliminating cancer by destroying all of its victims, or jailing them with lepers, somewhere in the deep South Seas. Politicians and soldiers want to stop war by winning or making a reasonable peace. Doctors want to muffle disease by curing. And yet, they seem to believe—doctors, politicians, and statisticians—that the only way to decrease death and destruction involved in motorcycling is either to abolish the machine or severely limit its use. This point of view has been proven invalid with alcohol and marijuana, and there is no reason why it should even be considered with respect to motorcycles. There is no reason, in fact, to accept the testimony of a few highly touted non-motorcycling experts before hearing a competent defense of two-wheeled machines.

Besides, does danger always justify retreat? We are not turtles and cannot live our lives in fear of statistics, avoiding all activities calculated as the easiest in which to die. If so, we could never go out of the house. But then, how many thousands of people die in fires in their homes each year? We could stay in bed; but if we accept on statistics alone the fact that motorcycles are dangerous, then we must conclude that lying in bed is the most dangerous activity of all, since the majority of Americans seem to die there.

Twenty million Americans are zipping and zooming across country and city, over mountain and meadow on motorcycles. Hundreds of thousands of parents start their children on motorized bikes at seven, eight, or nine years of age. Thousands of grandparents visit their families and travel from one end of the country to the other on two-wheeled machines. Motorcyclists **come from many** different states and cruise in many different directions. They are younger and older and darker and lighter than their contemporaries. They practice different religions and some practice none at all. They ride different kinds of motorcycles, and ride for different reasons. But to the man—or to the machine—on one point they all agree: with proper preparation, cooperation and care, the motorcycle is potentially the safest vehicle on the road.

PROBLEM: *The number of people killed or injured on a motorcycle during the past decade has doubled. . .*

But during the same period the number of motorcycles registered in the United States has increased from 600,000 to 3.5 million. There are six times as many motorcycles registered today as there were a decade ago and ten times as many riders. In California alone, the state with the largest cycling population, as well as the highest rate of fatalities, motorcycle registration increased 128 percent from 1964 to 1969, while the number of serious injuries and deaths went up only 48 percent. There were 496 motorcycle accidents per each 10,000 machines in 1964, according to California Highway Patrol Commissioner Harold W. Sullivan. There were 321 per 10,000 five years later. Nationally, registration went up 17 percent in 1971, while fatalities increased only 4 percent.

No one should die because of automobiles, airplanes, snowmobiles, jeeps—or motocycles. But anyone can manipulate numbers to make things seem worse than they really are.

Professor O'Mara chose to compare four-wheeled and two-wheeled vehicle fatalities on a per-mile-traveled basis. But many cyclists think this an invalid way of looking at the situation. First, at the time of his study, at least one-fourth of all motorcycles were used strictly for racing or off-road riding. Most of these bikes don't have odometers. The miles logged by such machines are 1,000 times more dangerous than those recorded by their brothers on the road. Yet, O'Mara included the deaths from such activities without having any measure of mileage.

Second, at the time of the O'Mara study, motorcycles were used primarily for short trips. Very few riders could afford to leave their families for a month to travel across the country.

They chalked up hazardous city miles, primarily, while mileage figures for automobiles were inflated by traveling salesmen and the millions of families on vacations and weekend junkets.

In fact, one of the reasons motorcycle fatalities and accidents are decreasing at such a phenomenal rate today is because more and more men and women are beginning to take the time to discover the joy of traveling cross-country. Touring bikes are heavier. With wider tires, they have a much more secure grip on the road. Powerful engines make heavy bikes able to respond quickly in dangerous situations. Professor O'Mara was reacting to the lighter bikes—little Hondas and Yamahas—which today are not used on the street with nearly as much regularity. In this affluent society, the trend is toward bigger, more expensive machines.

True, one person died in 1971 for each 1,500 registered two-wheel machines compared to one death per 2,000 autos. But these figures are misleading. The law requires registration of all automobiles, but motorcycle registration is not mandatory. In most states, if a motorcycle is not used on public roads it need not be registered. In a few states, cycles need not be registered at all. There were approximately 3.5 million registered motorcycles in 1971, but at least another 3.5 million off-road and/or nonregistered machines, cycle industry officials estimate. There were more than a million trail bikes sold in 1971 alone, not counting mini bikes or racing machines, by far more dangerous than regular motorcycles. Thus, by substituting a far more accurate figure for motorcycles, the ratio between bikes and fatalities is reduced more than 50 percent, far below that of the ratio of deaths in automobiles. Motorcycles are obviously dangerous. But are they as dangerous as automobiles? Are they as dangerous as the public has been led to believe? There is ample evidence for serious doubt on both points.

PROBLEM: *A motorcycle is the most deadly vehicle on the road and this ghastly characteristic is inherent in the machine. For stability and security, motorcycles cannot compete with the automobile.*

Admittedly, motorcycles cannot compete. Cars are more comfortable, much faster, and easier to operate. While a cycle can do little damage to an automobile, it can be smashed and torn by a four-wheeled two-ton machine. Just because Joe Frazier and Rod Laver are both athletes doesn't mean Frazier can compete in a tennis court or Laver should fight Muhammud Ali. And the fact that motorcycles and automobiles are both self-propelled vehicles doesn't mean they both can or should perform in the same way. An automobile is not better than a motorcycle, nor is a motorcycle superior to a car. They are different vehicles, operated by different people, for similar but hardly ever the same purposes. Nor do cyclists want to compete. Just as truck and bus and Volkswagen drivers, just as all drivers, they want no more than an equal share of the road.

More than three-quarters of all motorcycle accidents are caused by automobiles—by drivers unable to, or who refuse to, see motorcycles. By drivers who do not accord them equal respect or recognition on the street or highway.

Although cyclists are at a slight disadvantage in poor weather, even Dr. O'Mara admits that road conditions and weather have "about the same relationship to cycle accidents as they do to all motor vehicle accidents."

In fact, on a motorcycle, a much more maneuverable vehicle, a rider has a much greater opportunity of avoiding danger—open manhole covers, potholes, children running suddenly into the street.

The motorcyclist also has fresh air on his face to keep him awake and alert. He has both hands and both feet on the controls all at the same time. He has two sets of brakes, in case one fails. He doesn't have his arm around anyone. He is not concentrating on the radio, talking into a tape recorder, having an interesting conversation, glancing at a newspaper, or smoking a cigarette. He is just driving. The demands of the machine will not permit him to relax. All of his concentration and effort are directed toward the problems and challenges of the road.

PROBLEM: *The motorcyclist is continually exposed to the injurious forces of the road. He has no seat belts, no doors, windows, bumpers, or chrome, no protection of any kind.*

In head-on or high-velocity collision, the rider is hardly ever thrown into the object he has hit. He is catapulted over the handlebars, sometimes as much as ten feet in the air and 100 feet away. People in an automobile accident, however, have shattering glass, steering wheels, dashboards, open glove compartments, windshields, and bouncing passengers to contend with. A cyclist may be lucky enough to land somewhere soft, may be lucky enough to keep himself intact. But for the victims in an automobile accident, like soldiers trapped in a collapsing bunker, there is nowhere to go, nothing to protect them, nothing to do except wait and hope not to die.

Automobiles are magnificent manifestations of American technology. American four-wheeled machines are, in fact, made too well; they are far too comfortable for our own good. Packed so snugly in these luxury machines, we develop a false sense of security. Sinking into soft foam-rubber seats and listening to our reverberating sound systems, it is very difficult to realize the intimate proximity or imagine the possibility of injury or death. A driver is wearing bermuda shorts, perhaps a T-shirt; his wife is modeling hot pants, or buried underneath a loose-fitting dress. They have unbuckled their seat belts, or slipped off their shoulder harnesses. They are driving, talking, watching the country go by. It is very cozy, but very dangerous.

An intelligent cyclist, however, aware of his vulnerability, is prepared for disaster and ready to react. He is wearing heavy boots, leather pants, jacket, and gloves. He is wearing a helmet capable of withstanding a 100 mile per hour collision or the weight of a three-ton truck. He is far from safe—no one can ever be totally secure today— but his chances for living or escaping serious injury are much better than those of his adversaries, snug in a car.

Yes, we have all seen motorcyclists riding in bathing suits and bare feet. We have seen them without helmets or boots, riding fast, without caution or care. But they are neither intelligent motorcyclists, nor intelligent persons. Riding a motorcycle without proper protection is like skydiving without a parachute or playing hopscotch in a minefield.

PROBLEM: *But if motorcycles are so safe and secure, why are there so many serious injuries, why are so many of our young men and women still dying on two-wheeled machines?*

According to the American Motorcycle Association, 72 percent of all automobile-motorcycle accidents are caused by the automobile. And a 1969 California study of collisions involving motorcycles and autos indicates that the motorcycle was at fault less than 39 percent of the time.

In addition, the United States Department of Health, Education and Welfare, in a 1967 study, showed that 70 percent of all motorcycle accidents occurred on borrowed or rented machines, and 20 percent of all motorcycling fatalities happened the first time a person rode a motorcycle. A 1965-1966 survey in Washington state showed that 29 percent of cyclists involved in fatal accidents did not own the machines they were riding. In a 1968-1969 North Carolina survey, 23 percent of all cycle fatalities were on borrowed bikes, and a Minnesota hospital study of 123 riders, seriously but not fatally injured, indicated that 70 percent of the victims were riding someone else's machine.

The evidence is clear: dead or injured cyclists, lucky enough to escape the wrath of automobiles or their drivers, were victims of their own stupidity.

Hardly anyone drives an automobile without first receiving proper instructions, practicing in parking lots, driveways, city parks, and uncrowded residential areas. Yet that logic escapes some motorcyclists. They seem to think that riding a motorcycle is somewhat of a cross between riding a bicycle and driving a car—master one and you've mastered them all.

Except for minor differences, automobiles have become fairly standardized. But motorcycle manufacturers have a tendency to work apart from each other, usually in secrecy. As engines become more sophisticated, and body styles more attractive, each manufacturer clings to his own individual method of vehicle operation.

Some British motorcycles are designed with shifting mechanisms on the right, braking controls on the left. Japanese bikes offer the opposite selection of controls. Some two-wheeled machines have hand shifts, most are shifted by the foot. Some bikes have different shifting patterns, and varying locations for the clutch. Lights are turned on by buttons, hidden switches, and keys. Some handlebars are positioned to force the rider to sit up straight, others are placed to make the rider crouch low. The weight of a motorcycle varies from 200 to more than 1,000 pounds.

Part of the fascination of motorcycling is that each bike can be a new challenge. It takes hours of practice and care to learn to master each size and weight and kind of machine. And yet motorcyclists seem to think themselves invincible and indestructible. Overconfidence is a common cause of death.

There are usually compound injuries leading to death from a motorcycle accident. Often, because of so many bruises, fractures, and broken bones, it is difficult for doctors to determine the fatal blow. But in more than half of the cases where documentation is possible, death was attributed to head injuries. And yet, many motorcyclists in the United States do not wear helmets regularly.

The most painful kind of motorcycle accident is when skin has been sliced and shredded, rubbed into sand, mixed with mud and dirt and filth. Doctors in emergency rooms in hospitals wash out such injuries every day. They take tweezers and pull from raw, bleeding flesh bits of dirt and gravel and twigs. And yet only a fraction of all cyclists invest in and wear riding suits and leathers, knowing full well that much pain, to say nothing of dangerous infection, could be avoided by doing so.

Motorcycles are potentially the safest vehicles on the road. Unfortunately, many motorcycles are operated by men and women who consider safety secondary, who think that common sense applies only to the four-wheeled, common man.

PROBLEM: *But if the evidence is so clear, if we know exactly why most people are killed or injured on motorcycles, why isn't something done about it?*

Motorcycles are dangerous. No one will debate that. But how dangerous and for what reasons? Wars and automobiles, airplanes, mad dogs, and dark alleys off metropolitan main streets are also dangerous. But the politicians in Washington fight a different battle than the soldiers who labor in Vietnam. The physicians in safe hospitals in Saigon see a different war than those surgeons working on the front.

And so it is with motorcycle injuries and fatalities. The professors and the politicians read from graphs and charts, draw conclusions from statistics poured from tireless computers. The doctors see only one by-product of the motorcycle—the end result of the unfortunate few, sometimes packaged only in a soggy wrapper of blood and guts.

Could it be that the experts have allowed the charts and graphs to fog their view of what is real and what is not? Could it be that doctors are allowing their personal feelings to far outweigh professional prognosis? Many cyclists believe this to be true.

Twelve

In 1962, reportedly, there were 6,363 known drug addicts in the United States, 47 percent of whom, according to the Bureau of Narcotics and Dangerous Drugs, were black Americans. Seventy-five percent of the total lived in slum areas of large cities, 7 percent were ex-convicts and approximately 3 percent were American Indians. By 1969, reported drug addiction had increased more than 1000 percent and deaths resulting from drugs had multiplied at least tenfold.

And yet, except for those families intimately involved with the death and misery wrought by narcotics, hardly anyone cared. Hardly anyone paid attention until law enforcement and public health organizations revealed that more and more young people were dying of dangerous drugs, especially middle-class whites.

"The hard, cold truth about drug addiction," said Dr. Milton Halpern, New York City's Chief Medical Examiner, in the February 24, 1970 issue of Christian Science Monitor, "is that death is increasingly the end result. In 1950, the number of New Yorkers who died from drug addiction was 17, by 1961 it was 275, and by last year [1969], it had grown to 1,100, of whom 224 were teenagers, including 20 under the age of 15."

"Heroin is probably being sold," said The New York Times, on February 7, 1970, "in almost every public high school in the city, in many junior high schools and in several private and parochial schools."

Drug addiction did not snare only a certain kind of young per-

son. Narcotics pushers are not selective. They will sell to who-
ever will pay. More and more teenagers from suburban high
schools were embracing drugs—the children of executives,
scholars, and highly-skilled, well-paid, blue-collar workers. By
1969, there were almost 45,000 known drug addicts under thirty
years old, at least one-fourth of whom were from middle-class
homes.

But not until the victims were clearly identified and verified
did the media take a firm and powerful stand against drugs and
that faction of organized crime that sold them. Not until then
did federal, state, and local law enforcement agencies begin to
actively seek out, capture, and convict drug pushers, smugglers,
and synthetic drug manufacturers.

It is unfortunate, but true. Nothing can be reformed or improved in America until the right people are harmed for the
wrong reasons. The man in the ghetto and the ex-convict have
no voice, no strings to pull in the legislatures, no pressure to
wield in the press. Children are as important as their parents.
Parents are as important as who they know, where they live, and
how much financial influence they can exert.

Prior to 1966, it was generally assumed that only a certain
type of person rode motorcycles. In 1964, the Hell's Angels
raided and reportedly raped two young girls in Porterville, California. In 1965, the Lynch Report documented the grisly and
sadistic activities of motorcycle desperado bands. In the same
year, Wiers Beach burned. Fear, not sympathy, was the domi-
nating public emotion related to motorcyclists, until Professor
O'Mara came to Washington and presented the results of his
study.

The motorcycle, once identified with the black leather jacket
crowd, had become something of a status symbol, he said,
because the machines were easily obtained by America's un-
usually affluent youths. A motorcycle used to cost an average
of $1,500 or more, but now various manufacturers, particularly
the Japanese, offered machines that would cruise at fifty miles
per hour and reach that speed in seconds for only $300. Some
cycles could be purchased in discount stores for much less.
Hundreds of thousands of American youngsters, richer than three-

quarters of the world population, could pay cash outright for such vehicles, others could arrange installment loans, and thousands more could rent two-wheeled machines.

"A most distressing fact," said Drs. Dillihunt, Maltby, and Drake in the *Journal of the American Medical Association* in 1966, "is that the group involved [in motorcycle accidents and fatalities] are young, otherwise healthy persons. This is not an epidemic involving the aged or infirmed—rather it involves a group of young, healthy people who must be regarded as a most important group in our society."

But Louisville surgeon James C. Drye was much more concise: "The individuals who are being injured are largely high school and college people. They are not leather jacket boys."

At the peak of the Hell's Angels scare, in 1964 and 1965, the cycle fatality rate had increased more than 40 percent in less than three years. But not until there came an understanding of the kind of people mostly being killed and injured on motorcycles, did the American public, largely through their legislatures, react.

Although Professor O'Mara had unfairly condemned all two-wheeled single track machines, he did have some valid arguments. The availability of the light-weight, inexpensive motorcycle, and the inadequacy of its construction, were partially the cause of this great increase in injury and death. But motorcyclists, and the motorcycle industry, equally shared the blame with federal, state, and local law enforcement agencies. And O'Mara condemned none of those.

In 1962, 12,751, or 71 percent, of all public high schools in the United States, offered driver training courses. Not one devoted as much as an hour to motorcycle operation. At the time of the O'Mara study, the federal government and three-quarters of all the states had absolutely no legislation governing the use, purchase, or operation of a motorcycle.

Half of all motorcycle fatalities were traced to head injuries —and yet hardly anyone, including those racing professionals under the sanction of the American Motorcycle Association, was required to wear a helmet. More than a fourth of all fatalities were attributed to lack of riding skill—and yet few riders were required to take a test or obtain a license to ride a motorcycle.

Any license would do—expertise with an automobile, truck, or tractor—would deem you officially capable of riding a two-wheeled machine.

But O'Mara's study and the reaction of the press influenced people to pressure for reform. Although little was accomplished on the federal level, almost every state legislature managed to push at least one motorcycle safety bill into law. Despite the increase in motorcycles, the number of deaths dropped from 2,050 in 1966 to 1,950 in 1967. By 1970, there was a 21 percent drop in fatalities from the 1966 figure.

And yet thousands of people are still needlessly injured on motorcycles every year and fatalities each year are slowly increasing. Is this because of the phenomenal growth in motorcycling? Perhaps. But more so because of the tendency of a comfortable society to exploit itself; because a fickle society tired of a crusade before it hardly got started.

Like a wave, proposals for new legislation thundered with powerful force against the legislative beach. And just as quickly, the wave receded, leaving a residue of disorganized and deceptively dangerous junk.

Halfway measures reap halfway results. No farmer has ever grown a full and healthy crop by fertilizing only part of his field. And no law or guideline that is partially articulated and half-heartedly enforced can yield maximum results. Since no action was initiated on the federal level (The National Safety Council did take a federal helmet law under advisement as a result of the O'Mara study), each state tried to quell the clamor for motorcycle safety in its own unique way. But the kind of laws enacted reflected the mood and attitude of the strongest lobbying force in each state capital. The results might be compared to a game of Scrabble with all of the vowels missing.

There is no uniformity. As late as 1969, 16 states did not require a special motorcycle driver's license. But 34 states did. Nor were age minimums for cycling clearly articulated. In some states they might be lower for motorcycles than autos, or related to the size and weight of the machine. In 1965, 27 states allowed fourteen-year-olds on the highway riding motorcycles. But such cycle riders were not permitted to drive cars.

Rearview mirrors are required throughout the country, except in Idaho, Indiana, Utah, Arizona, Pennsylvania, and Wyoming. With the exceptions of California, Washington, D.C., Illinois, Iowa, Mississippi, Montana, and Wyoming, all the states have some type of helmet law, although it varies widely from state to state. Except in Wisconsin, Arkansas, and Tennessee, crashbars are considered ineffective.

A cyclist cannot carry a passenger in seven states, must ride with his lights on in six states, and must have two rearview mirrors mounted on his machine in three states. Handlebars cannot be higher than the rider's shoulders, no matter who is riding, in two states. And in ten states, handlebars can be no higher than fifteen inches above the cycle's saddle.

But this lack of uniformity is only part of the problem. Cyclists suffer from the idiosyncracies of local law makers who enact half-witted, incongruous criteria. In Michigan and Washington, legislation requiring eye protection while riding at speeds higher than 35 miles per hour has been enacted. In West Virginia, goggles are required in the city of Charleston only. And in Indiana, goggles must be in the cyclist's possession—although he need not wear them.

In Montana, helmets are required in Billings and Great Falls; in Nevada they are required in Carson City, Las Vegas, and, for persons under seventeen, in the remainder of the state. In New Mexico, helmets must be worn by cyclists under eighteen, in Oklahoma by those under twenty-one. In Idaho, if a person travels at more than 35 miles per hour in posted areas, he must wear a helmet.

We ride a terribly dangerous and frustrating legal maze. Motorcycles under five BHP (brake horsepower) are not permitted to enter freeways in Florida, Hawaii, Kentucky, Ohio, Tennessee, West Virginia, and Mobile, Alabama. But to ride a freeway in California, a cycle must be more than fifteen BHP. In Illinois, Iowa, and Nevada, a motorcycle must not exceed the minimum speed on interstates. In Colorado, motorcycles are not permitted in wilderness areas, in New Jersey on the Garden State Parkway, and in Michigan, on limited access highways if the bike is under 125 cc.

And motorcyclists have given the "Vague Award" of the decade to Massachusetts and New York State. Motorcycles are permitted on some parkways in the Boston area, reports the American Automobile Association, and some motorcycles are permitted on the New York Thruway.

O'Mara had successfully scared the American public into action. So action was taken and Americans were placated. Soon there were other issues, the war in Vietnam, the unrest on college campuses, and drugs, to direct public wrath away from motorcycles. But the link between motorcycles and safety was never completed. We had gone halfway and then dropped the ball to start a new game. The cyclist was like the tenant evicted from his apartment for harboring pets—after his dog had broken loose and run away. The chain to which a motorcyclist's freedom was linked to his safety hung loose on both ends.

There are more than 2,000 motorcycle clubs and organizations in this country which, at least on a limited basis, bring two-wheeled enthusiasts together. And yet the motorcycle is such a diversified machine, offering so many ways in which cyclists can play apart from one another, that their relationship is semi-cordial at best. Motorcycling's objectives—the quest for both safety and freedom—are not contested. But the methods utilized to achieve such objectives, and the extent to which each group is willing to compromise, are bitterly, unyieldingly and continually debated. There has never been a group able to marshal the strength and influence of all motorcyclists, and until that happens there can never be standardization of laws, there can never be equitable and sensible laws. And the organization that must inevitably carry the torch is necessarily the AMA. Although it represents only 130,000 riders, a fraction of all of motorcycling's vastly growing population, it is by far the largest and most skillfully organized motorcycle lobbying machine.

At the time many of the laws were originally enacted in the 1960s, the American Motorcycle Association, then called the Motorcycle, Scooter and Allied Trades Association, was largely administered by a collection of Harley Davidson motorcycle executives. Consequently, there was prejudice, hardly subtle, against all motorcyclists not operating American-made machines. During the 1950s American riders with a preference for British bikes were obviously harassed by officials at AMA-sanctioned racing events. In the early sixties, the AMA turned against Japanese machines. And since most laws and criticisms were aimed at lighter-weight motorcycles, usually of Japanese origin, and most definitely the cause of the decreasing American-made share of the motorcycle market, the AMA played a passive role. Had it exerted its power and influence then, had it put forth an effort to organize the energies of motorcyclists before many of the bills were turned into laws, motorcyclists might not be facing such severe and possibly insurmountable problems today.

But during the past few years, the AMA has changed its leadership and its focus. It has become an independent organization, devoting more energies and resources toward helping those cyclists—the majority of all cyclists—who ride on the street. For the first time, the organization is concentrating not especially on selling motorcycling or administering racing activities, but on educating lawmakers.

"We must have legislation that is not detrimental to the interests of the cyclist, but at the same time, could be called 'responsible' legislation," Russ March, director of the AMA, has said. "We've got to talk personally with legislators, point out to them what kinds of laws we need to make motorcycling safer. We've got to clearly explain to them why we're against certain laws and, on the other hand, why certain laws should be passed in spite of the fact that we don't particularly like them."

The AMA retained Bill Low, former campaign advisor to the Republican National Committee, to help instruct smaller cycling groups on how to operate efficiently and effectively in the local political arena. The organization began a public service television campaign designed to reach more than seven million viewers. Its members have gone into New Jersey and a number of other states and deliberately broken laws considered prejudicial to motorcyclists just for the opportunity of fighting them in court. They have approached state legislators sponsoring bills unfair to motorcyclists and, by amassing evidence and gathering electorate power, often convinced lawmakers to amend or cancel pending legislation.

In Texas, the AMA successfully lobbied for a bill to have motorcycle highway speed limits made uniform with those for automobiles. In California, the organization successfully muffled a bill which would have required motorcycles to run only with lights on.

The AMA has established a full-time legislative department, and started massive letter-writing campaigns aimed at previously uncontested anti-motorcycling legislation. And representatives of the AMA are in Washington regularly, pushing, pressing for and against pending legislation, documenting their positions with evidence and testimony from experts.

But they are working with a minimum of resources, time, and popular support. And they are working against the often insurmountable odds against change—never popular or successful in this or any other country. Consequently, they have more than just a long way to go. It is a journey with, under the present circumstances, no achievable destination.

Thirteen

Laws. They are the bulwark of society for those who support them. But to those who fight against them, laws are our weakness. There are motorcycle interest groups throughout the country fighting for stricter laws. Others want more relaxed laws. Still others are pushing for the enactment of legislation they particularly support, or for the abolition of legislation they find particularly offensive. Motorcyclists reflect as many different points of view as there are different motorcycles and special ways to ride.

Most are convinced of the importance of helmets, yet some are unwilling to accept a law that will force them to wear one on the grounds that telling an American what to wear is a violation of the rights granted by the Ninth Amendment to the Constitution of the United States. Helmet laws have already been repealed in California and Illinois for that reason.

Some cyclists point to the results of a mandatory helmet law in New Zealand which, according to government officials there, has cut motorcycling fatalities in half. The federal Department of Transportation is considering the sponsorship of similar legislation. But the AMA is not in favor of it, claiming that the same job can be done through an intelligent, high-saturated publicity program focused on the values of wearing protective headgear.

Many motorcyclists debate even those values. They claim that helmets are more a hindrance than a help. Being able to hear cars coming up behind you in dense fog or heavy traffic is extremely important, they say. And helmets muffle sound. Furthermore, at

137

slow speeds on a very warm day, the rider becomes uncomfortable, often irritable, all of which correspondingly decreases his riding efficiency. A few cycling interest groups even doubt the motives of those legislators pushing for mandatory helmet controls.

"If saving lives was the real intention of these laws," said *Popular Cycling* magazine in 1971, "far more could be saved if automobile drivers were forced to wear safety helmets. Many more car drivers are killed each year by head injuries than motorcyclists. The only problem here is that our legislators would he attacking a majority group and the screams would be heard coast-to-coast. Can you imagine a woman paying $20 to $30 to have her hair done and then having to put a helmet on to drive home?"

Other people against cycling legislation hold the manufacturers responsible:

"We have questioned the motives of manufacturers and have criticized them for what we feel may be their selfish part in the constant outpouring of certain anti-personal-freedom bike laws," editorialized *Easyriders* magazine in 1971. "By doing so, we have automatically cut off any hope of receiving future advertising from them—for the name of the game is to brown-nose them, glorify their products editorially, and in return receive a share of their huge advertising budget every year.

"But we decided, screw it, we would rather jam an altered bike, customized the way we want; wear a helmet when we want to, not wear one when we don't; fight for right and screw hypocrisy."

Nothing is sacred in the helmet dispute. No group can be counted on to think or react in a particular or logical way. Even the majority of helmet manufacturers, specifically those of high quality safety helmets, are against compulsory helmet laws. They say that they want to manufacture a superior product but that mandatory helmet laws would be a boon to unscrupulous manufacturers of inexpensive and low-quality products that would, at the slightest impact, shatter or crack. To compete, they don't want to be forced to produce junk.

For every law governing motorcyclists there are thousands of objectors, hundreds of experts who will prove its inadequacy and invalidity. Some states require motorcyclists to ride with their lights on, hoping that will increase recognition and awareness on the highway of the man on the two-wheeled machine.

"But," says Ed Youngblood, director of public relations for the AMA, "what of the legal ramifications? If a car does hit a motorcycle, one of the first things to be knocked out are the lights. Thus, the automobile driver could claim and probably prove that the cyclist did not have his lights on. We would be at fault in virtually every case."

Rearview mirrors, at least in a four-wheeled culture, seem a reasonable request. And yet in some quarters it is one of the most bitterly contested cycling safeguards.

"Believe me," says Theresa Wallach, author of *Easy Motorcycle Riding*, "having a rearview mirror on a motorcycle is one of the most incorrect and criminally wrong bits of advice that anybody could tell you.

"A mirror mounted on the handlebar, the steering control of a motorcycle, is as useless as if a car's mirror were attached to its steering wheel. Unless you're going in a perfectly straight line, no mirror is in focus, is it?"

There seems to be no answer. No matter what is proposed there are waves of objections. The opposition whines on irritably, seemingly with no end.

A cyclist's greatest joy might be in riding with his wife or girlfriend. And a passenger is in as much or as little danger as the rider. Crash bars are good looking, and possibly helpful at slow speeds, but often buckle or collapse under high stress. Goggles and leathers are all right. But again, why should someone legislate what we can and cannot wear? Why should we be permitted to ride some roads at seventy miles per hour and prohibited on others with a maximum of 65? How can we, as taxpayers, be prohibited from any of America's roads? Why can't we adjust our handlebars to the position most comfortable to us? Why can't we have as many rearview mirrors as we feel we need? Why can't we design our machine any way we want?

It is most definitely a question of how much freedom a human being can handle, how much freedom a democratic country can afford to provide.

But it has never been our idea or our practice to make all Americans totally free. There are rules for walking the streets, flying airplanes, driving cabs and other motorized machines. There are laws against murder and rape and robbery. Although motorcyclists can and have claimed that they have been subject to discrimination, they are not totally immune; they cannot escape all legislative restrictions. There must be some measure, some line drawn, between where freedom leaves off and anarchy begins.

And that line must be drawn by the federal government. No motorcycle interest group, including the AMA, has the power. No organization could marshall the influence to bring together representatives of all major cycling interests. In Washington the Department of Transportation could nominate a committee composed of these representatives, equally balanced with doctors and statisticians, known for their expertise in the transportation safety fields. The objective: to standardize the laws, to articulate clearly and finally, exactly what will be expected from a person riding a motorcycle, to safeguard constitutional rights without sacrificing life and limb.

The Uniform Vehicle Code, annually amended by DOT, sets forth a comprehensive program of laws governing four-wheeled vehicle operation, safety, equipment, manufacture, and sales. These are not federal laws, but they are well-defined and intricately articulated suggestions for four-wheeled vehicle legislation that have been adopted almost verbatim by all states. The government does not force each state to comply with the principles set forth in the Uniform Vehicle Code, but it is specific about reasoning and intentions, as the code's "Foreward" indicates:

"The Uniform Vehicle Code is a specimen set of motor vehicle laws, designed and advanced as a comprehensive guide or standard for state motor vehicle and traffic laws. It is not based on theory; it is based on actual experience under various state laws throughout the nation. It reflects the need for uniformity in traffic regulation throughout the United States and, to this end, serves as a reliable, contemporary guide for use by state legislatures . . . ."

Among the 284 pages of the Uniform Vehicle Code, a little under two pages are devoted to motorcycles. Just two, under Article XIII, "Special Rules for Motorcycles." The government suggests that motorcyclists ride only on permanent seats, that they not ride side-saddle, that they not pass in the same lane occupied by the vehicle overtaken, that they do not cling to other vehicles —information that any seven-year-old hobby horse rider could articulate just as succinctly, advice that anyone not planning an early death would surely follow. As to equipment, the government suggests footrests (it would be impossible to ride a motorcycle any distance without them) and handlebars no more than fifteen inches above the portion of the seat occupied by the operator. The government recommends eye protection and helmets as well.

But what about rearview mirrors? Isn't the ability to see behind you at least as important as the height of the vehicle's handlebars? What about leathers? Isn't the rest of your body just as important to protect as your head? What about rider training? Isn't a comprehensive program of methods of testing and licensing as essential to the cyclist as it is to the auto driver? What about equal treatment? Shouldn't the government at least consider the possibility of allowing cyclists on all public roads, at least on federal highways, and permitting them to ride at will and at the speeds legislated for cars? What about uniformity?

Says the "Forward":

"Certain portions of the Code set forth rules of the road—the things that people shall and shall not do as they drive or walk. If the public is to understand, remember and observe these rules in moving from state to state, they should be exactly the same, word for word, in every state. Such uniformity also makes easier the task of police officers, judges, traffic engineers, motor vehicle administrators and educators. The language of the code has been tested by long experience and there is no need for deviation.

"Substantial, but not necessarily verbatim, uniformity is a clear necessity in the chapters of the Code dealing with motor vehicle equipment, because vehicles are designed for use anywhere in the country."

It isn't as though the federal government or, more specifically DOT, is prejudiced against motorcyclists, but this token attempt at including two wheels in a four-wheeled uniform code is surely an abdication of responsibility. In a uniform code, motorcycles and riders would receive attention equal to that given cars and drivers. As an alternative, a separate code, based on adequate research, articulation, and development should be worked out for two-wheeled machines.

DOT is obviously aware of the inadequacy of cycling legislation and the lack of uniform laws from state to state. Ignoring the problem will hardly stimulate solutions. Only an outright confrontation will bring feedback, discussions, agreements, compromises, and eventual results. DOT, simply by recognizing and publicizing the motorcyclist's problems, by registering concern, would legitimize motorcycles and add needed weight to the AMA's state-by-state lobbying efforts. That would be a good beginning, but only that.

In 1971 and 1972 DOT invested $2 million on two prototypes of automobiles designed for total safety, but did nothing about two-wheeled safety. DOT claims that the ideas set forth in the Uniform Vehicle Code are merely suggestions, that it can't force any state to comply with them. Yet seat belts, seat belt warning systems, anti-pollution devices, increased safety measures such as turn signals have been demanded from Detroit auto manufacturers and required on any auto imported into the country. instead of ignoring motorcycles, can't DOT act as positively on the riders' behalf?

If all drivers of four-wheeled motorized vehicles are required to have a license then there is no reason why this law cannot be extended to riders of two-wheeled vehicles. The tests required before a person receives such a license should be standardized and improved as well. In Pennsylvania, a cyclist is licensed if he can make an emergency stop and maneuver his cycle at five miles per hour around a series of pylons set up in a parking lot. Some states merely ask the cyclist to beep his horn, blink his lights, and stop and go to earn permission to drive a two-wheeled machine. These tests are hardly measures of skill and ability in traffic or high speed situations. The beep-blink tests would hardly be adequate in any state to authorize automobile operation.

With its considerable weight and resources, DOT, working with cycle manufacturers and riders, could certainly design a suggested motorcycle-riding training program and procedure for licensing that most states would readily adopt. DOT could require all dealers to offer a training program, at a fair charge, to all novices purchasing two-wheeled machines. Its endorsement of such a program would help convince instructors and administrators of driver education courses in high schools, colleges, and other institutions to offer a motorcycle option in conjunction with the standard auto criteria. There are a number of organizations, such as the Scouts and the Shriners who do offer motorcycle training programs, but unless a large and powerful institution, such as DOT, concerned with the public welfare, supports and pressures for such reform, more and more Americans each year will continue to be injured and to die needlessly.

And the machines must be standardized as well. If automobile controls—steering wheel, clutch, brake, gas pedal—are always placed in the same general area, then there seems to be no reason motorcycle manufacturers should not be required to follow a similar procedure. It would not be difficult, if given the same amount of time allowed to Detroit auto manufacturers to develop anti-pollution devices, for motorcycle manufacturers to design operational controls that would fall into a standardized pattern. Again, by ignoring the evidence and the need DOT is abdicating responsibility.

And what of the roads on which two-wheeled machines must travel? Highways have been designed for buses, trucks, and automobiles. With steel-grated bridges, grooves cut in the road to increase automobile traction, the lack of adequate shoulder areas, all roads seem designed to be hazardous to the motorcyclist's equilibrium. DOT should take definite action to suggest highway designs that take all vehicles into consideration.

All vehicles should be permitted to ride all roads. Certainly there are small motorcycles that cannot carry a passenger safely at very high speeds. But there are also automobiles, out-dated rattletraps from another age, newer Volkswagens, Fiats, and Corvairs, that are equally unsafe at seventy or eighty miles an hour. None should be permitted the freedom to endanger the lives of other people. And to legislate against one hazard, while ignoring another equally dangerous one, is indeed an injustice, not to mention a violation of an American's constitutional rights.

Finally, motorcyclists require not only public recognition, but some means of identifying themselves at a distance. Admittedly, considering the motorcycle's vulnerable electrical systems, blazing lights might not be the answer. But surely in this rapidly advancing technological society, motorcycle manufacturers could develop some way of safeguarding lighting systems against breakage, or suggest some other simple way to easily identify the man and his machine. Most motorcycles are not manufactured in the United States, as are most automobiles on American roads.

But America represents the biggest motorcycle market in the world, and no manufacturer would dare refuse a DOT edict.

It seems odd that the only definite action taken by John Volpe, who became Secretary of Transportation in 1969, was against motorcyclists and, in a very strange way, against uniformity of motor vehicle laws for cycles.

A number of state supreme courts have ruled the Uniform Vehicle Code's helmet provision unconstitutional. It might seem, then, that the only course of action would be to decide whether it is an important and valuable idea, and if so, enact it into law on a federal level. The AMA or some other responsible motorcycling organization or individual could then test the law before the federal supreme court. One way or another the idea of uniformity could be achieved.

But DOT seems utterly opposed to standardizing the helmet law even though it is probably the most important and bitterly contested part of the debated motorcycle legislation. Secretary Volpe, it appears, prefers to fight each battle on the state level, and avoid a resolution of the problem.

When Connecticut's 1967 helmet law, which was in compliance to the Uniform Vehicle Code, was repealed, in compliance with the wishes of the people, Secretary Volpe said, according to the Boston *Herald Traveler*, that "he has 'no patience with the attitude' of those who are attempting on the state level to repeal laws requiring crash helmets to be worn by motorcyclists. He will do everything in his power, he said, 'to keep those laws on the books, even if it means withholding highway safety and federal aid highway funds.' He has the authority and 'will not hesitate to use it,' he declared."

After a resolution in protest to Volpe's threat was presented to President Nixon by the Connecticut State Assembly and, in return, Mr. Volpe's position was once again articulated by the DOT, newly elected Governor Thomas Meskill responded:

"Connecticut could not stand the loss of these funds.

"I am sympathetic with those who wish to see this law repealed because of the design and weight of the safety helmets, and will work to have a more acceptable helmet approved by government officials. In the meantime, however, I must veto this legislation."

There can be no doubt. Instead of confronting the problem and resolving it in one way or another, instead of complying with the wishes of the people the agency is proported to serve, DOT resorted to methods that could be defined only as extorionate in nature. As of January 1972, there were anti-helmet groups actively lobbying in 43 of our 50 states. Might Volpe's tactic, for which there seems no logical explanation, be initiated 43 more times?

The Connecticut Motorcycle Association based much of its campaign against helmets on the premise that the USA Standards Institute Specification for Protective Headgear for Vehicular Users, Z-90, provides less than minimal protection for the motorcyclists involved in an accident. The helmet laws, with Z-90 Standards as a guideline in the Uniform Vehicle Code, the Association reasoned, as outlined in the Uniform Vehicle Code, endorsed the products of disreputable discount stores and manufacturers. Shoddy companies manufactured cheaper, though unsafe, products, and could drive the better helmet manufacturers out of business—those that followed the Snell Memorial Foundation's recommended standards, which is about 50 percent higher than the Z-90—and subsequently increase, rather than decrease the loss of lives caused by head injuries.

Here again, at the risk of being repetitive, one must point out that DOT could take an active and responsible position. Instead of rejecting the wishes of motorcyclists, DOT officials could re-examine the Z-90 standards, which were established as far back as 1965, and perhaps more thoroughly safeguard the lives of those people who choose to wear protective headgear.

DOT could even go so far as to conclude that helmets are less like clothing and more comparable to fenders and bumpers and chrome. As with seat belts, the agency could require that a helmet be included with the purchase of every machine. Helmets could even be designed with eye protection built in. A DOT requirement of this kind perhaps is not as forceful as legislation, but it would have a psychological effect, persuading many more riders to use protective headgear. This way out is somewhat of a compromise solution that should be agreeable to both groups. And it would establish, once and for all, a uniform and consistent guideline.

For though we can require seat belts sold with each car and helmets with each two-wheeled machine, there is no way we can force people to use them. Certainly the line between freedom and anarchy must be drawn. But it should be managed with care, delicacy, and precision.

There is much the federal government can do, working within the structures of power, polemics, and politics, to keep a rather large portion of its constituency active and alive. But the ultimate responsibility for survival, whether it be war, motorcycles, or pollution, must be delegated to the individual. Each man must be his own strongest link between death and life.

Fourteen

Motorcycles were invented a thousand times. They were invented in tool sheds and vacant lots, and in earth-walled basements illuminated by the pale yellow of flickering kerosene lamps. Motorcycles were put together in the rear of printers' shops, in newspaper offices, behind taverns and livery stables and candy shops. They were manufactured by the calloused hands of farmers, the fat mitts of merchants, and by the long, trained fingers of draftsmen and engineers. Motorcycles were invented on Sundays after church and evenings after dinner when the children were tucked in bed and the women sat by the stove darning socks. The evolution of the motorcycle was no different from the evolution of any other sophisticated, highly-complicated device: they were conceived and fashioned by men schooled in experience, whose resources were ideas, whose rewards were hope, and whose virtues were conviction. Men working independently without benefit of telephone or technical journals or prototypes of the failures or successes of their contemporaries.

The first spark plugs were bigger than baseballs, carburetors were made from tomato juice cans, seats were leather-wrapped planks. And gasoline, for those who used it, was purchased at the drug store by the pint. But the best of our technology seems to have developed in a similarly independent, crude fashion. Teamwork and mass production must always be prefaced by the loneliness of motivated young men, dedicated to a device, hell-bent in an anonymous crusade to succeed.

And the way to succeed in the development of self-propelled road vehicles in the middle of the nineteenth century was to utilize steam. Steam-propelled locomotives for cross-the-nation railroads. Steam could power paddleboats on the Ohio and the Mississippi and ships on the open seas. And steam was the form of energy used to power the oldest self-propelled land vehicles now existing in the United States.

Water for the Roper Steam Velocipede was contained in a hollowed-out slab of wood on which its inventor, Sylvester H. Roper, first sat in 1869. The boiler was below the seat, the chimney behind it, and when it operated, the Velocipede barreled along at five miles per hour on wooden-spoked wheels with iron band tires.

The Long Steam Tricycle, manufactured in 1879 by George A. Long, still works. It is the oldest self-propelled completely operable road vehicle in the United States today.

Sylvester Roper used charcoal to heat water to make steam. Some men used wood chips, others kerosene or coal. But on July 10, 1883, for George A. Long's patent number 281,091, granted by the United States Patent Office, gasoline was specified as the major fuel.

It took only two more years for Gottlieb Daimler, a 51-year-old Cannstatt, German inventor, to introduce, along with gasoline as the fuel, the internal combustion engine as the power plant for most self-propelled land vehicles. Previously, internal combustion engines were considered too heavy and too weak to move a vehicle, but Daimler liberated the engine, miniaturized it, and devised a way to feed it gasoline through a surface carburetor. Paul Daimler, the inventor's son, became the first man to ride what is today commonly accepted as the motorcycle. He traveled three kilometers, from Cannstatt to Unterturkheim and back, on November 10, 1885.

After the ride, the elder Daimler tried to convert his motorcycle to a power sled, unsuccessfully. Like other technological pioneers, he had many more ideas than years in which to develop them. He dreamed of a power boat and a horseless carriage, and dedicated ten years to these projects while his motorcycle gathered dust and the less-sophisticated visionaries in other lands and faraway cities still toyed, futilely, with steam. Daimler was later sorry not to have realized the potential of the motorcycle and dedicated more time to refining it. But his work with the horseless carriage resulted, at the turn of the century, in an unique automobile that today is known as the Mercedes Benz.

No matter what the engineers will say, machines will never be entirely and consistently reliable, and into the twentieth century motorcycles were designed with unreliability in mind. The Brown Brothers Push Cycle, for example, although powered by a V-belt Direct Drive Engine, had starting pedals for emergencies—especially those occurring midway up a steep hill. George L. Holzapfel bought a Brown Brother's Push Cycle second hand in 1906, for $25.

"The sight of all the pedal gear and its accompanying chain offended me," says Holzapfel, "so I threw them away. Afterwards, I had to run with the machine to get it started, but this was not uncommon in those days. Longer handlebars, a modified seat position and footboards completed the major modifications. On the footboards, boxes for tools and books were mounted, along with a good-sized battery to lessen the intervals between charging."

There were no custom-designed factory specials at the turn of the century. The machines were only as pleasing as the modifications of their riders made them. You got nothing less than was necessary. But you expected nothing more.

George Holzapfel rode his Brown back and forth from home to London University from 1906 to 1910. After graduation in 1911, he went on a holiday to western England, about 200 miles:

"About 50 miles from my destination, I saw crossroads with a steep hill on the other side. I opened the throttle (about 45 miles per hour) and then noticed a coach with three horses about to cross. The brakes on the Brown were practically nil, though, and stopping was out of the question. It was either the leading horse or the brick wall. I hit the horse in the chest with my left shoulder. The motorcycle hit the wall and was completely demolished. Ironically, the horse was injured, but not I, and the owner of the coach charged me $25 to cover the injuries."

Those were the days of simplicity, when machines had token brakes and half-hearted gears and attracted attention with the rattles and roars of primitiveness. When a man cared for his vehicle and blazed his own highway. When you knew and everyone else knew that the only controls to count on were the throttle to keep you moving and your boots to make you stop. The days when lawyers still fought criminal cases and a man paid not for insurance policies, but (sometimes honestly, sometimes not) fairly for his mistakes.

Speed traps were everywhere. There were more speed traps in 1910 than there are in parts of the southern United States, the land of the speed traps, today. Some towns had ten miles per hour speed limits, and the police in one village in England— Stoney Stratford—waited hungrily behind buildings and trees on horses for a cyclist to exceed the six miles per hour law. It wasn't unusual for a cyclist to collect two or three citations a day. But that problem, too, was uncomplicated:

"Fortunately," George Holzapfel recalls, "the police were very reasonable. Fines were not always increased for subsequent offenses, and some of the police could even be persuaded to forget about the whole thing—*if* you could get one of them alone and *if* you could spare a few shillings."

Bribery: an international tradition. A link to the past and between every nationality. That, and man's feeling for space and freedom, his desire to take off on his own and roam:

"All a motorcyclist needed in those days was a good cycle, some tinkering ability, an oil stove, a frying pan, and a shotgun [for hunting]," says George Holzapfel. "It was a very happy life."

But simplicity eventually fades under the pressure of man's insatiable energies to create something better than people before him did. Problems are never solved—they breed other problems. Challenges are never completely met—they splinter into other challenges. Technology never rests—it multiplies into intricacies.

From steam to gasoline. From Roper to Long to Daimler. From the Clark Gasoline Tricycle, designed in 1897, to the E. R. Thomas Motorcar, the first commercially produced automobile in the United States. From the 1¾ horsepower Indian, designed by racer Oscar Hedstrom in 1902 to the 3 horsepower, 25 cubic inch Harley Davidson, *the silent gray fellow*, in 1903, and the 15.4 horsepower Pope, less than a decade later. From the seat-less Autoped Motorscooter in 1918, to the luxurious Simplex Servi-Cycle in 1935. These were years of technological pioneer-ing that the common man could appreciate and understand. Years before push buttons and power steering made technology a frightening mystery, years when hard work was symbolized by grease on a man's hands.

The Harley and Davidson families, a manufacturer most involved in the development of the early motorcycle, were known as good people who produced a reliable motorcycle that would last and last.

The early Harley Davidson Motorcycles were built in the evenings and on weekends by members of both families, aided by an unidentified German draftsman and a Scandanavian, Ole Evinrude, who was to become a successful manufacturer of outboard motors. In 1903 the Harleys and Davidsons took time to build a ten by fifteen foot wooden structure in the Davidson's backyard and the following Monday evening, with Harley-Davidson Motor Company freshly painted on the door, the company was officially in operation.

The first motorcycle to be produced in that factory was sold to a Mr. Miller, according to company records, who rode it for 6,000 miles. George Lyon bought it from Miller and logged an additional 15,000 miles. Then a Dr. Webster purchased the machine from Lyon and rode another 18,000 miles. Louis Fluke was to eventually buy the machine from Webster and add 12,000 miles. The last reported owner was Stephen Sparrow who was still riding when he last notified the factory that he had chalked up more than 32,000 miles.

That is the way all machines ought to perform, but somewhere the American industrial tradition of giving the public its money's worth was lost. Sometime, with technology multiplying to the beat of an expanding population, product quality and efficiency became secondary to the rate of production and appearance upon completion. Hardly a self-propelled vehicle today—automobile or motorcycle—will last for 83,000 miles, traveling roads far superior than those of fifty to sixty years ago. But those motorcycles Messrs. Harley and Davidson offered at the turn of the century for $250 were probably the finest ever made.

"The wheel base is 51 inches and the height 21½ inches and it is made especially strong to stand rough American roads. The motor is hung low in the frame and this together with the extention front forks, 2½ ins. detachable tires, spring seat post, and 3 coil suspension motorcycle saddle, make the Harley Davidson an ideal, easy riding machine for touring or general purposes." So stated the first Harley Davidson advertising brochure, issued in 1907.

Four Harley Davidsons were sold in 1903, and in 1904 the company doubled the size of its factory and turned out eight new machines. In 1905 production was doubled again and the following year the company moved to a new building, twenty-eight by eighty feet, hired five additional employes and, working through the pains and expenses of growing, produced more than fifty machines before the end of that year. The demand for Harley Davidsons was increasing so rapidly that little time could be dedicated to refinements of the new building. Once the framework was up, an adjacent railroad discovered that it was too close to the tracks. So Walter Davidson, along with "eight or ten other fellows picked up the entire shop and moved it back about a foot and a half."

Ten years later, Harley Davidson was producing machines at a rate of 18,000 a year. By 1916 the motorcycle in America, led by Harley Davidson and Indian, was well on its way to becoming modern man's replacement for nature's four legged horse. Then, in 1917, on motorcycles and on all sorts of motorized monstrosities, America rode into war.

World War I was good for the American motorcycle industry at first, especially since the British had stopped producing two-wheeled machines in 1914 and converted all their production facilities into plants for grinding out the tools of war. All Harley Davidson production efforts were devoted to military vehicles by the time America entered the war, and during 1917 and 1918, few civilian machines were sold. But the wartime boom for the American motorcycle industry was to turn into a long and debilitating peacetime bust.

Not only had consumers lost contact with motorcycles during the war years, but they had become acquainted with the autocar, the horseless carriage, especially with Henry Ford's black and inexpensive machine. A motorcycle with a sidecar could never provide the comfort and convenience of the Model T. The motorcycle truck couldn't hold a tenth of the weight or a twentieth of the volume that could be carried in a big-binned four-wheeled machine. The motorcycle, no matter what brand or modification, could never provide the prestige of a Desoto or a Chrysler.

And at no other time before in America's history could luxury be purchased so readily. Everybody seemed to be making money and feeding that money at a rate far greater than it was received back into the economy. With respect to transportation, why struggle with two wheels, most people reasoned, when we can afford four?

One might think that the depression of the 1930s was the best thing that could have happened to the motorcycle in America, but during the ten years prior to the stock market crash of 1929 motorcycle manufacturers had modernized their ideas and their products. In the 1920s and 1930s motorcycles became more expensive, more luxurious, and more powerful. Those few hearty souls that wanted motorcycles could buy the biggest and fanciest two-wheelers ever made before or since. But they could no longer purchase, with a motorcycle, inexpensive transportation. In 1930 one could buy a deluxe Harley Davidson or Indian or Henderson with a sidecar and all of the options to go with it for $2,000. Motorcycles were at least as expensive as automobiles, and often much more so. And people were choosing comfort and convenience over the Spartan attributes of two wheels, especially since the investment for both was equal. The whole industry couldn't seem to do anything right. Companies could produce excellent motorcycles, of course. But what worth has a good product that no one will buy?

There were many motorcycles in the Second World War— Harley Davidson sold 90,000 of them—yet they represented only a small portion of all of the vehicles produced by the American war effort. War II was a four-wheeled war: jeeps could handle almost any terrain and carry guns, supplies, officers and ammunition faster and farther. War II was an eight-wheeled war: men closeted in tanks fired at others closeted in tanks, ironclad fortresses that could gallop over barren sand and rock-knuckled roads. War II was a three-wheeled war: hundreds of troops could be transported in flying baggage cars that needed wheels only to take off or land.

Nor did the boom of the economy at war's end help the motorcycle. More motorcycles were sold, of course, than at any other time in the previous two decades, but sales increased far below the percentage of increase in automobile sales. And some of the people purchasing motorcycles were plainly the wrong kind of people—according to many other people—the greasers and the hoods, the jobless who jockeyed about the country causing panic, and diminishing respect for the machines they rode.

This wasn't all true, of course; the outlaws represented a very small percentage of those men and women who rode two-wheeled machines. But the truth in fact has little weight or importance compared to the truth that most people believe— the riot in Hollister, California, Frank Rooney's short story, Marlon Brando as "The Wild One."

The history of the motorcycle from 1920 to 1951 reads like the book of Job. Companies folded—Henderson, Yale, Merkel, Minnesota, Pope, Thor—one, sometimes two, at a time.

In 1953, because of continued financial trouble, the Indian Motorcycle Company of Massachusetts closed its doors for the last time. Its exit from business left Harley Davidson the surviving motorcycle manufacturer in America. As its predecessor, the horse, the motorcycle was relegated for the most part to those well-heeled sportsmen who preferred to play only with the most expensive of toys. And to those few cowboys who refused to allow technology to extinguish tradition.

Fifteen

Motorcycles were re-invented in 1947 by Soichiro Honda, a five-feet, four-inch Japanese mechanic who worked his way in school through the eighth grade. His story resembles the traditional pattern of American success, except that it occurred in the Orient, and without American help.

When the first automobile clattered into the obscure village of Komyo, 150 miles southwest of Tokyo, a little second-grader ran after it. He followed it through the town, then down to the main road. And when it was finally out of sight, he turned and walked back to his parents' house, a boy bewitched. "When it stopped and oil dropped on the road," Soichiro Honda said many years later, "I smelled it and dipped my hands into the dirt and just breathed."

Some men, if they are very lucky, will actually confront the crossroads of fortune and mediocrity. It is not easy to pick the right road and the opportunity comes only to a dedicated few. But for Soichiro Honda that day the short cut to fortune and perhaps immortality rolled out in front of him like a bulldozer clearing debris for a great highway.

At age five, Honda would stand for hours at a rice mill, tapping his foot to the beat of a diesel. At eight, he bicycled ten miles to see his first airplane. At ten, he was building and selling bikes made with self-forged frames and scavenged wheels. At twelve, he invented an improved bicycle foot brake. At thirteen, he dropped out of school, and the next year he received his first patent and profit for the invention of an improved wheel with wire spokes. At age twenty-one, master mechanic Honda opened his first garage, at Hammasatsu, and became known as the man who could fix the unfixable.

And he not only fixed, but continued to create. He put motors into skiffs and suddenly they were power launches. He bolted an old Curtis airplane engine into an Oakland chasis and had a racing car nobody in Japan could beat. He made 100,000 piston rings of his own design until finally he developed the finest ring in Japan. And the country's army bought his entire and continually increasing output every year. Through his whole life, Honda's favorite toy had been one his father gave him when he was three years old: a pair of pliers. By the beginning of World War II, he was a wealthy and successful young man.

It has been said that Japan won the war when that nation lost it. Honda, however, received little help from the victors—except for the bomb that demolished his piston ring factory near the close of the conflict. He was then forty-one, his money almost gone. But by now, his creativity had matured, polished with continuing persistence, refined with the trials of experimentation, failure and success.

First, Honda purchased 500 war surplus radio generators and attached them to bicycles. These were hardly efficient machines —a rider had to pump twenty minutes to start one—but in a country with little transportation, they were more valuable than gold. When the war surplus ran out, Honda made his own engines and frames. By 1949, the model that would sire all machines called Honda was zipping along the production line. It could go 45 miles per hour for 200 miles on a gallon of gas. And it looked like a motorcycle. It was not a scooter or a reject from a bicycle factory. Painted red, black, white, and blue, it was called the Dream. By 1950, Honda was making 3,600 motorcycles a year and two years later he was employing 1,000 men in a factory 100 times larger than any he had had before. The Japanese Dream was actually the American Dream come true.

In 1959 Soichiro Honda decided to invade the staid American motorcycle market. The year before, Harley Davidson, the only remaining American motorcycle manufacturer, accounted for 70 percent of all the motorcycles sold in the United States.

From beginning to end, it was a David and Goliath match and Honda lost the first round.

"At first, people laughed," says Mat Matsuoka, director of public relations for Honda Motorcycles. "They said the Honda would never sell and that he would save a lot of money by going back home. Indeed, in the first year, there were only 167 units sold."

People stopped laughing two years later when Honda sold almost 100,000 machines. But the shock did not set in until about the middle of the decade when Honda accounted for more than 63 percent of all the motorcycles sold in the United States. From a standing start, sales revved up to $32 million by 1963 and almost $70 million a year later. Although Honda's percentage of the American market had decreased by 1970, because of the influx of so many new brands, and renewed enthusiasm for the older ones, Honda still held more than half of the United States motorcycle market. By 1974 or 1975 the company is expected to sell close to a million machines in this country every year. And America accounts for only 25 percent of all Honda sales.

But what Honda did for Honda benefited the entire motorcycle industry. The offspring of the pioneers who had spearheaded the development of the motorcycle, lacking the blood and guts of their grandparents, lay in a forty-year limbo. BSA, BMW, Triumph, Norton, and Harley, reasoning that they had no future except that which was based on their past, produced the same motorcycles every year, hoping not necessarily for an increased sales curve but at least a level one.

But Honda stimulated change. Although Harley lost is dominance of the American market, slipping in half a decade to about 5 percent of all bikes sold, its gross sales increased from $20 to $50 million. Two other Japanese manufacturers, Suzuki and Yamaha, soon grabbed a share of the motorcycle bonanza. By 1964, their U.S. sales totalled in excess of $30 million. Sales of all makes—Honda aside—jumped 125 percent from 1962 to 1964. And Honda was directly responsible. No other genius need be named.

At the end of World War II there were fewer than 200,000 motorcycles registered in the United States. Fifteen years later, there were fewer than 400,000—far below the increase in other motor vehicles. But during the 1960s, motorcycle registration jumped 279 percent while that of automobiles went up only 40 percent. By 1964 there were 960,000 registered motorcycles, in 1966, 1.4 million, and by 1971 nearly four million.

A number of states do not require motorcycle registration and in no state, as of 1971, did a person need to register mini-cycles or any other cycle not used for street riding. Some motor-cycle magazine editors estimate that there are at least double the number of unregistered machines from the number of regis-tered ones.

"Sales figures," says Charles Clayton, publisher of *Cycle News,* "are rather jealously guarded. No cycle manufacturer wants the big money people to know just how good business really is."

There were 1.3 million motorcycles sold in 1969 and 1.7 mil-lion in 1970. And what has stopped the industry from growing any more phenomenally, according to Clayton, "is the pure incapacity of manufacturers to fullfill the ever-expanding de-mand. From 1968 to 1970, almost every motorcycle manufac-turer in the United States, Germany, Japan and Great Britain, has been producing and selling at capacity and increasing that capacity at the rate of twenty percent a year."

The downward turn of motorcycle sales at the end of 1966 and into 1967 was caused, according to some experts, by over-saturation of the American market, somewhat of a backlash from the enthusiasm stimulated by Honda. Others attribute it to the attack of "those frenetic safeniks" like O'Mara who trans-formed two wheels into a technological evil. Some people blame the popularity of the compact car. And a surprising number of cyclists attribute it to the cyclist's most bitter enemy: helmet laws.

"More than anything else," says Ed Youngblood, director of public relations for the AMA, "it was the helmet laws. The helmets took the fun out of riding motorcycles. The guys that had been riding motorcycles for decades plainly decided that they would rather switch than fight."

In 1970, motorcycle sales started to rise again, working against the natural downward trend of the Nixon administration's econ-omy. Motorcycle unit sales doubled that of 1969, and dollar sales were up twenty percent over 1966, the previous record year. "Most of these buyers are new riders," said Youngblood, "people who have never experienced the joy of riding free and helmetless in the wind."

"Cycle sales are almost too good," said Cook Nielson of *Cycle* magazine. "Some distributors are backed up on orders six or seven months. We can't even get some new models to test."

"Previously," said *Forbes* magazine on June 15, 1970, "the excuse often given for buying a lightweight cycle was commuting utility. But now, customers desire all styles and models from putt-putting Honda mini-bikes at $250 each to imposing 1,200 cc Harley Davidson Electra Glides at $2,300."

"But this time," says Cook Nielson, "I think the cycling boom will stick. The market has matured."

And so too, it seems, have buying patterns. Before 1964 a large percentage of motorcycles were sold during the first half of the year, especially in the spring when the weather was good. But since 1965, cycle dealers have generated profits even when there was snow on the ground. In most northern states, nearly half the gross sales are made during the second six months of the year.

Motorcycles are big business in this country, but few people think of it as a business at all. It is difficult to conceive of such an anomaly as a money maker, unless you own a motorcycle yourself and realize what you pay. If you do not visit cycle shops, you do not know about backlogs and waiting lists, and the men and women standing in line, just for the privilege of plunking down their money and riding away.

It seems as if America has Marshall-planned half the world. But the debt owed by Japan has, through the work of Soichiro Honda, been partially repaid. Honda seems to have been able to do all the right things for the motorcycle industry. There was nothing truly remarkable or ingenious about his methods. But it was as though, from Japan, Honda could sit back and see and understand the problems of the motorcycle industry while the more established western cycle manufacturers could not.

For decades, the American consumer has been harried and deceived by both legitimate advertisers and persuasive con men. But coming out of the Eisenhower recession, Americans fell into a period of cautious buying. They became wary of spending unnecessarily and had, most recently in the case of the Ford Motor Company's Edsel, demonstrated their power of rejection. There had to be a reason for America to switch to motorcycling at about the time President John Kennedy took office. And in America, money is usually the answer.

You could buy the Honda 50 cc dream machine for less than $300 in 1960 when most of the other motorcycles available cost $1,500 or more. You had your choice of six snappy colors and three different models while the total model and color count for most other motorcycle manufacturers usually was no more than two or three. The people riding Hondas could travel at 55 miles per hour for 180 miles on thirty cents worth of regular gas. For the first time in perhaps half a century, America was actually getting its money's worth in a mechanized motor vehicle.

Said the director of a prominent British motorcycling firm after examining the Honda product in 1961: "When we stripped the machine, frankly, it was so good it frightened us. It was made like a watch and it wasn't a copy of anything."

In 1954 Honda had taken his machines to the Isle of Man in the Irish Sea, site of the most important of cycledom's Grand Prix road races. But when he set up in the pits he realized that the average European racing machine had three times the power, model for model, than his own two-wheelers could deliver. He withdrew from the race and toured Europe, foraging competitors' motorcycle parts for testing and comparison at home in Japan.

In 1959, returning to the Isle of Man, Honda's machines won the sixth, seventh, and eighth places in the 125 cc class. In 1961, he entered five motorcycles in both the 125 cc and 250 cc classes and won the first through fifth places in both events, establishing eleven new track records. And in 1966 the Honda became the first motorcycle ever to win in a single year the manufacturer's team prize in all solo categories—50, 125, 250, 350 and 500 cc.

Honda not only established the market for smaller two-wheeled machines, but led the way for other motorcycle manufacturers to begin manufacturing their own inexpensive products. In 1964 Harley marketed a $225 lightweight and in 1969, BSA revealed its $260 Ariel 3. And in 1970, when the market turned from smaller to heavier, more expensive machines, Honda still maintained prominence. That year, the 750 cc "Four" was introduced—a motorcycle that generated eight more horsepower than a showroom Volkswagen, that could be cruised from shop to highway at a vibrationless 125 miles per hour—and it won the Daytona 200, America's classic road racing competition.

Honda had translated the American consumer's austere stomach grumblings and quieted them with a menu of economy and precision. He had transformed a need into a product, an almost unbeatable product. Then he swept away the final barrier—the one remaining link to the American public's resistance to buy:

"We had to work at changing the image of motorcycling," says Mat Matsuoka. "We did this by taking the showrooms out of the garages, making them a place for the entire family to visit and generally cleaning up the entire presentation. We made them look more like automobile showrooms."

Then, for the first time in the history of motorcycling, the mass media came into play. What Honda spent on advertising in the 1960s has hardly been equalled by many other large motorcycle manufacturers even with the inflated prices of today:

"Honda took out advertising in *Life* magazine," said Matsuoka. "It was the first time a motorcycle group had advertised at that level. It was a significant investment in the neighborhood of $40,000 and it staggered the industry.

"Then in 1964 and 1965, Honda co-sponsored the Academy Awards on television and this suddenly snapped a lot of people to attention, their thought being, 'Wow, if they can afford something like that, they must be for real.' As a result, we began to have a stream of visitors wanting to go in with us on promotions—groups such as Hilton Hotels, Pepsi Cola, Laura Scudders and some airlines, just to name a few."

Today, there are more than fifty motorcycle manufacturers and thousands of motorcycle distributors, dealers, and accessory manufacturers. The hotrods of the forties and the custom cars of the fifties were as fadish as hula hoops, as parochial as professional wrestling or roller derby. But because of Soichiro Honda, motorcycles today are representative of our culture, of an enthusiastic and active modern age.

Sixteen

Think of touring bikes as Cadillacs or Lincolns, off-road cycles as Jeeps or other four-wheeled drive vehicles. And street cycles, depending on the weight or size, run the gamut, Fords through Chevys, Mercuries to Buicks.

Touring bikes are graceful on smooth concrete, but awkward and difficult to control on rough terrain. They are designed to stick to the road and hold the rider comfortably for long distances at highest speeds. To obtain these features, quick maneuverability and off-road durability are sacrificed.

The off-road rider must expect to fall, and he needs a machine light enough to maneuver easily and to lift up by himself, yet strong enough to withstand continuous beating. Dirt cycles have upswept exhaust pipes, lower gear ratios for pulling up hills rather than cruising and tires designed to dig into mud or loam or withstand the continual pounding of rocks and ruts.

Dirt bikes can be ridden on the street or highway but, like Jeeps, are limited by lower speeds and minimum comfort. The gear ratio can be changed with a street sprocket and tires switched. But it takes hours of work. And the smoothness provided by street or touring machines cannot be equalled.

Street cycles—commuting machines—have higher gear ratios, smoother tires, and a dual exhaust system placed lower and parallel to the road. This closeness to the road makes riding smoother, but the pipes are more vulnerable when the bike is dropped. Street cycles can be used sparingly and carefully on rough terrain, as can Fords and Chevys, but forks and shock absorbers are not designed to take much bouncing and beating. Tires are made to glide, not dig. Remember that a street machine is geared for speed, the trail machine for power.

Racing bikes are, for the most part, like racing cars—high performance machines that belong in a high performance track.

Before buying, decide how you are going to primarily use your motorcycle, and select your bike with that as your guide.

The second most important decision is the size of the engine you want to pull you. In most cases, engine size equals power potential, equals weight of chassis, equals comfort, equals cost of the machine. Most motorcycle brands cost approximately the same—it is the size of the engine that makes the difference.

Motorcycle engines are rated by volumetric displacement of the pistons in cubic centimeters (cc). A rough equivalent is between eight or ten horsepower for each 100 cc.

Motorcycles can be purchased as small as 50 cc or as large as 1,200 cc. To a point, the more powerful—depending on the way you use the machine—the better off you are.

Cycles under 100 cc are valuable for teaching children to ride. Remember that the bike is balanced and controlled with the body, and that a twelve-year-old can easily learn to maneuver a lightweight bike. But such motorcycles lack the power and substance for traffic. The increase in motorcycle fatalities in the middle of the 1960s can be directly related to the sudden popularity of the lightweights. Most manufacturers are now phasing out lightweights for street riding.

Such cycles, however, are excellent for off-road use. You can haul them in the bed of a station wagon or hooked onto the back of a camper. They cost from $300 to $500 for street models, and from $400 to $700 in off-road designs.

Street cycles from 101 cc to 175 cc are fairly safe for teenagers and women who ride primarily in residential areas, commuting back and forth to school or the supermarket. A man or woman weighing more than 150 pounds should turn to machines in the 176 cc to 250 cc category. They are inexpensive (from $550 to $750) and weigh under 250 pounds. For adults, these motorcycles are best for first learning to ride. They are easy to maneuver, yet heavy enough to simulate the real motorcycle experience.

And the real motorcycle experience for the street rider begins at 350 cc with a machine weighing more than 300 pounds and powerful enough to hold its own on parkways and freeways. The middleweights can grip the road in heavy winds and are built with stamina to cruise at high speeds for 50 or 75 miles at a clip. Tires are wider and seats made for more comfort. Although it is possible to travel cross-country on these machines, it is both unlikely and inadvisable. But they are good for short-range safaris and weekend outings of a couple of hundred miles.

Off-road cycles at 101 cc to 175 cc are comparable to middleweight street machines. They have sixteen horsepower engines, five-speed gearboxes, plentiful low-end torque and waterproof ignition systems. They will go anywhere. And they will go anywhere fast. Off-road cycles of 176 cc to 250 cc provide a nice balance of power and weight. A good rider working a 250 can keep up with much bigger machinery. And an intermediate rider can have big-bike fun for less money. Off-road bikes from 100 cc to 250 cc range from $500 to as much as $1,000.

The 250 cc to 360 cc off-road category is for expert amateurs or professional riders who can handle heavy machines going very fast. At 32 horsepower, these big "stump-pullers" generate a maximum torque-pulling power—and speeds in the low eighties. The average machine of this size costs more than $1,000.

The top-of-the-line off-road bikes—those from 360 to 500 cc— are magnificent machines. They are fast, well-balanced, and almost indestructible. A novice can probably handle a powerful street bike. But in the woods, a 500 cc road bike, piloted by a rider without years of training and experience, is a ticket to a broken leg. Or a smashed collar bone. They are just too spirited, too much machine for the common man to handle.

Street cycles of 361 cc to 500 cc are probably the best small bikes for long trips. They cruise easily at sixty miles per hour— all day—and are light, easy-to-handle, and smooth riding. Their 35 horsepower engines deliver sixty miles per gallon and speeds in excess of 100 miles per hour. Average prices range from $900 to $1,200.

Although every man cannot afford them, the poor man's super bikes, those with 501 cc to 650 cc, are hearty and fast. They accelerate, brake, and handle almost as well as the real superbikes (651 cc to 750 cc), and they cost as much as $200 less, or about $1,300 to $1,500.

But the real superbikes are the best and the fastest machines made. They cost anywhere from $1,600 to $2,500 and are probably more machine than any man will ever need—no matter how far, how long, or how fast he wants to travel. These motorcycles are built to last for a long time, and they are designed to maintain their value and their thrill. Superbikes can log 100,000 miles without a major overhaul, and men have coddled and beaten the same machine for decades. They are the best machines and the best bargains for touring, if you can afford one.

The "hogs" some people say, are owned by hogs—in the sense that anyone wanting or needing 900 cc or 1,200 cc must be something more than just a glutton for comfort, speed, and thrills. Harley Davidson monopolizes this category and offers stock machines for more than $3,000. They weigh 700 pounds or more and you've got to be better than just good or experienced to ride them. They are the SST's, in size and power, of the motorcycle industry.

There are still a few single-cylindered motorcycles available. A single is cheaper to purchase and easier to maintain. But multiple cylinders produce more power, and are easier to start and more economical to operate. Most new motorcycles have twin cylinders, but some companies are producing threes and fours. Generally, the cyclist who wants to ride should buy a twin. The cyclist who appreciates tinkering more than riding would be happy with a single.

There are also two and four-stroke engines. The crankshaft makes two revolutions for every power stroke in a four-stroke (or cycle) and one revolution for every power stroke in a two-cycle.

As a result, two-cycles tend to use more gasoline and oil. Spark plugs don't last as long. Two cycles are noisier and harder to tune, require frequent carbonization, and the gas and oil must be mixed together, although many modern two-cycle designs automatically tend to the mixture. In addition, there is no valve gear to malfunction as in a four-cycle. Nor are there camshafts or pushrods. All this makes the two-cycle most appealing to the mechanically disinclined. Because of its simple construction, it is also less expensive to purchase.

Four-cycles are more reliable and substantial machines. They are suggested for long trips and can be counted on for steady performance. While two-cycles are best in high-power situations, four-cycles will respond as expected in any gear, or at any speed.

Most two-cycles have five forward gears. Four-cycles need only four. The two-cycle ride is a harder ride—but ease of maintenance and initial cost might, for many riders, make the sacrifice worthwhile.

You can debate brand names for decades, generating a lot of heat without the benefit of much light. But a motorcycle is only as good as the man who is selling it and the service he can offer you. Choose your dealer first. Then select from whatever brand of machines he sells.

Motorcycle dealers are not unreliable by choice. The factories they represent are at least as busy as they are—probably more so—and are much more concerned with putting together and moving machines than in supplying training for mechanics or replacement parts. Dealers bear the brunt of the criticism that should be leveled at the manufacturer.

So instead of shopping first for motorcycles, shop for dealers. Talk to the owner, examine his parts inventory, try to come to some conclusion about the ability of his mechanics to service your machine. If he carries more than one brand of motorcycle, buy from his primary line. On this line, he will give more competent service, be better stocked with parts, and be more concerned with maintaining good will with the factory and his customers. If you plan to tour, buy a popular brand, so that service facilities and parts are available in all major metropolitan areas.

Used motorcycles fall into two general categories: bargains and nightmares. It's not unusual to find an almost new machine in good condition, selling for hundreds of dollars less than its original price. There are many ninety-day enthusiasts who tire of riding or are petrified with fear of the machine after spilling in traffic. There are also riders genuinely in need of money, which is not uncommon these days.

But along with "Smilin' Bob" and "Honest Honus" of used car fame are the cycle shysters who beat hell out of machines and unload them on unsuspecting novices after a year. Or those riders who decide to unload their machines when they begin to need extensive repair.

If you can't take an experienced mechanic with you, then look for cycles less than two years old. Motorcycles age quickly. Unless you are buying a touring bike, don't buy a machine that has logged more than 10,000 miles. Don't buy a used bike that doesn't look as if it has been maintained well.

After test driving the bike, drain the oil. If it is dirty, the owner has probably not cared for the machine. If there are bits of metal on the pan, he has probably used it hard. Have the spark plugs been recently changed or are they black and gritty? Is the drive chain well lubricated? If not, look at other machines. If the tires are nearly bald, add at least $50 to the purchase price for a fair set of replacements.

If you know little about the workings of a motorcycle and the bike you can afford must necessarily be more than two years old, visit a dealer. You'll pay top dollar, but if you select a reputable dealer you'll probably get a thirty-day guarantee. And at least he might feel a moral obligation to help you if anything goes wrong after the statute of limitations runs out.

A buyer can also choose between a chain or shaft-powered bike. Except for the number of wheels, shaft-driven bikes have engines very similar to those in automobiles. A shaft-driven engine looks very much like a Volkswagen engine minus two cylinders and a cooling fan. The bike is powered by a rear wheel which pushes the driveshaft. One advantage of a shaft over a chain-powered engine is that a drive chain is quite vulnerable. It must be lubricated, for when it is dry it can snap and get tangled in the spokes of the cycle's rear wheel. The shaft eliminates this worry.

But whether to buy a shaft or chain-powered machine is really not a difficult decision to make. BMW and Moto Guizi are the only manufacturers offering a shaft design. And it is available only in high-powered touring models. Also, many bikers consider the experience of a shaft-driven bike too much like riding an automobile. BMWs and Guizis lack vibration, caused by the chain, and provide a quiet, super-smooth ride. But for those who require ultimate touring comfort and have the money to pay for it, they are the machines to buy.

Companies specializing in motorcycle insurance base their rates on engine size and the overall value of the machine. For 50/100/10 liability insurance, you will pay $40 up to 100 cc, $50 up to 200 cc, $60 up to 360 cc, $70 up to 500 cc, $80 up to 1,000 cc, and $90 for the super-super bikes.

Collision, theft, medical payments, and uninsured motorist policies are also available. Medical coverage can be purchased for both rider and passenger. Most auto insurance companies will write motorcycle insurance, but their reluctance is reflected in their rates—usually higher than those companies specializing in two-wheeled machines. Motorcycle insurance companies have few field representatives and finance plans. They work with a low overhead and are able to offer inexpensive, although sometimes unreliable, service. Complete minimum coverage on a rider on a medium-sized machine costs around $250. Not insuring the passenger, the more vulnerable of the two riders, would decrease the charges by almost half.

All AMA members are covered by a special group insurance policy, and it is worth joining the organization just for these benefits. Injury received at any AMA sanctioned event, whether the member is a competitor or spectator, is covered up to 75 percent for all medical expenses—to a maximum of $10,000. In case of death or dismemberment, a $5,000 benefit is paid. An AMA member, riding a motorcycle anywhere in the world, but not in competition, receives $1,000 benefit in case of death or dismemberment. The medical protection coverage of this policy is only $25 deductible for any injury.

Seventeen

Pretend you are teaching your son. The motorcycle is a weapon and he is a rookie and you are a top kick master sergeant, drilling on the use of a powerful, rapid-fire M-16. To the boy the motorcycle is a toy, and he is young and impetuous, and you must make him play with caution and respect. The motorcycle is fun, and he is hungry for thrills, and you must feed him a balanced diet of knowledge and guidance before he can successfully digest the road. The best way to learn how to ride a motorcycle is to pretend, or, in fact, to teach one of your children how, or to imagine you are instructing someone you love. For your sight may be at stake—or his. The loss of an arm, the loss of a leg, the distortion of your features. Castration. The motorcycle may very well be potentially the safest vehicle on the road, but it is also potentially the deadliest.

Memorize the machine first. Although no one can ride a motorcycle without his eyes, without concentrating on the road and the traffic signals, the cars behind and in front, the actual operation of the machine is blind. Like an exercise in braille, the cyclist must learn to read the controls without seeing them.

Push the bike to its center stand and ask your boy to mount the machine. Then begin:

"The handlebar grip on the right-hand side is actually the throttle. It serves the same purpose as a gas pedal on an automobile. Your bike accelerates as you turn the grip toward you.

When turned the other way, speed is reduced. The lever right above the throttle is the front wheel brake."

"What's the lever," he asks, "above the left grip?"

"That's the clutch. You must squeeze that lever every time you shift gears."

"Shift gears . . ."

"If you hook your heels firmly on the footpegs, the gear shift lever will be right above your left toe. Starting in neutral . . ."

"How do I know where neutral is?"

"Eventually, you'll know by feel, but for now, there's a small green spot on your speedometer that lights up in neutral position. Starting from there, you push the shifting lever down with your toe to go into first gear. As you pick up speed, you lift the lever up one notch with your toe. Now, you're in second. Then higher one notch for third. Still higher for fourth and even higher for fifth gear. Each time, before you change gears, you squeeze the clutch.

"Of course, motorcycles aren't yet standardized. Some manufacturers have put shifting mechanisms on the right foot side. Your bike has five gears, but some have six and others have only four. Some motorcycles have an opposite shifting pattern: first gear up, and then four down. But the method of operation is the same. The lower gears are used to build up speed or climb steep hills, the higher gears for cruising at fast speeds."

"What's on my right foot side?"

"The rear brake pedal."

"Both feet and both hands are always busy."

"Right. But never rest either your feet or your hands on the controls. You steer and balance a motorcycle by applying pressure and weight at any of these four positions. Besides, you don't want to accidentally engage any of these controls. And if you allow your feet to hang free, there's a possibility of hitting a rock or bump. You could break your ankle."

"OK. When do we start?"

"Before you learn to ride, you've got to learn to start the machine."

"That's easy, all I do is press the starter button, put the bike in neutral, and give it some gas."

"Well, you're right and you're wrong. That's the way to use the electric starter, but many motorcycles don't have electric starters. Your bike, like most, has both a kick and an electric starter. So you might as well learn how to start the hard way first. What happens if your battery is low or your electrical system fouls? If you know how to use a kick starter, you can still operate the machine. Otherwise, you could be stranded with a dead battery. And gasoline stations or the AAA as a rule don't service motorcycles.

"You should standardize the starting procedure. Do it the same way all the time so you don't forget any of the steps. Get back on the machine and turn on the gas. Unlike an automobile the fuel must be manually activated for a motorcycle. Look in the manual to find out where the fuel pet cock (sometimes also meaning gas cap) is. Next, turn on the ignition and make sure the cycle is in neutral."

"All right . . ."

"Press lightly on the kick start pedal and open your throttle slightly. Then throw your weight on the kick starter, kick down as if you are trying to smash the pavement with your boot . . . ."

"Wow, listen to that!"

"OK, with the machine started, let the kick starter up slowly. Don't let it snap up or you'll wear out the starting mechanism. Then turn the machine off and practice. Make sure you have memorized the controls and know exactly how to operate and start the bike."

An infant stands before he walks and walks before he runs. There is a natural progression in mobility, a way of stacking the knowledge from each lesson learned onto the previous one. The sink-or-swim philosophy guarantees that you sink. The rider who jumps on the motorcycle before he knows his machine is as foolish as the soldier who has not studied his weapon properly. The way to learn to ride a motorcycle is from the beginning. Slowly. And with patience. There are no alternatives or exceptions. That is the only way to be fairly certain of staying alive.

We are in a parking lot, or a big back yard, or a quiet, seldom-used residential street. It is warm today, and the road surface is dry, even the puddles from yesterday's rain have almost entirely evaporated by now. The boy is wearing his leather pants and jacket and his new white and orange helmet, and we are sitting and watching as he practices coordination between clutch and throttle. It can be likened to trying to catch a football while eating an ice cream cone; there never seem to be enough hands at first. He squeezes the clutch lever closed, shifts into first gear. Then simultaneously and slowly, he increases throttle speed and releases the clutch lever. When done successfully, he is underway in about a second. Then he stops and starts again.

In any situation, there is only one way to stop: quickly squeeze the clutch lever to disengage the clutch, shut down the throttle, push on your rear brake pedal first, then squeeze your front brake lever. This process must be accomplished almost, but not quite, simultaneously. Always use both brakes. Neither is strong enough to safely control the weight of the rider, let alone a machine with both rider and passenger. Neither provides a secure balance. Squeezing only the front brake might lock the front wheel, which can cause the rider to fly over the handlebars. If you use the back brake alone, the cycle could fishtail. The brakes are designed to be effective together. At 50 miles per hour, a cycle, braked correctly, needs 175 feet to stop. An automobile needs 243. Since you brake from the rear first, many riders get in the habit of relying wholly on the rear brake. But both brakes must be used for maximum efficiency. Adding the front brake increases stopping capacity by 70 percent.

We draw a line with a stick in the dirt or chalk a line on the pavement. The boy is to use this line as a reference to determine actual stopping potential. He accelerates up to thirty miles per hour and, when the front wheel reaches the line, brakes as quickly as possible. Then we measure the distance between the line and his stopping point, repeating the process until he can stop the machine in the shortest possible distance without skidding or spilling. We experiment at different speeds until he learns maximum stopping control, and has a good measure of stopping capability.

We depress the clutch lever, twitch the throttle, and tap the gear down. The bike clears its throat and winds down. Depress, twitch, tap second gear. We roll slowly now, step on the rear brake, squeeze the front, toeing up into neutral as we glide to a stop. The neutral light flickers above our speedometer and the machine rests its thunder between our legs. When the stop light changes, we go again, easing into a secret rhythm. Like surfers, we ride each wave until momentum is barricaded by the beach, we ride and ride . . . .

He keeps practicing how to begin moving. When his engine stalls, you tell him he hasn't fed it enough gas. When he takes off too rapidly, you tell him he's feeding too much gas. When he bucks forward, he is letting his clutch out too quickly. Keep reminding him to squeeze in the clutch before stopping because that action deactivates the rear wheel, the main power generator.

Tell him to increase his speed after a while, just enough to shift into the higher gears. The owner's manual will tell him at which speeds to shift to second, third, fourth, and fifth. For a smooth shift, squeeze the clutch lever, turn the throttle off, then shift. Then release the clutch lever and feed gas.

Convince him that he must move at minimum speeds at first. If he has not had previous experience on a two-wheeled vehicle, he will have to concentrate not only on the process of operation, but maintaining balance as well. If the bike begins to tilt, instruct him to turn the front wheel in the same direction. Turning it in the opposite direction will shift the weight of the rider and vehicle too abruptly.

To test his sense of balance, drop objects such as sticks and stones and cans here and there and make him pick them up while moving, without allowing his feet to leave the footpegs. As he improves, place smaller objects, like quarters and dimes on the road surface. Tell him he can pocket whatever he picks up without losing his balance or having to drag his feet.

In an automobile with a standard transmission, you can come to a stop in any gear. But motorcycle transmissions are not designed that way. Even if they were, part of the skill of riding a motorcycle is being in the right gear at the right time. Often the margin of safety is contingent on how quickly the cyclist can avoid a dangerous situation. So the cycle must have a potential power spurt at all times. Which means that downshifting is important when coming to a stop.

If you are going 25 miles per hour in third gear while accelerating, then while decelerating you should be in third gear when moving at approximately the same speed. Since you are riding in lower, more controllable gears when downshifting, remember that your engine must work harder to maintain speed. So the rider must feed a little more gas each time he is downshifting. The process is simple.

We are riding at forty miles per hour in fourth gear. We see a stop sign ahead. We slow down to thirty and shift into third gear, opening our throttle just enough so that our engine speed (rpms) is high enough to match the road speed. We slow down to twenty and repeat the process. The gears are slowing us down, not the brakes. When we stop at the sign we shift into neutral and wait until we can move forward. We should not shift into neutral too early for we lose the possibility of acceleration if needed.

Learn to use the gears. Downshift to gain additional power while climbing a hill. Merely feeding more gas in a high gear will not do the job and will put unnecessary strain on the engine. But never downshift into a speed higher than the maximum allowed in a gear as outlined in the owner's manual.

Sooner or later, he will fall. Many accidents can be avoided, but eventually he will make a mistake, or the bike will, or a pedestrian or motorist will, and the cyclist dumps his machine. It often happens when the motorcycle is at its least stable position, in a turn when a machine is not perpendicular with the road. So tell your boy . . .

"Look, you don't steer a two-wheeled machine with the handlebars. It doesn't function like a steering wheel of a car. The only time to use your handlebars to steer is at low speeds. You steer by leaning into a turn and manipulating your stationary controls."

"You mean the footpegs?"

"The footpegs and the handlebar grips. The idea is to lean your body into a turn. The sharper the turn, the farther over you will lean."

"In which direction?"

"The direction in which you are turning. You see, when you lean, you unconsciously put pressure on the handlebar grips and footpegs in the direction of the turn. By leaning into a turn instead of steering into one, your wheels are traveling in a straighter line. The bike has more road stability."

"But if I'd lean my bike over when I'm not moving I'd fall down."

"Yes, but the outward centrifugal force caused by your lean

is counterbalanced by the downward pull of gravity. At some traction point, depending upon your speed, and sharpness of turn, the two forces will equalize."

"Huh?"

"Forget it."

"Actually, I really can't see why the motorcycle doesn't fall anyway. I mean, it's only got two wheels."

"Right, but if you put a top on the ground, what happens?"

"It falls over."

"All the time?"

"Not if you spin it."

"And it is the same principle with the motorcycle. The spinning wheels produce a gyro-stabilizing action. As long as a wheel or top can spin rapidly it will resist any force that tries to divert it from its course."

To increase cornering proficiency, space cans or other objects on two parallel lines about five feet apart, leaving about twenty feet between each can. Then make him practice weaving in and out between the cans without knocking them over. Place out-of-bounds lines around the course so he is forced to weave sharply. Keep time with your wristwatch until he becomes satisfactorily efficient.

"OK. I understand the principle of controlling the motorcycle. Now tell me how I actually make that sharp corner or turn."

"As you approach the curve, slow down until you are a little bit below the speed you need to safely make it. You'll learn this with experience and practice, but in the beginning be over-cautious. Go slower than you need to. Make sure you are in a gear that will allow you to accelerate out of the turn. If you have to downshift to reach the gear, do that before the turn, not during it. Downshifting in a turn might unsettle your balance.

"The best advice I can give you is to not turn too sharply. Try to go into the turn wide, and come out of it a little more than half a lane's width from oncoming traffic when the turn is completed.

"But still, there's a difference between making a left and a right turn. When making a right, even though you are driving on the right, you should ease out toward the left-hand center of the lane. Then lean. That should put you in about the middle of the road you are turning into. But if you start too close to the right hand edge of the road, you could lean too hard and smash into the curb. Or not lean hard enough and drift into the opposite lane. By beginning a little over to the left, a margin for error remains.

"You should make a left, however, from the left-hand side of the lane because, in this case, you are banking away from oncoming traffic and you need ample drifting room so you don't crash into the curb."

"Are you ready to ride by yourself now?"

"Yeah."

"Scared?"

"Nope."

"Well you should be. Don't forget that you're pretty vulnerable, even though you're wearing a helmet, leathers, and bright colors. Don't forget the invisible man."

"Who's he?"

"You are. Drive defensively. Watch the eyes of motorists when you can or the front wheels when you're passing a car, or the wheels of cars in oncoming traffic when you're passing an intersection where they could turn. Assume you are invisible to the motorist. He can't see you. You don't know what he's going to do, but you do know that he doesn't see you. Develop a paranoia. Expect every automobile door you pass to open right into your gut. Remember that all motorists are blind and crazy. You can count on them only to do the unexpected."

"But what happens if I *do* fall?"

"Pick yourself up."

"Seriously . . ."

"OK. Usually it happens so quickly that there's very little you can do. Of course, if you see a car coming right at your head or leg, then sure, get the hell out of the way. Jump off. But at high speeds, things will happen too fast. Besides, in those situations, you will doubtlessly be knocked off the machine. Your best bet then is to tuck yourself into a ball and roll to the ground. Don't try to break your fall with your hands, or you'll break them.

"At slow speeds or in heavy traffic, try staying with your machine. Jumping free might put you right in front of a moving car. At least with your bike you have more visibility and weight. And more protection. You won't be dragged very far at 20 or 25 miles per hour either. The bike will stop soon after it makes contact with the road surface."

"What bothers me a lot is starting on a hill. I keep drifting backwards when I take my foot off the brake, before I can get it moving forward in gear."

"In this case, stay in first gear with the clutch lever pulled in and your foot brake holding the bike. When the light changes and the traffic begins to move, keep holding the motorcycle with your brake. At the same time, let your clutch out, feed some gas. Don't release the brake until you are assured of immediate forward motion.

"And incidentally, keep in the left half of the lane whenever you're riding. Then, if the car behind you wants to pass, he's got to go in the opposite lane to do it. Otherwise, with you too far to the right, he might decide to try to squeeze in beside you. And if there's any oil dripped from trucks or cars on the road, it should be right in the middle. That's the slipperiest part of the road.

"And don't let cars intimidate you. Hold your position on the road. Don't go too fast, but maintain normal speed. The motorist doesn't know what you're planning to do if you go too slow. All he knows is that he doesn't want to be behind a tortoise. You are riding a licensed motor vehicle. Treat it like one."

From the boulevard onto the freeway, we trumpet each gear. We slide down a few inches on the seat so that our ass is positioned above the main power plant and our head is tucked under the heavy thrust of wind. Our knees and thighs wrap around the neck of the bike like strangler's hands. Our plug into the external world works loose. We are wired for dreams, running, and riding.

Stupid questions:

"Can I wear sunglasses instead of goggles? Can I wear tennis shoes instead of boots? Do I ride with my knees stuck out? Do I sit far back in the seat? Should my passenger sit far away from me to give me room to operate my controls? Should I try to jump or force my way over an object in the road? Can I hook packages onto my handlebars? Should I try to dodge puddles? Can I pass directly on the center line, rather than having to move into the opposite lane?"

Intelligent answers:

"No, no, no, no."

Sunglasses are certainly better than no eye protection at all. But they don't effectively stop the wind from streaming into your eyes and with it, dirt and grit. In either case, tears form and blur vision. Sunglasses are no substitute for goggles or shields. Tennis shoes do not provide the protection of good, heavy, high-topped boots.

A rider uses his knees to control the machine. When turning, he should push against the rubber pad on the gas tank with his knee in the direction of the turn. At the very least, flapping knees will decrease balance and increase wind resistance. At the most, those knees could be amputated by a close-shaving car.

A rider sits far back in the seat only at high speeds. Hunching over, rider and machine take on the shape of a bullet, significantly cutting down wind resistance. By shifting his weight above the back wheel, the power wheel, he is also assured of additional road traction. In the city, at slower speeds, where balance is much more difficult to maintain, the rider sits forward on the seat, closer to the machine's center of gravity.

Although some male passengers might not like to cuddle with their best male friends, intimacy is perfectly acceptable on a motorcycle. It is, in fact, desirable. The closer the two passengers sit together, the easier it is for the rider to balance the machine. The ultimate traction point is at the center of the rear wheel. Control of any weight behind that point diminishes as it extends further back. Passengers should keep their feet on the footpegs rather than the mufflers, tuck their knees in, and lean slightly in the direction in which the rider leans.

When riding over railroad tracks or a severe bump, stand on the footpegs, bend your knees, use them as springs. You will not be jolted that way, nor will the shocks or front forks be put under unnecessary stress. Never plow into a big object. If you can't go around, stand on the pegs and ease the machine over. A motorcycle's wheels are delicate. You can carry a spare tire or wheel in an automobile, but not on a cycle. With a broken spoke or bent rim, the cyclist is stranded.

A cyclist should carry an extra inner tube, however, and a patching kit just in case of a flat tire. Also a portable tire pump can usually be fitted under the seat or rear fender. A cycle should be outfitted with a compact tool set, extra brake and clutch cable, a chain breaker and links (in case the drive chain snaps), and spare spark plugs and clutch lever. (One lever is actually temporarily exchangeable with the other, but it is best to buy the clutch lever because the rider can stop the machine using the rear brakes; without a properly operating clutch, however, the bike is immobile.) You also should carry an extra headlight and rear light bulb and some raingear. This equipment is suggested for day-to-day operation. More equipment is advised for a long trip.

Packages should be carried on a luggage rack extending behind the passenger's seat or attached to the seat with an elastic "bungie" cord. Remember the maximum traction point. Keep heavy packages as close to the center of the rear wheel as possible.

Some automobile drivers have fun hitting a puddle at thirty or forty miles per hour and splashing pedestrians. It is not nearly as much fun on a motorcycle, however. Cyclists often forget that they too are as vulnerable as the pedestrian and they can get just as wet. And heavily splashed water could damage the electrical system of the engine if the cycle is running extraordinarily hot. Puddles also conceal oil and grease and, most especially, deep potholes.

Don't suddenly swerve around puddles or make a dead stop in front of one, especially in heavy traffic when cars might be passing or breathing close behind. Go through fairly quickly, but always cautiously.

Don't rest on the shift lever or on any control until you are ready to activate them. Don't pass or ride directly on the center line until you are ready to die.

Off the freeway, it is not hard to find the right road. We see it from the top of the mountain or when looking up from a knoll in the valley. It curls like a corkscrew, like rawhide the road wraps around the hill. We ride with our bodies. Downshifting, we slow for the curve, sailing into it, feeding throttle about halfway through, so we can accelerate onto the straightaway. When there is an obstruction, a patch of sand or puddle of oil, we let up on the lean enough to go around it on the outside. We don't want to jerk our bike too sharply and lose that precarious point of balance between traction and full flight. Our bodies work up a rhythm as we rock down the hill, kicking down, leaning left, toeing up, leaning right. Like kites, we sail on, sail down, rolling and riding.

Snow: Colorado— north

We rolled into Walsenburg, Colorado, where we met the girl Delilah and her little boy Timothy with the brown angel's eyes.

"What do you think about," said Delilah, "when you ride your motorcycles all day?"

"I don't know," Burt told her, "I know I think about a lot of things, but I can't remember any of it after the ride is over."

It was dark in the cafe and, after the bright, hot sun, we could hardly see the girl, sipping Coca Cola and talking across the table.

"We would go with you in a minute," said Delilah, in her Mexican-American voice. "If you asked us, we would go away with you, me and Timothy, in a minute."

"Both of us are married," we told the girl who worked in the cafe during the day as a waitress in the summer, and in the winter went to school and worked at the cafe at night.

"I wouldn't go if it would cause you trouble."

"It would be impossible."

Her hair was long and black, and the colored lights of the jukebox were mirrored in the silken strands. There weren't any people in the cafe, only the little man with the mustache at the far corner of the bar.

"I want to go to New York. We have friends in New York. You could drop us there. I once saved enough money for a bus ticket to New York. But that was when Timothy got sick and I had to spend it for medicine. The doctor didn't cost, but the medicine was more than $100."

The little man at the far corner of the bar was sipping beer and watching us. He was not watching all of us, just Delilah.

"We're not going to New York," said Burt.

"I wouldn't mind going to Los Angeles."

"We're on motorcycles," I said, "and we're riding north."

The man with the mustache finished his beer and slid off the stool. "See you later," he said to Delilah.

"Don't do anything I wouldn't do, Juan," Delilah said.

"I'll remember that," said Juan.

"We better be going too," Burt said.

"Yeah."

"We would go to Los Angeles, but not unless you asked us," said the girl who would be only seventeen that summer.

We slept hard that night in a cabin that had weathered many winters and shrunk in the hot summer sun. We awoke with the morning streaming through the cracks between the wood of the cabin.

We rode north on the superhighway that cuts a clean white line over the southern Colorado plain, stopping once to snap pictures of each other, sitting on our motorcycles, with Pike's Peak silhouetted behind us against the sky. Burt had a camera mounted on the handlebars of his motorcycle, but it was unreliable because of the vibration of his machine. He had another camera in his saddlebags. Burt had made his saddlebags from large, army surplus ammunition boxes, and had bolted them to the back of his bike.

After looking at Pike's Peak and smoking cigarettes in tribute to it, we moved on.

At a gas station near Denver, we met two cyclists from San Francisco heading for New Orleans. "I was riding near Provo, Utah," said the one who was an electrical engineer. "There was a car with a man and his wife and a kid in front of me. The guy kept motioning me to pull up beside him. When I did, the kid dumped the contents of an ashtray in my face."

"You better be careful," said the other cyclist, who had just graduated from UCLA, "everybody hates motorcyclists, except other motorcyclists."

Everybody was writing our obituaries that summer.

We stopped at Shelby's BMW Motor Works in Denver to have my cycle serviced. Shelby is one of the old-time masters whose mission in life seems to be to achieve mechanical perfection. He used to build electrical equipment for the University of Denver and work on BMW's for extra money on weekends before becoming a dealer. He has developed a number of electrical gadgets with which to tune motorcycles and his workbench looks like the cockpit of an airplane. You could watch him work through a window in a showroom that led to the garage. Shelby's wife managed the parts department at the motorcycle shop, assisted by his daughter.

We spent a pleasant afternoon at Shelby's, talking to people who dropped into the shop. There was a fat, bearded fellow from New York City who had recently completed graduate school at Denver and was heading for California with a friend to start a stereo shop.

"I was in San Diego last week," he said, "and my partner and I went to a police equipment auction. They were selling a bunch of old, beaten-up stuff, radios, cars—and plenty of motorcycles."

He filled a brown cigarette paper with pipe tobacco, tapped the clump of tobacco to a line extending the length of the paper, and then rolled, licking the ends of it.

"Some of the cops were standing around their old motorcycles. It was like they were dogs or horses, or sons going off to war, and the cops were saying good-bye to them. They were very sad. I'd guess these bikes were about five years old, so conceivably the same cop could have been riding the same cycle for five years." He lighted his cigarette and pulled smoke from it.

"All of a sudden, this whole contingent of Hell's Angels came walking in. They looked as grimy and mean as they're supposed to look. I've never seen Hell's Angels before, but these guys had on greasy Levis and leather jackets with the skull and crossbones painted on the back. They looked as mean as the movies make them out to be.

"They outbid everybody, bought every one of those police cycles up for sale, paid cash, took them out of the cops' hands, loaded them into their own truck, and drove away. The whole thing didn't take an hour.

"Those cops were dumbfounded. I mean, man, they really looked stunned. They knew that someday they're going to end up arresting or chasing after the riders of their own old bikes. It was really great to see."

We left Shelby's later that afternoon. He had delayed all other work to service my bike first. Most good shops will extend a cross-country biker that courtesy. It's not a good shop if it won't.

I had been to Wyoming before, once on an assignment for United Feature Newspaper Syndicate to retrace Ernest Hemingway's steps during the decade in which he had spent his summers there. Hemingway had written portions of *Farewell To Arms, Death in the Afternoon,* and *Green Hills of Africa* in Wyoming. Most of the time he stayed at the Nordquist ranch in the Clarks Fork Valley near the northwestern tip of Wyoming. For a couple of summers though, he remained further east, in the Big Horn Mountains, near Sheridan.

Wyoming is the kind of state in which it is easy to be a Hemingway. There's plenty of game and plenty of mountains and wilderness to hunt game in. There are 300,000 citizens of Wyoming, carbon copies of no one, people who are not lonely being alone, whose joy in life comes from fishing, hunting, and riding a good horse. Many rodeo on Saturday nights in the summer, sit and watch the cattle grazing, or the deer—sometimes even moose—that trot by their porches on Sunday, sucking on pipes and sipping coffee. The day of rest in most of Wyoming is, quite literally, the day on which people rest. Wyoming, I think, is the kind of place America was supposed to be, thirty or forty years ago.

But it is changing. That is probably one of the reasons Hemingway eventually moved into Idaho. As is usually the case, the natives are not changing it, the visitors are. The camper corps roll in from the East, Midwest, and Far West, choking the roads with mobile living rooms, with bathrooms and kitchens and televisions inside. The campers have money and the money brings the big-time merchants. Both of these predators bring wealth and construction. Both leave small animals killed by building machines, or crushed by cars. They bring bulldozers to make big hotels; they leave dead fish floating atop the water of polluted streams. They bring credit cards and travelers' checks; they leave lakes bottomed with beer cans, shotgun shells, plastic plates. They bring prosperity, but in their wake, they leave destruction.

The people who come to Wyoming to appreciate its beauty are, each year, depreciating it ever more. And Wyomians seem unable to cope with the difficult dilemma of civilization known as progress. They are well aware of their fading lifestyle, and are guarding what remains of it with a fervor laced with fear.

Most of the young people leave early for school or jobs in the highly populated states. Neltje and John King, however, are among the few young people who have migrated there. Neltje bought the Sheridan Inn, once the home of Buffalo Bill Cody, and restored it with the help of the ladies of the Sheridan, Wyoming historical society. Everyone seems to have a fine sense of history here, and the old people, who in metropolitan areas often go unrespected, are treated like the wise men of Indian villages.

We ate beef raised on the King's ranch and took coffee by the fireplace talking of motorcycles and Wyoming winters, while Burt snapped pictures of Neltje, leaning up against the brick of the fireplace, her face shining in the soft lights of the glowing coals. She is the perfect-looking Wyoming woman, the way I think many women once looked before the Wild West was tamed. She is tall, very lean, very dark, with long black hair hanging in a braid down her back. It was the summer of 1971 and we were at a ranch near Sheridan, Wyoming, but watching her lean up against the fireplace, blotting out the images of Burt and John, it seemed like a century ago.

I remember how nice it was to sit in a living room once again, sip brandy and be with people who weren't strangers. I listened to the sounds of the children playing, then folding up in their beds to sleep. Burt, Neltje, and John were talking, but I thought past them. I could hear their voices and scattered words, but not what they were saying. I do not have any children now at home, but I thought past that possibility, too. I cannot picture myself as a child; I can only think of myself as I am now. Yet I felt like a child, looking into the fire, listening to the voices, sounding far away. I played games with my eyes and the fire, closing my eyes just enough so that I could see the fire, without seeing the fireplace or the brick hearth. The flames flickered through a sea of black, and I experimented, letting in varying intensities of the light made by the fire, to see the effect. I did this for a long time, feeling very much like a child, a little boy growing tired before bed. And I was. We had ridden our motorcycles from state to state, like children, exploring new neighborhoods and mysterious backyards.

It was late when we left the King's, and there were no lights on the road that led back to town. The early morning chill of the mountains is drier and more penetrating than the cold of the day, and we shivered in our seats, while our headlights bounced off the blackness of the heavy night. Even with our high beams blazing, we could see very little in front of us. It was quiet. We could hear deer rustling on the side of the road and the cattle moving about, grazing in the dark.

When talking about mountains in Wyoming, most people refer to the Tetons. The Tetons are memorable because they look the way mountains are supposed to look—exaggerated peaks, very black against the blue sky, splotched by snow. The Tetons are impressive, but the Big Horns are the softest and most articulate mountains I have ever seen. The peaks, unlike the arrowheads of other mountains, are rounded dull. The trees are spaced apart so that each is individual and can be seen from almost anywhere. The water that rushes through the Big Horns is cold, but not so cold as to hurt your head when you drink it. The cliffs jag out from the sides of the mountains like plateaus and display the treasures of nature, golden cinquefoil wildflowers, purple lupine, red and blue prairie lillies. The road that swirls through the mountains winds up and down from the top to the base of the valley. You can look down into a magnificent bowl of green and yellow and brown. You look up at the pine and the aspen that climb the side of the mountains and stand solid against the pale sky.

I had seen the Big Horns before, but Burt had not, and he breathed them in, thinking he would never see them again. He stopped again and again at the lookouts on the tops of the mountains to take pictures and to groan at the colors and shapes. On the motorcycle, we could smell the mountains and Burt would sometimes ride off the road, toward the most enticing of the smells. The flowers were sweet, the pine strong, like good antiseptic. Burt would scramble up the ledges on the side of the road and throw rocks and sticks toward the bottom. He weaved on his motorcycle along the road, his whole body trembling. I have seen people affected by drugs before; their movements are usually slow, often jerky. Burt was caught not by a drug, however, but by the spirit of beauty.

That day, I feared that Burt was not going to make it off the mountain. There were times when I thought he was going to throw himself into the valley, just for some kind of sated sacrifice to its beauty. I tried to make him go quicker, but he ignored me. I kept passing him, hoping he would follow, but he never did. I don't think he knew I was even there. We made it through the Big Horns eventually, down the final grade, and onto the flat road beyond, although the aftertaste of my fear still lingered.

We left Cody, Wyoming, at five A.M., winding high into the rusty Shoshone Mountains. At a diner near the Montana border the temperature was 24 degrees, and the wind was blowing hard from the northwest. We were into the sixth week of our journey, near the middle of July, when it started to snow.

At the diners and lodges spaced along the road, Burt ordered scalding cups of coffee, simply to soak his hands in them. I sat on my cold hands, or buried them in my warm crotch when we rested, and frequently waitresses had to unclasp our helmets and pull off our gloves. We bought new gloves at each stop, but the snow repeatedly soaked them, and the cold wind froze them to our hands.

We steered with one hand and warmed the other by bending over and clutching the hot exhaust pipes. Our gloves would steam and sizzle against the exhaust, but after a while, I could hardly feel the warmth.

Sometimes, when I pounded my hands against the gas tank—when I punched the gas tank as hard as I could with my fist—I could feel them hurt, but the pain was dulled by the cold.

The wheels of our motorcycles cut squiggly lines through the new snow as we pushed along. I could not hear the wheels crackle against the loose asphalt lying on top of the road now that we were running on the bed of snow. So hard was I concentrating on riding in the snow that I could hear nothing but Burt's motorcycle whining behind.

I had never dreamed of riding a motorcycle in the snow. It would be damn crazy to ride purposely in the winter, when the thermometer dips way below freezing and ice sheets the main roads. The fact that it was not too unusual to find snow high in the Montana mountains early in July did not soothe me.

Yet I never thought of stopping. If Burt considered stopping, he never mentioned it to me. We made it through the fog in the Shenandoah, the wind and sand of Texas. We made it through all that rain. We hadn't expected snow, but we hadn't expected all the rain and wind either. The plan was to push on, to experience everything. It seemed silly to hole up somewhere. We were short of money and the thought of getting snowbound didn't appeal to me. We had started this trip on motorcycles and had no intention of abandoning them until there was no other alternative.

I was leading and the snow was getting ever deeper and more treacherous, yet I rode progressively faster as we wound up and down the mountains. I don't know if I was going faster out of fear or excitement, if I was running from the weather or was spurred on by it, but the harder the snow came, the faster I pressed along the highway. I watched the road ahead, fascinated by the way my front tire cut a narrow black line in the white powder, like a crayon in cotton.

The sheets of snow caked on my shield. I rode with one hand and gloved the shield with the other—back and forth I wiped, like a car's windshield wipers, pushing away the snow to see, seeing to go ever faster over the road. I was going very fast, although I don't remember how fast. I was passing cars and trailers. I rode the white line, squeezing between the cars that were ahead, and the cars that came toward me from the opposite lane. Burt was somewhere behind, although I could not see through the ice that froze away his reflection in the mirror.

I did not think of cracking up and dying, but was preoccupied with the tragedy of not having grandchildren. I do not have children, nor any prospects right now, but was very sad over not having grandchildren. I made up a song about not having grandchildren and sang it to the cars I passed as I rocketed up the road.

I was not afraid. Never have I felt more rational, articulate, philosophical, more competent or capable. Yet, all along I knew, as I wound faster and faster, always faster around the snow-clogged mountains, that I was moving with the courage of fear.

More than anything else, fear was the overwhelming reason I rode this motorcycle. Maybe this is not true for everybody, but right then, for me, I was convinced it was. Not just today in the snow, but any day, in any weather, fear turns men to two wheels. Fear of getting too old. Fear of losing attractiveness. Fear of people higher up. Fear of a world too complicated. Fear of a world never seen. Fear of the ghosts that haunt at night. Riding a motorcycle eases the fear for some men. For me, on that day in the snow, I was held together by the courage brought on by the awareness of the fear.

At one point, I stopped at an outhouse, a shack sagging under the weight of the snow, to rest. Burt pulled in beside me, but we didn't talk. We walked down the hill from the road toward the building. We went inside, took off our clothes and wrung our underwear out. We smoked cigarettes, inhaling the foulness of the outhouse, trembling in the cold corner, nude.

Caution replaced courage later when we moved on. The rest and the warmth made us more aware of our vulnerability, and we rode carefully. Near Yellowstone we saw two cyclists who were stranded after skidding across the snow and into a ditch. It was too cold to stop.

We plunged into the Tetons. The snow dissolved to rain. The roads were black and shiny, spiraling up and down the mountains. Forgetting caution, we ran from the cold, searching for the sun, going too fast, and getting tired, ever more weary, leaning drunkenly into semi-circular bends, when Burt lost control and dumped head-on into the side of a rocky hill.

I heard the metal of Burt's machine scrape against the asphalt and clatter against the rocks like a cupboard of pots and pans flung to the ground. In my mirror, I saw the bike, a dangerous island with Burt riding the side of it, shooting a stream of golden sparks along the asphalt, splashing against the wall of rocks that made the hill.

Then I dropped my bike. I was running before the bike hit the ground. It caught my leg and I went down. I scrambled up and fell down again. I pawed at the ground till I pulled my leg out. Burt was wedged between the rocks and his machine.

Burt got up. "I'm all right," he said.
I pulled his cycle up, but he sunk back down to his knees.
"You all right?"
"I said I was all right."
"But you're bleeding."
The road had ripped through the canvas rainsuit with the rubber lining and the Levis under them, and scraped away his skin.
"It's okay," he said, "I've lived through worse."
"You were lucky."
"I know."
He was covered with mud, and there were cinders stuck in the mud, but he wiped most of it off. Then he slapped his gloves against his good knee, shaking the dirt from them.
"Wow," I said, watching him.
"Yeah," Burt smiled.
"What happened?"
"I don't know. I think I got too tired. Maybe I went to sleep. I don't know. Maybe I was thinking about something. I don't know. I can't remember anything about it right now."
"You were lucky."
"The wheels just slipped out and I was on the ground. I wasn't even scared. Anyway, I'm all right."
"You were lucky."
"I know."
We moved on for a few days, but the trip was over. Burt's bike was not in good shape. My left hand was frostbitten and although I could use the hand well enough, I could not feel it. I could drive the motorcycle, but without the feel of the controls it did not seem the same. Burt was already late getting back to work, we had lingered longer than planned. We could have continued, but we were finished. The trip had taken on a pleasant rhythm, a lot of good things had happened, yet we were waiting for some kind of ending befitting it. The snow was the last act of our cross-country play, climaxed by the courage of fear we found to move through it.

I hardly talked to anyone on the way back, except for those people in restaurants, motels, and gas stations you need to talk to. It was time to duck inside of myself, time to synthesize my thoughts and impressions for when I would be facing my typewriter at home. I wanted to work on establishing a distance between myself as the protagonist of the adventure and the writer who articulates it. A writer needs that distance. He must be able to pull back from the situation about which he is writing, and observe himself as other men would. For this, he needs self-imposed solitude.

It takes three days by motorcycle to ride the superhighways that lace together the states from Wyoming to Pennsylvania. From South Dakota to Iowa to Illinois to Indiana to Ohio. From toll booth to toll booth at 85 miles per hour. Howard Johnson's to Stuckey's, bitter coffee, burnt hamburgers, corn in the fields, rain in the morning, television at night.

Then it was over. Cross-country on a motorcycle, six weeks of a dream. It took six weeks to get there; it could have taken six years. It took six weeks of riding, and in the epilogue of the dream, three days to get home.

I have taken shorter trips since, of course. From Pittsburgh, I've traveled to New England, and to Ohio, West Virginia, and Washington, D.C. I have seen Burt and we have talked. He is sculpting full-time now, has another woman who understands him better, and a new Honda 500 that can take him around the world and back—twice. I have been dreaming too, dreams of two wheels and one man, winding like a blackbird over roads that lace together forgotten worlds. I have been dreaming and dreams, after all, are what motivate man.

I shall go across the country on a motorcycle again. Perhaps I will ride a different way, perhaps I will ride over a different country, but I will ride the long road on two wheels again, for there is nothing I know that will replace the joy of it. There is nothing quite like cross-country motorcycling that reconciles man's spirit, which is indestructible, to machines, which are inevitable, to the land, which is indefinable. There is nothing as brutal, as beautiful, as thrilling, as austere.

THE LAND

Eighteen

Short of flying great distances, short of swimming the seven seas, there is nothing the dirt riders cannot do or haven't done. Up canyon walls, down narrow mountain halls. They are technological camels in the desert, motorized alligators in the swamp. Like drills, they mole through marshes; like pogo sticks, they leap boulders and rotting logs. Snow soothes their hot brows, rain lubricates their muscles, lightning cuts a path for them through the night. Short of producing an earthquake, there is hardly anything mother nature can do to stop them. Including earthquakes, there is hardly anything she hasn't tried. They are called dirt riders, but they are actually argonauts of the muck and mud.

A different kind of competitor from a professional racer, dirt bikers are mostly amateurs and mostly ride on weekends. Dirt bikers are usually family people. Mothers, fathers, and children will often have their own machines and race in separate competitions. Dirt bikers are usually more diversified people and they are traveling people. They find their action in many forms, and in many different places.

The *scramblers* compete on a smooth-surfaced dirt course with up and down hill sections, left and right turns and ski-like jumps. The *motorcross*, a more sophisticated kind of scramble, is held on unimproved terrain, on a course not longer than two miles. The men who ride motocross can expect almost anything. Hidden pools of water, trees, and rocks. Mud and more mud. Fifty percent of the riders won't finish an average moto-cross, and those who have spilled or stalled on the way are perhaps the most frequent and frightening of obstacles to those who have not. Three heats, or "motos," are held for each engine size. There is a winner in each class, as well as an overall champion.

The margin between excellence and mediocrity is often in blasting off the line. All motocross races employ the European start: motor running, gearbox in neutral, hand on your helmet. The idea is to watch the tip of the flag man's flag. The idea is to go like hell when it moves. Often, the best riders are the best cheaters. They find a place, far down the line from the flagman, and creep their bike slowly forward with their feet. Or sometimes they put their bike in gear and their foot on the clutch cable on the side of the gearbox, chiseling an edge on the dropped flag.

On take-off, the veteran riders rev their machines high so that the rear wheel breaks contact with the ground and digs them away quickly. The less experienced riders will sometimes not generate enough starting rpms. Consequently, their rear wheel bites, their machines rear up in front like frightened stallions, wasting precious seconds off the line.

If the track has been used before, then hundreds or thousands of bikes have traversed it. They will have worn in a groove of perhaps a foot or two feet wide and the smart riders, even if it means not having an initial lead, will keep their wheels true to it. The skilled rider shoots for victory when the groove runs out. One must use the work of others for momentum before pioneer-ing with a thrust of his own.

The dirt rider is an intelligent man and a physical man. There is hardly a muscle, hardly a nerve that isn't strained to its tautest. He is a blood and guts, bowl-em-over kind of man. Courageous is perhaps an incomplete way of describing him. Trials and *enduro* riders, especially, would more aptly be labeled spartans.

A trials course is usually laid out in a loop of about ten miles. There are sections of the course, usually about four feet wide, marked off by lines of lime or tape, and each rider must ride in them without putting a foot down for balance, dropping, or stalling the bike, or crossing over the markings. Checkers watch the riders and award penalty points when they make mistakes.

Each competitor travels the track three times. There are four classes—novice, junior, and expert, and a separate class for women and children.

An enduro is perhaps a little tougher. Aside from the usual mud, hills, and swamps found in both activities, sections of public roads and highways are included. Which means that a machine, although outfitted for mud and misery, must also be street legal. Either activity, trials or enduros, is nothing short of diabolical.

In 1972 the American Motorcycle Association sponsored 27 national enduros from the 100-mile Stone Mountain National in Dalton, Georgia, to the two-day 500-mile Greenhorn National in Duarte, California.

If 200 riders start, then maybe twenty will finish. If it happens to be spring and the sun is shining and the leaves and early blossoms are painting the world gay, most will not notice. All they will see are dead-end canyons, walls of thorn bushes, mountain paths winding interminably up interminable mountains. All they will do is dance and bulldoze, pick and push their way through it. Dance and doze, that is the rhythm.

Discounting the day, it is often what they don't see that will hurt them. The sadists who design the course camouflage mud holes, tree stumps, or road wrinkles with pretty green leaves and crisp yellow straw. There are even specially selected pools of tired, stagnant water with stuff less substantial than ooze lining the bottoms. About half of the course is usually over virgin terrain. The other half might have been blazed once or twice before by Land Rovers, Jeeps, or more probably, by men on foot. Scored roughly like a sports car rally, enduro riders are awarded 1,000 points at the starting line and try to run the course at a prescribed average speed. Points are taken away from early or late riders at checkpoints along the way.

The riders who compete against each other are forever ripping down directional signs so that the men behind them become temporarily lost or hopelessly delayed. Some, it is rumored, never return.

And if two days and 500 miles are not enough, then the English and Spanish offer six-day, 1,500-mile trials for the super spartans. For each day the rider is given a different course and, like the enduro, is scored on his average time, often around thirty miles per hour. A point is lost for every early or late minute.

For a six-day trial, the rider must carry all tools, replacement parts, and survival equipment with him. And he must maintain his machine during the actual daily competition—not before or after it. In some trials, a rider is alloted two minutes to change a tire, perhaps three minutes to repair a broken clutch or brake cable.

Emsworth, Pennsylvania. Nothing country. Where the landscape has been butchered by phantom strip miners. Where the hillsides spread wide their raped crotches. Where the speedway juts out at the far edge of a poor gray excuse for a park.

"Where else you gonna get a hill like this?" says an official with a yellow and red "Leap n' Linx" badge sewed onto his shirt. There is a clear imprint of a hand sopped in grease on his knee, but except for that blemish, his overalls are virgin white. "That hill is 110 foot high and about 72 degrees straight up. Nothin' to laugh at."

And except for some beer-can suckers standing behind the plywood barrier below the hill, nobody is laughing. Although the atmosphere is no match for the sobriety of the countryside, everyone is seriously toiling with their machines or discussing in earnest the Everest of the day.

In the pit area, a few bikers are working on their machines, changing sprockets, disconnecting lighting systems, fenders, and license plates, checking carburetor settings, painting racing numbers on the pie plates pasted to the front of their bikes. Everyone seems to be sharpening the edges of tire cleats.

Traction. A precious grip on mobility. One man is painting his tires with his girlfriend's hair spray. Another rider is heating and reforming tire cleats with a blowtorch. Lots of people have built fires, and the women are sitting around them on newspapers warming beer-can-cold hands, while the shapes of their asses gradually make impressions in the mud.

And the pits are really pits. No clubhouse area, paddock, or riders' quarters. The men's room is as close as the nearest tree. Bring your own toilet paper. You can shower if it rains. Bring your own soap.

"This isn't mud," says one rider standing in line at the registration trailer, "this is quagmire."

"Why does it always have to rain before a climb?" somebody mumbles the most repeated rhetorical question of the day. "I lose a boot every time I take a step."

Cars pulling trailers loaded with bikes move past the registration line. Pickup trucks with bikes. A few cars with bikes hanging precariously out of trunks, but mostly you think that the best thing for the automotive people in Detroit are the motorcycle dirt machines that aren't registered for the road. There seems to be a truck or trailer for almost every bike. Sometimes there are two trucks, one hauling motorcycles, the other for riders, mechanics, girlfriends, and relatives. People have come all the way from Lansing, Michigan; Indianapolis, Indiana; Zelienople, Pennsylvania; and Cumberland, Maryland. They hang together in their groups like unbroken six packs of beer. There is little horseplay though because, to them, motorcycle hillclimbing is serious fun.

The hillbusters are the mountain tamers of motorcycling. Since the turn of the century they have competed against both time and gravity. Without pickaxes or ropes, they scramble or fight or persist or claw their way from a dead start up hills that most men could not climb without crawling. Hillbusting has never been an especially popular phase of motorcycle dirt competition, but it has always had its following.

Even in the early days, the champion hillbusters weren't very well known. Hardly anyone will remember Orie Steele, Dud Perkins, Wells Bennett, Earl Buck, Sam Parriot, TNT Terpening, because men are vulnerable and inconsistent and machines are destructible and just as inconsistent. But free of dozers and dynamite, the hills will outlast time.

In the early days, every state had its unclimbable hill. In Massachusetts, it was Enfield; in New York state, it was Egypt or Port Jervis; in Oregon, Wagner's Butte in Corvalis; and the all-mighty in California was the great Capistrano. Yet nothing could or will ever equal the supreme test of persistence and skill: Muskegon in Michigan. From bottom to top, Muskegon was almost 300 feet high. The last seventy feet, say some of the old timers, were like a vertical wall. Muskegon was so steep that riders and machines had to be lowered down by an automatic logging cable. Muskegon was so dangerous that once making the hill, a rider had to use all cunning and stamina to stop the machine before slipping down the other side—and dropping into the depths of Lake Michigan.

At the far edge of the pit area, some of the Leap n' Linx people are revving their machines up a half-hearted hill in practice. It isn't much of a hill, but from the bottom, the bikes bellow to one another like timber cutters' ripsaws; from a dead start, their riders build up revolutions, pop the clutch, and let-er-rip.

The riders are as mature as 56-year-old Clem Harper and as young as 12-year-old Kenny Cline. They are wearing almost anything you can think of for protection: skin pads, shoulder pads, and knee pads. Many of those who didn't brace with protective gear last week do so this week, wearing arm casts, leg casts, and ankle casts. The wounded ride or walk around the pit area, oblivious to their disabilities.

The fanatical hillbusters have their own special hill machines and use them only for that purpose. Some of the bikes have less than a couple hundred miles on them which, up and down hills, is a lot to gather. A few of the bikes are fancy, chopped low, and quilted with chrome. Most, however, are derelicts, leftovers of many different machines, wired and bolted and stitched into one. They look like Siamese triplets, some of them, with Honda engines, Bultaco forks, Harley tanks, and bicycle seats. They are light-weight and built low to the ground. Everything not needed, including the kick starter, is stripped from the machine. For maximum lightness, some bikes are fed from nothing more than a test tube full of fuel. All that is added is a kill strap—a piece of rope attached to the rider's wrist and hooked to the ignition so that an out-of-control-machine will die before it stampedes into the crowd. One of the earliest champion hillbusting machines was the Excelsior Motorcycle, manufactured by Igantius Schwinn, who eventually found more profit and pleasure in making bicycles.

The motorcycles trudge up to the starting line like grumbling legionaires. One at a time. Men in leathers or sweat pants, white helmets with peaked visors. Men in blue jeans and quilted nylon coats and boots strapped tightly around their ankles, buckled high up to the knees. One after another they try the hill.

"All right. Git 'er in there. Git 'er lined up. Numba wun fuh fuh. McMasta fum Detroit."

All motorcycle race announcers seem to sound as though they come from the South. Even if it is only south Philadelphia, they all display their Georgian twang.

"We sure do 'preciate you fellas comin' all the way fum Mich'gun to see us. McMasta on a Kawaaaaaasakeeee. Git 'er in there, McMasta. Sure do 'preciate them boys comin' all the way fum . . . Git 'er in there McMasta or we'll have to disqualify . . . ."

The bigger bikes are most exciting. The bigger bikes, 500 cc and above, will usually make it up the hill. Trophies are awarded to those busters that scramble up the fastest. As machine size increases, times drop from seven plus seconds to under 4.5 seconds, a good score. Smaller machines don't usually make it up; they are judged by how far they go.

McMasters is on a 125 cc. He wheels his bike in, kicks it started, then pulls the kick starter off and throws it behind him. He leans his back wheel against a plywood barrier, revs his machine softly—whaaa, whaaa, whaaaaa—pops the clutch slightly, and lets the back wheel cut a starting edge in the dirt. He sees the groove up ahead of him where the other bikes have climbed. He will have to follow this groove if he expects to make it to the top.

"Cut eeem loose," the announcer says, and the kill-strap checker taps McMasters' shoulder.

WHAAAAAHHHH WHAAAAAAA WHAAAAAAAA WHAAAAAAAAAAAAA!

McMasters pops the clutch and lurches forward up the groove, shooting clots of mud back behind him at the checker. The key to climbing is to keep your front wheel down and McMasters shimmies his crotch from the seat to the gas tank and presses his weight against the handlebars. A quarter of the way up, the bike rears up on its back wheel, but McMasters throws his chest on the front bars and pushes it down.

Don't die on me, baby, please don't die.

But the bike sings its swansong like a trumpeter out of breath. McMasters claws with his boot heels for additional footage, then the bike collapses under him. And together, faster than slow motion, and slower than real life, they roll in unison back the way they came.

"Fuhty tooo feet fuh that boy. Fuhty tooo feet. Git the next rider up heah. Git 'er up. Git 'er up. Git the show on the road.

Don't be a toad. Git 'er going, git 'er up."

"Thought I was going to make it," McMasters gulps "Damn. Damn."

"You got 42 feet."

"Damn, I don't want 42 feet. I want to make it, I thought I was going to make it."

"How did you know?"

"I don't know. I just knew it."

McMasters made 27 feet on his second run. The best time of the day was produced by Pappy Kerns on his blue, metal-flaked 650 BSA. Pappy cut his own groove twice behind the plywood. Then he went up the hill in 3.49 seconds. His wheels never touched the ground. Nobody cheered when he came back down. Hillbusters are the Quakers of dirt competition. Weakness is tolerated, but excellence is expected.

Barstow, California. Thanksgiving Day weekend. Desert and desert. Far away a glass blue Pacific shatters against a bone white beach. Far away, 161 miles, the slot machines and tinsel of Sin City, Las Vegas, will be the oasis for those riders who choose to rip across the hot plain.

The San Gabriel Motorcycle Club first organized the Barstow to Vegas Cross-Country Desert Run, the world's largest motorcycle race, in 1967. Three thousand riders, headed by top professionals, tailed by the rankest amateurs—together like a flick of thunder—scamper across the desert for a piece of the checkered flag.

Roughly 10,000 people each year come to see them off, in vans and mobile homes, pickup trucks, campers, buses, cars, helicopters, and motorcycles. All up and down the Las Vegas freeway, motels are flickering red, green, and blue, no-no-no, beside their vacancy signs. And the California highway patrolmen, sweating under wide-brimmed hats and stuffed with an early turkey, are struggling to free the Minneola Road off-ramp from congestion. It is hot.

Side-by-side, footpeg-to-footpeg, the riders are set up in a line that waves down the desert for more than a mile. The wind is blowing up scrims of dust and sand. And to keep from running into one another coming up to the line, the riders have their lights on. Some riders are wearing wetted-down kerchiefs over their faces, desperado style, to keep their throats moist through the early dust when all the bikes blast off together.

A black smoke bomb pops and inks the sky like an octopus' excrement darkens water. Everyone barks his engine to life and straddles his machine. When the ready flag tips a few minutes later, officials on the starting line signal the riders to kill the engines and get ready to go.

When it's missing, that's when you hear the noise. And you hear the desert wind and the way the wind lifts paper-thin layers of sand from the dunes and paints the riders' colorful nylon and leather outfits gray. Like statues so still, their legs raised and in limbo beside their kick starters, poised for action.

The lights from the motorcycles look like yellow tulips running down the edge of a sidewalk of a long gray street. The scrub and the rocks and the bumps below the hill where the smoke bomb blasted are merely shadows. The greasewood bushes, joshua trees, and yuccas dot the brown with green. Yet even the colors are in shadows. The rabbits and the ground squirrels hop beneath the shadows. Everything seems a shadow after all the noise has been replaced by silence under the windy heat.

Then the flag drops. The riders kick over the start levers and explode across the desert in a tidal wave of noise and thunder and vibration that is far too deafening to hear or feel. It is something you remember later much more clearly than you will remember the winner, the weekend in Vegas, or the heat of the race.

Unlike the Barstow Run, the Baja in California pits motorcycles against all sorts of motorized all-terrain vehicles over a 557-mile course, although motorcycles, because of their durability and maneuverability, are most often the highest finishers. There are also hare scrambles in the desert, shorter races, usually held on a fifty-mile loop, which the bikers circle twice. Although desert racing is quite popular, it is obviously limited to the southwestern sections of the United States. But most other forms of off-road motorcycle competition can be found in rural pockets and suburban patches all over the country.

On the same Sunday afternoon the Leap n' Linx held their hillclimb, there was a motocross in Murraysville, Pennsylvania, 25 miles to the southeast. Seven miles from Murraysville, in New Alexandria, Keystone Raceway is sponsoring a scrambles. Thirty miles further east, in Johnstown, there is another motocross. And a hillclimb 35 miles past Johnstown in State College, Pennsylvania. From Emsworth going west thirty miles, the Sunset Riders had their first scrambles of the season at their Chicora, Pennsylvania farm. Thirty miles to the south in Greensburg, there is another hillclimb and motocross. In most directions from most large cities, men, women, and children compete regularly on Sunday afternoons, on motorcycles, off the road.

No one can say how many dirt machines there are and how many people race with them. But is it certain to be in the millions. Dirt bikes need not be registered. And they are often former street machines junked and legally long gone. In certain parts of the country, dirt cycles sell three to one over street bikes.

The number of dirt machines increases the farther west you roam, where there is more reliable weather and larger tracts of wilderness areas. There are more adults, more families, competing on a regular and organized basis in professional and amateur off-road motorcycling events than in any other sport in the nation.

That is because dirt biking is the last haven for those contemporary young men and women who feel that golf and bowling and television baseball are poor excuses for exercise, a boring and feeble kind of fun.

Nineteen

In dirt riding, falling down and getting back up and falling again is the rhythm of life. Dirt riding is for the young man to whom bruises are badges, to whom satisfaction is earned through the use of razor-sharp reflexes, to whom spirit and a reluctance to accept defeat are often more valuable than sheer riding skill.

"Now look, Dad, the first thing to remember is that there's no shame in falling, as long as you get up again. And little danger, at least compared to the consequences of falling on the street. Besides your boots, goggles, helmet, and leathers, get yourself some elbow and knee pads. The elbow and knees are vulnerable in a fall. It's best to be prepared. Now, when you're ready, meet me at the field down the road."

The trail bike is not easy to ride. The seat is not as comfortable as a street or touring bike. The back tire is oversized, bumpy, and hard to handle because of its thick, square cleats. On the road, a trail bike rides like a car fitted with studded snow treads. It also has to be shifted more often because the machine is geared low for maximum traction, and has nothing resembling a comfortable cruising gear.

But we make it down the road and turn off at the field. The boy is waiting. These kids today have a kind of leering way of smiling when they know that they know more about something than their parents. We resist the temptation to tell him to shut up before he even begins talking and then we listen.

"There are a couple of things to learn about stopping in the dirt that are different from street braking. First, we rely much more on the front brake. Lots of people hesitate using the front brake on the dirt because they're afraid the wheel will lock. But there's really little danger, if you use a light and delicate touch."

"So I should apply the brake slowly?"

"But not too slowly. Apply steady pressure until right before you think the wheel is about to lock."

"How do I know that?"

"Practice. Start at slow speeds and keep practicing, gradually increasing your speed until you can come to a safe stop at any speed."

Learning to stop in the dirt is like moving to England and learning to drive on the left side of the road. But we practice and get to be fairly good. The difficult part is to convince yourself that the front brake is a control like any of the other controls, that there is nothing to fear. The fear, of course, is that should the wheel lock, we will be thrown forward, over the handlebars.

"Now the next thing you have to learn," he says, "is making a fast corner. Remember that trails are cut much more sharply than streets. And there are always obstructions—big rocks, logs, tree stumps—to dodge. A lot of the skill has to do with how you maneuver your weight. This is probably the single most important thing to learn about trail riding. For you," he says, glancing up at our belt buckle, "it might be a problem."

"All right. That's not funny."

"Seriously, when you want to cut a fast corner, you've got to get your weight toward the center of the machine. So slide forward up the seat before you get to the corner. At the same time, slow down to the speed at which you want to turn. Now, as you hit the curve, lean in the direction of the turn."

"OK. Except for moving forward, that's the way a street rider would take it."

"Right. Except there's more to do. You take your inside foot off the peg and kick it out and forward. Now, put all of your weight on the outside peg. Your weight on the outside increases your traction and, on the loose dirt, you're going to need all the traction you can get. One more thing. Never apply the brake once you're into the turn. Take it smooth."

"I see, its the same as in street riding."

"Right. You're correctly leaning into the turn, as all cyclists must do. But, by the same token, your weight on the outside peg is pressing you back into the turf. Sort of nailing you down. This is important because the dirt is unstable. A few pebbles or a clump of mud could make that back wheel slip out."

"Is that all?"

"That's all about fast corners. Slow corners are an entirely different proposition."

"That doesn't make sense."

"It does if you remember that speed is usually a stabilizing factor on a motorcycle, so you are more prone to fall the slower you are going."

"So what do I do differently?"

"At a low speed turn, you leave the seat completely and stand up on the footpegs."

"I don't like doing that. The seat sort of gives a good feeling of security."

"But by standing, you're actually safer because it keeps your center of gravity low."

"What do you mean? If I'm standing, that puts me up higher than before."

"Yes, but you forget that by standing, your weight is on the footpegs. If you were sitting, your weight would be on the seat."

"I see."

"You've got to think much more carefully about what you're doing. Trail riding is not as relaxing or as easy as road riding. But it's also more fun and more challenging."

"All right. What else?"

"Standing on the pegs during a slow turn also makes it easier for you to maneuver your weight and control your body. So get up on the pegs, press your knees tight against the bike. Then, at the same time, lean the bike toward the inside of the turn—and bend your body slightly toward the outside. The weight of your body on the opposite side is the stabilizing factor. Remember, you've lost the stabilization that comes naturally from speed. So you have to provide something to replace it."

"Hell, this isn't motorcycling, it's calisthenics; it's physical torture."

"This is nothing," he tells you, smiling.

We approach the hill and examine it closely, visualizing from that jumble of rocks and puddles and trees the best path to the top. Sometimes there is no best path. Sometimes there is no path at all. But we size that up before we get there, before we hit the hill. And we hit the hill hard. Speed and momentum are our biggest assets, so we try to generate as much as safety will allow. We shift down into second, usually the best gear, low enough for biting traction and high enough so that we're not forced to downshift in mid-climb because of lack of speed. As we reach the hill, we stand on our footpegs and push our weight where it is needed, toward the front of the bike. Then we dig.

"You made it!"

"What did you expect?"

"Well, that was a pretty rough climb."

"The climb doesn't bother me. What scares me is going down the other side."

"Just remember, when going down, to keep standing on the footpegs, but shift your weight to the rear of the bike. Always think of your traction points. You apply your weight where traction is most needed. On the front of the bike going up a hill, on the back of the bike going down. You've got plenty of traction on the front wheel when going down because that's got the weight of the bike behind it. So shift yourself to the back. And keep your speed under control so you don't have to make an abrupt stop. It's better that you keep rolling smoothly, and don't use your brakes at all. But if you have to, brake with the front."

"Why the front?"

"Well obviously, I just said that was where the weight of the bike is. Secondly, it's operated by a hand lever, so your feet can remain steady on the pegs. And finally, going downhill the rear wheel locks very easily if the brakes are applied too hard. Of course, don't use either brake if you can help it, if you're in the middle of a turn."

"What happens if I don't want to go up or down a hill, but just sort of ride across its slope? I want to run against the grain of the hill, in other words."

"Right. Here again you have to stand on the pegs and squeeze your gas tank with your knees. You should move your body—remember it is often the stabilizing factor—to the downhill side of the bike. But put your footpeg weight on the uphill side of the bike. At the same time, try to hold the bike as vertically straight as possible. Steadiness is the most important thing to remember here. A steady posture, a steady bike, and a steady speed. If you have to change speed by shifting, do it gradually and smoothly. Otherwise, your wheels are going to slide out under you."

If you don't mind getting wet, it is not difficult to cross a stream. The best place to cross is where the water moves fast, because the loose mud or sand is usually carried away by rushing water, leaving a firm bottom. After finding a good place, we stand on our pegs and shift our weight a little to the rear. We want our front wheel light and loose for it is apt to hit an invisible rock or stump, buried in the mud.

Where the ground is soft, we must shift our weight even further to the rear. A brisk speed is important, for it enables us to stay on top of the ground rather than digging into it. The faster we go, the less likelihood the rear wheel will be buried. This means a loss of mobility and requires more power to propel the bike forward. As your rear wheel spins in the mud, you dig a deeper grave into which you and your bike will die.

"But what happens if I do get stuck?"

"You're in trouble. Most of the time you just have to physically push your way out. Your only option is to suddenly slam your body back to the rear, at the point at which you feel yourself getting stuck. This might provide enough instant weight for your rear wheel to bite. If it works, shift into the next highest gear and build up more speed so that it doesn't happen a second time. Always try to keep moving."

"What else about dirt riding?"

"About the only thing you don't know now is how to get over big logs and rocks. Not that you know everything. Experience is what you need most now—and plenty of patience and spirit."

"Forget patience and spirit and tell how to get over logs and rocks."

"OK. You've got to stand up again and shift your weight to

the back of the machine. Try to approach the object, whatever you're going over, at a reasonable speed. Don't try to smash your way across or your wheels will buckle. Let's say you're heading for a log. Approach it as squarely as possible, head on. When the front wheel hits, pull up on the handlebars. That will take the impact stress off the front wheel and help it to ease over smoothly."

"Sounds easy enough."

"That's only half the process. Remember, you've got two wheels. As soon as your first wheel rolls over, move your body forward a little. That will lighten the weight of the rear wheel when it comes over. You would use this same technique for smaller rocks and bumps when going up a hill."

"There's a lot to remember."

"Oh. Something else is that you should always try to remain relaxed and comfortable when your rear wheel is skidding. Remember that you're on loose turf and your rear tire is naturally going to slip all over the place. The natural tendency is to tighten up and put your foot down for balance. That's both dangerous and incorrect. It's incorrect because it retards balance and rhythm. A rider could go on skidding indefinitely after a few weeks of practice, but touch the ground once and he'll spill all over the place. It's dangerous because if you use a foot for a kick stand or training wheel, it could easily be lopped off or broken by a rock or a tree. Just try to stay relaxed and confident, and close in to the bike. You're always the safest if you stay with the bike."

"That's it?"

"Theoretically that's it. Or at least that's enough for the beginning. The rest comes with experience and time and practice. I think you've got a lot of potential if you worked hard at it."

Big man.

Twenty

It was noon and Red Madison left the Indian to cool under an awning of lodgepole pine. Then he walked over to the rim of the road to look down the mountain. From there, he could see the snow and the pine trees climbing up the slopes of the other mountains, and the line of the road below that rimmed the lower edge of all of them.

Red Madison lit his cigar with a match scraped against the side of his boot and sat under the sun, smoking and thinking and watching the wind whip clouds of red dust over the baking upper plain.

He leaned back, sucked the tip of the cigar wet, and blew out white smoke. From where he lay, the trees towered above him, leaning inward at each other, their tops forming the bushy green crotch of a gigantic multi-legged man. It was hot but the breeze that whipped the dust cooled his face. It was quiet, for the birds were not singing; but he could see them sitting in squat cottonwood trees.

Red Madison, on his way to a job on a ranch near Billings, had left Sheridan, Wyoming, early that morning, cut north through the Big Horns, then dove like a swan into the blue big sky that bordered Montana.

The morning was cool and Red Madison had floated through it. The Indian's eye had cut a yellow path through the darkness cast by the great mountains. Red's heart had tightened in excitement as he trumpeted the Indian over the roads that corkscrewed to the clouds, then whizzed on the wide highway that roped straight across the prairie.

He had stopped at a cafe near Red Lodge for hot cakes and coffee, and had found the trail he was now on a few miles out of town. He remembered the area from thirty years ago when he first came to Montana and what a thrill it had been to climb with his friends and their bikes up and through the mountains.

That was when there were many trails like this one and many other gypsies to ride them with. And no one dreamed, with the way the world was moving from depression into war, that the supply of good roads or the number of gypsies would ever diminish. You could ride into a town, find the local cycle shop, and more than likely there would be someone there you'd know. Or you'd know someone he knew. And soon there would be talk of a hill, or a special road and the doors of the shop would quietly close. Then suddenly there would appear another couple of bikers, and you'd kick down together and pick up a couple more before you'd hit the edge of town.

Before you knew it, you were one of a dozen in the thunder, and there were no helmets to cut out the noise or mufflers to shut out the foul gasoline smell. There were no fences or police or diners or gates or hippies, and whatever road you hit, you owned.

A man on a Harley or an Indian or Henderson, blowing out seventy big horses, pushing a 1,000 pound machine, could intimidate all but the impregnable persistence of time.

But that had all changed. Even though he returned to this part of the country every year most of the people Red once knew had gone. The people that were left had withered on their porches or in the dirty corners of the towns like forgotten fruit. The nice towns that once had as many as seven saloons lining a lone main street had turned to the tourists and the tinsel. The mountains that had kept the tourists out of the fertile green valleys with their clear lakes had been severed by gigantic corporate cleavers—steam shovels, drills, buzz-saws. The lakes that had glinted silver in the sun, with hardly a reason to ripple, were bottomed now in beer cans, despoiled by men hauling stainless steel bungalows. The ranch at which Red had worked for the past twenty years was soon to be taken over as part of the federal government's wilderness reclamation process.

So he had found this old, red road, a few miles out of Red Lodge, Montana, and followed its bumps to the plateau at the summit. It was the last time he would see this mountain or any other mountains in this part of the country, and now, sitting on top of it, Red Madison felt sad. The wind leaked this sadness in a whine through the trees.

Red tucked the cigar into the side of his mouth, took off his leather riding jacket and laid it on the ground. He was not tall, but his shoulders were large, which made his whole frame seem a lot bigger. He looked like a young man, from behind, except for his hair, which was short and speckled gray like the bristles of a painter's haphazardly cleaned brush.

From the pocket of his jacket he pulled a camera, and walked back over to the edge of the mountain to click shots of the valley and the little ranches nestled like pebbles in the sea of yellow and green below.

Then he picked up the jacket and walked back to where the pine cooled the Indian, laid the jacket down with the camera on top of it. Opening the tool box under the seat of the motorcycle, he pulled out a set of wrenches, wrapped in grimy oilcloth, and spread the wrenches over the oilcloth on the dirt near his camera and coat, selecting two. He had purchased his fiberglass saddlebags ready-made, but had devised a way of connecting them so that they could come off in less than a minute by unloosening four screws. He quickly unbolted them, and laid them one at a time beside his camera and coat. Then he went around to the front of the bike and started taking off the head-light. That was not as easy because of the electrical connections, and the wrenches clattered against each nut. When it was finally disengaged, Red wrapped black electric tape around the bare exposed prongs of wire. The rear light came off also, but much easier, then the rear view mirrors on both sides of the handlebars.

He wheeled the bike away from the cool pine, back under the hot sun, puffing some more on his cigar, swallowing its juice. He inhaled a few times and watched its smoke, then dropped it and ground it with his heel into the dirt. He picked up his leather jacket and put it on.

The bike ignited on the first kick and startled the quiet mountain, the leaves seemingly pricking up their ears. He got on the bike, arranged himself on the seat, pushed off the center stand, kicked down into first gear, and eased out onto the ragged prairie.

Suddenly, he was flying and his shoulders were so light he could hardly feel them. The Indian bellowed as it bounced over the sage, and folded down the yellow grass on either side of the wheels.

Oh my God, Red said to himself as his boots scraped the ground, and he fed more fuel with his wrist through the throttle. "Oh my God," Red said aloud, as he hooked his heels on the footpegs, pressed his knees hard against the tank. He felt the breath of the wind. He felt the hard rubber handle grips scratch his palms, the roughness of the road jounce his kidneys.

Red cranked on the accelerator and shifted into second and then cranked some more and squeezed into third. He jetted off across the prairie for a while, breathing in the red dust that the wind and his wheels were kicking up, and then coughing it out again. He trampled the sagebrush at first and then started playing looping games around each clump. With the back of his hand he wiped the dust that mixed with his perspiration off his brow.

He ran out of prairie and dropped down a steep hill into the trees, the shade and the coolness splashing him like water. He swam in the shade for a while, darting around the bushes and trees and following what looked to be a horse riding trail through the forest. Even in the patches of mud, he kept his feet on the footpegs and his back arched straight, and varied his speed to match the turns and the terrain by kicking down and up into gear, without using his brakes. He took a long, banked downhill to the left, shooting clots of mud with his wheels behind him and splashed head-on over a stream.

His mind had dropped out and left him hanging in the sensation of the ride, but the sound of the splashing water and the feel of it on his hot legs brought him back. He turned off the throttle and kicked down from third to second to first, then circled a clump of bushes and went back to the bed of the stream. He paralleled the stream, riding on the dry crust beside it, following its line as it jagged through the trees.

From his position on the bike, Red could look down and see the geysers of sand made by the fish and the rushing water. Red thought he could smell the water, it looked so fresh and pure, and he knew he could smell the animals that each night drank there. He turned into the stream at a place where the bottom looked solid and went over to the other side. Then he turned back around, splashing through the water again, dragging his hot boots in its coolness. When the water seemed to be running out of the forest, trenching a plain, Red turned away, and cranked the bike on.

He hadn't the slightest idea how long he had been riding, the bike had hummed him numb, but the sun still splattered its gold through the trees.

Up ahead, the forest thinned out and wound into a wide, deep wash of parched prairie dirt. Red slid as far back on the seat as he could without giving up control of the handlebars. He had to get up on top of the dirt, he knew, otherwise the weight of the bike would sink his wheels in. Gradually he turned on more power and shifted through to his top gear. The wash ran for at least a couple of miles, curving every several hundred feet, but Red could follow the line of it comfortably, and he rested as he rode. Periodically he would veer off the wash to try out the hard, banked ground on either side. But there were too many rocks to dodge and the loosely packed dirt in spots was far from trustworthy. He leaned back into the wash and rode it out.

He had traveled in what seemed like a circle and over to his left he could see his awning of pines. Red was up higher than the island now and, turning toward it, he went down a narrow slope of about ten feet, which cut off his vision of the trees. Then he went up a hill and he saw his pines again, then down the other side of the slope, they were lost. Before he knew it, he had run into some "whoop-de-do" jumps—a series of brief hills, about 25 feet apart. He cranked on, climbed the hill, and disconnected from the ground, landing about four or five feet down on the other side of the next hill. He stood up on his pegs and wedged his hands tightly against the handlebars so that his arms shot straight out from the handgrips, and cranked it on some more. Each time he hit the top of a hill, his wheels left the ground and his stomach ricocheted into his throat. Each time he landed, he was climbing again, his kidneys almost bouncing in the dirt.

There was no greater feeling Red Madison could remember than the up and the down of the whoop-de-do. His stomach tightened and his heart beat hard, and he saw himself streaking through the sky, floating silently through that part of the universe where there was no gravity nor civilization to build gates and tall buildings or concrete roads.

So when he hit the rock, knuckling from the hill, he forgot to roll up in a ball, or throttle down, or brace himself or look to see where he was landing. He was still floating above the trees and hanging in the clouds when he smacked into the ground.

It didn't jar Red Madison, though, and he couldn't quite remember why he was there or what had exactly happened. He was up like a shot from the dirt, running to rescue the Indian, wailing on its side against the hill. He pulled the bike up and scrambled crazily on, kicked down and charged up the hill, blind to the tweaked handlebars on the bike and his own scraped and bleeding hands. He took an indeterminable number of whoop-de-doos more, using as a directional reference his awning of pine while the wind chorused his excitement.

The hills ran out and he was over the prairie again, grounding down the sagebrush with the wheels of his machine. He was under the awning of pine and over the carpeted needle floor past his saddlebags, emerging out the other side.

Suddenly, there was a large, steep hill in front of him, and above the peak of the hill's slope there was shelf. The hill ran up about 100 feet and the shelf stood about twenty feet behind it, and maybe five or six feet higher, Red judged. Red wished he had his camera and the time to take a picture of the hill because he instinctively knew he was going to jump it before he even went through the process of deciding.

He was going so fast and it was so surprisingly near that the hill came up on him long before he was ready. But he managed to shift into second gear, pull the throttle on full and hit the slope head-on. He managed to do that. He managed to slither forward toward his gas tank, lean his weight on the front wheel, and lift the wheel up over the ridges and ravines carved by water into the hill and the rocks knuckling up through the dirt.

Red Madison was at the top of the hill before he remembered hitting the bottom and starting up. He skimmered across the grass near the peak of the hill and was almost in the air before he remembered reaching the top. When he ran out of ground, he pulled back hard on the handlebars and stood straight up on his pegs. Then he waited, leaning backwards on a cushion of air, and he waited, until somehow he found himself rolling down the tongue of the cliff he had just jumped onto, and into the mouth of the woods behind it.

He stopped his bike, leaned it against the tree and followed new tire tracks back up the shelf. He lit a cigar and sucked the end of it wet. His stomach was heaving and his mouth was breathing hard, but the pounding in his brain was winding down.

He looked over the cluster of pines where his saddlebags lay, past the prairie and down into the invaded valley. The wind took the smoke from his cigar and whisked it toward the distant brown mountains, ringed with snow. The sun felt cooler in the late afternoon, while Red Madison watched down the wall of the mountain, his heart singing the frenzy of his last great jump.

Red rode down into the valley, then through the town, then out onto the flat road beyond. Off to his right, he could see the yellow stubble of grain, edged all around by sagebrush. The sun glowed orange in a deep blue Montana sky. A vague, early moon hung up above the mountain. Red wiped the dirt and slivers of dried grass from his neck and shoulders. He stopped for gasoline and went to the bathroom, washed out his cuts, bought a package of cigarettes and smoked one of them, sitting on his bike at the edge of the station, watching the country rest.

It looked the same, but it was different. It sounded the same this late afternoon with the birds rustling the trees and the marmits and jack rabbits crackling the underbrush, but Red knew that faceless voices lied.

Chewing on the filter tip of his now dead cigarette, Red kicked the Indian started. He revved the Indian once or twice to get it warm, the call answered only by its own echo off the mountain.

Red pulled on and buckled his helmet, kicked down and moved out onto the smooth road. The white line of the road sliced straight ahead of him, so Red cranked on the throttle and the Indian bellowed in reply. He kicked into second and the Indian barked. He kicked into third and the Indian wailed. Red Madison was skimmering across the gray road, racing the white line that raced through the center of it. He kicked into fourth, leaned forward over the handlebars, cranked on full, synchronizing the beat of the bike with the rhythm of his own heart.

Then they moved that way up the straight smooth road, neck and neck with the white line that sliced through it, two wheels and one man silhouetted black against the orange globe sky. Two wheels and one man fading slowly into the mountains, their shadows gradually swallowed by the crevices of time.

Twenty-one

The gypsies are mostly gone, Red Madison is faltering, and the motorcyclist sits at the crossroads of life and death, strumming his engine and awaiting his future. It is a precarious position to be in. Trail biking is the fastest growing outdoor sport in the nation. A survey in California of 300 random bikers showed that they owned an average of 1.5 trail machines per man. Sales of dirt bikes in some parts of the country are ten times higher than street machine sales. Many executives cite woods riding as the primary reason for the current boom in the motorcycle industry. And yet, Red Madison's last jump may be the trail biker's swansong. For no matter how popular it has become, trail bikers are riding the edge of the cliff of extinction. Neither Marlon Brando or Sonny Barger, neither the burning at Wiers Beach or the Porterville Run, have tarnished the image or threatened the life of motorcycling as much as those men who ride a roughshod rape over the land.

Unwittingly or knowingly, motorcycles steered by the wrong hands into our diminishing wilderness areas can and have done irreparable damage.

A motorcycle passing through pliable clay or mud, deep in the forest, may leave a mark that remains for twenty years or more. That track churned into the side of a hill could cause an erosion process that will permanently change the shape and substance of the land.

A motorcycle's knobby tire, ripping over the topsoil, not only scars the landscape, but redistributes the layers of soil nature has carefully blended. Vegetation will not prosper in impotent earth. Animals will not live without a plentiful supply of green food.

"They're doing tremendous damage to the high country," says Colorado State Senator Joseph Scheiffelin. "Anything that grows over timberline—a little bush or plant—is going to take five years to come back."

Because of its ability to crawl into isolated areas, the low-polluting motorcycle engine can harm plants and animals that have not developed any resistance to carbon monoxide and lead.

"I have owned property [in the mountains]" wrote a Colorado state resident to the state legislature, "for some time and during the last several years have watched with dismay as the wildlife has been driven further into the mountains—probably to their death and eventual extinction—by fools on their machines."

A motorcycle carrying a soldier with a submachine gun mounted on his handlebars is a justifiable weapon of war. But when a hunter with a twelve-gauge shotgun chases down wild animals until they are too confused to hide and too exhausted to retreat, when he runs them until their tails are about to fall off and their guts well up in their rasping lungs, and then shoots them, he is no more a sportsman than the man who slits the pig's throat in a Kansas City slaughterhouse.

"If you have a large area, without woods, say 60,000 acres, this inaccessibility contributes to the survivability of game populations, like deer and bear", said Ralph Barick, an official of the North Carolina Wildlife Resources Department.

"But when it becomes easier for hunters with rifle scabbards hanging from their handlebars to cover more ground, the game becomes more vulnerable to the gun."

A motorcycle dropped in the water can season a pure mountain stream with oil, grease, and gasoline. A motorcycle trashing through dry leaves or through high, sun-parched underbrush can drop a spark that will swallow an entire forest in flames. A motorcycle can debilitate a wildlife preserve, can rape nature's purity, and grind the earth into decay.

In a 1970 article in *Motor Cyclist* magazine, Tom Moss reported with shock and disgust the ravages of motorcycle vandals riding the Mojave Desert in California.

He discovered a little cemetery where men were buried who

had died while working on the pipeline that brings water from the Owens River to Los Angeles. He saw how ghouls had dug up some of the bodies and destroyed the graves, and motorcycle tire tracks were everywhere, evidence that men with bikes had helped awaken the dead.

Moss went next to Jawbone Canyon and saw buildings, water tanks, mining machinery and transportation equipment—riddled with bullets. And more motorcycle tracks. He saw cyclists with wire cutters slicing through fences and riding indiscriminately over private property. He heard tales from shop owners forced to close their businesses because of looting by cycle riders. One shopkeeper could account for $2,000 to $3,000 of merchandise stolen by gangs of men on two-wheeled machines.

Unfortunately, Moss' experience is not unique. From all across the country come reports of rampant ecological destruction by men and motorcycles. Dirt roads leading up into the hills or down into canyons have been mutilated by motorcyclists doing stunts. When it rains, erosion sets in, ruining the roads, making it impossible to traverse them.

Many of the game birds have been driven from the deserts and the marshes where men ride. Motorcycles, dune buggies, and other all-terrain vehicles rip up the low brush near the ground where quail, pheasant and chucker nest. The birds are run down, frightened to death or frightened away, never returning to hatch their eggs. Many that remain see their eggs crushed by spinning cleated wheels.

To some, there is nothing more exhilarating than a romp in the wilderness on two wheels. But as with many hallucinatory drugs—and a cyclist let loose with the wind and without restriction is indeed on a high—the release and freedom can become too hard to handle. The exhilaration, in fact, can become distorted, breaching that line between joy and sadism, self-expression and savagery.

In Wyoming's Grand Teton National Forest cyclists have been seen throwing lighted flares into gopher holes. In Montana they have been caught emptying left over gasoline into streams where animals often drink.

A forest ranger in West Virginia observed two cyclists attaching ropes to an animal's legs and driving off, each holding an end of the rope, in opposite directions. And in his article, Tom Moss recalls one acquaintance whose pleasure was derived from running rabbits down in the glow of his motorcycle headlights late at night.

Only a small minority of motorcyclists take part in such gory rituals. But unfortunately predators are always more clearly remembered than doves.

And that is why the trail rider is balancing himself on the rim of oblivion. Because every day more and more off-road vehicles hit the dirt, and concerned citizens, property owners, sportsmen, and conservationists everywhere consider them no less than assassins of our wildlife, storm troopers of the wilderness.

Throughout the country, stringent laws are being enacted to limit the use of two-wheeled, off-road machines.

And that is why the trail rider is balancing himself on the rim of oblivion. Because every day, more and more off-road-vehicles hit the dirt, and concerned citizens, property owners, sportsmen, and conservationists everywhere, consider them no less than assassins of our wildlife, storm troopers of the wilderness.

Throughout the country, stringent laws are being enacted to limit the use of two-wheeled, off-road machines. In the 1971 session of the California legislature, there were 210 separate bills concerning motorcycles, many designed to ban motorcyclists from the back country. In Colorado in 1971, a bill was narrowly defeated that would have limited motorcycles to marked wilderness trails. And each year the bills become more numerous while the legislators and their constituents become more adamant. They want, they demand, they beseech, they implore that the wilderness be safeguarded from this senseless destruction.

"The key factor here is noise," according to Russ March, national director of the American Motorcycle Association, in an interview for *Bike and Rider Magazine.* "The public is rapidly getting fed up with it and the trail rider gets perhaps more than his share of the blame. Motorcycles—so goes the public thinking—equal noise: ergo, the trail rider is an undesirable character. He's accused of tearing up the land, but actually, if the complainer would stop to think for a minute, he'd realize that what he's objecting to is the noise the trail rider's bike makes. Motorcycles in general have been blamed, rightly or wrongly, for most of the noise we hear in our residential areas. Irresponsible riders roar madly up and down residential streets. Others go crazy in vacant lots surrounded by houses in which people are trying to find a little peace and relaxation. The trail rider, even though he may never ride within a mile of a residential district, gets his share of the blame for those irresponsible activities. Ecologists like to accuse the trail rider of destroying the land. Actually, as I said, its more likely that they just don't like his noise. The same is true of groups like the Sierra Club, and horseriding and hiking clubs. They can't stand the noise, but think they're reacting to land destruction."

There can be nothing more deadly and destructive to our wildlife than the motorcycle, most responsible and logical trail riders, industry representatives, and lobbyists would agree.

But, they also wonder, what about snowmobiles, even more efficient in hunting animals because they maneuver with precision through heavy snow where wildlife is at an even more lopsided disadvantage?

And an unmuffled snowmobile produces 103 decibels of noise at fifty feet compared to the motorcycle's 90. The threshold of pain from sound at fifty feet is 120 decibels. Yet, a pneumatic drill generates 130 decibels and a hydraulic press exceeds 140. From the inside of a DC-6 airliner, passengers are tortured with 100 decibels of sound each moment of flight. An underground train, a hard rock band, an opened sports car, all generate more decibels than a motorcycle churning at reasonable speeds through the woods.

There can be nothing more deadly and destructive to our forests than the motorcycle. That is possibly true. But what about all-terrain vehicles that have three to eight wheels to crush underbrush, or dune buggies that lack the maneuverability to skirt loosely packed hillsides and valuable patches of flowers and vegetation?

Motorcycles eat the land with a spinning, chopping rubber cleated wheel and press down on topsoil with as much as 500 pounds. Yet, four-wheel drive Land Rovers or Jeeps or Scouts are triple-ton tanks that demolish the countryside with spinning claws ten times the size of some cycles and twenty times more powerful. Although a motorcyclist can skirt certain vulnerable wilderness areas, a four-wheel drive vehicle operator has been born and bred on the principle that what you can't go around, you can always plow through.

Certainly, legislation has been proposed in many state capitols to limit the freedoms of other off-road vehicles. But not nearly to the extent to which motorcycles have been attacked.

And there are reasons for this, according to motorcycle industry officials, unsound but obvious reasons. First, motorcycles for decades have represented destruction and evil to a naive public deceived and aroused by an over-anxious press. The action against motorcyclists today is actually a reawakening of the unfounded fears and hatreds planted twenty years ago.

Second, and even more likely, say industry officials, motorcycles are the most conspicuous of all off-road machines. All-terrain vehicles (ATV'S), and snowmobiles, cannot be ridden in the street, so most people are not regularly made aware of them. Dune buggies are found mostly in coastal and desert areas. Jeeps are far from numerous; on the highway or street, they make little noise.

But motorcycles are everywhere, twitching in next door garages, barking down residential streets. And because they are the most conspicuous, they are considered the most destructive.

"Here's how it works," says Russ March. "John Jones was kept awake half the night last night by bikers roaring up and down the street in front of his house. Now today, he's just stopped to enjoy the quiet beauty of the desert. And suddenly, he hears it, way over there, barely visible, barely audible, three trail riders are ripping, roaring, snorting, buzzing along. And John remembers last night. He's edgy from lack of sleep anyway, and he begins to limber up that part of his vocabulary not usually heard in mixed company. These three trail riders have never been in John's neighborhood—and they never will be—but that doesn't matter. They're just three more of them blankety-blank clowns he wishes somebody'd turn a machine gun loose on. Look at 'em! Tearin' up the countryside like that! And John resolves forthwith to write a scorcher of a letter to his congressman. Result: another area closed to trail riding."

The letter referred to by March might stimulate support and cooperation at first—but in the long run no amount of letters will do much good. The conservationists and concerned citizens might force antibike legislation through state legislatures, but the laws that result will not be as easily enforced as they were made. Motorcyclists will not give up their territory and their fun. That is certain. Yet, just as certain is the fact that conservationists will not give up their attempts—not just to curtail motorcyclists in the woods—but to abolish them entirely.

The armies fighting for each group are forming now.

Twenty-two

Deep trenches will be dug into the lonely trails used regularly by woods riders, and covered with a screen of thin twigs, moss, and soft dry leaves. And when the unwary biker rides through, he will be swallowed by them.

Sharp spikes will be buried in the mud and loam under clean mountain streams at areas regularly crossed by bikers, and tires will be shredded like confetti.

Spark plugs and batteries will be stolen and gasoline siphoned from the trucks that carry the bikes and their riders to the edge of the woods.

Narrow wires will be tied taut, chest high from tree to tree, at the summits of high hills. And when riders come barreling to the top, they will be snafued and tossed backwards hundreds of feet down the hill, like men hitting a trampoline from a second story window.

High barriers of rocks and logs and mud will be constructed at blind spots on the trails and bikers will unwittingly splatter into them.

The soldiers of the Army of Ecology will carry out midnight raids to garages where trail bikes live, knife tires, slice cables and fuel lines, and feed sugar into gas tanks.

They will wait in ambush from cliffs looking down on narrow canyons and stone bikers when they ride through or hit them with bombs of green paint to simulate the blood of the forest.

A biker will be screaming down a trail he knows so well at

forty or fifty miles per hour, and when he makes the last corner and beats hell out into the clear at sixty or seventy miles per hour and still accelerating, he will see that the bridge he expected to roll over, ten or fifteen feet ahead, has suddenly disappeared.

It will begin that way.

Touring bikers are the more mature, less committed wing of cycling society. Although they have been threatened and cajoled, they have never felt the immediate pressure of extinction as trail bikers have. Because they are older and have been riding for a much longer time, they have learned to live and to cope with the hostility generated by their two-wheeled machines.

But dirt riders are young riders, generally more spirited and hot tempered. For too long, they have felt the criticism of ecologists, the discrimination of state and federal governments, and have stood by and watched while farmers, state forestry associations, and the Department of the Interior locked away the open territory over which they once rode.

Their ranks have significantly expanded over the past few years. Many of the people now riding trail bikes are veterans of the Vietnam war who were first hooked on motorcycles in Southeast Asia, where motorcycles are the primary vehicles of transportation, and where the size and quickness of your rifle is often the most impressive ticket to a safe conduct over the dangerous narrow roads.

So trail riders take to riding in groups of fifteen to twenty to protect each other, and carrying hand guns, mace, or knives in case they are attacked.

They storm the campsites of the ecologists late at night, knocking over water bags and supplies and kicking orange coals from the fire onto dry bedrolls, laughing when they ignite in flames.

The ecologists revert to nightly blackouts and build secret shelters in which to sleep. But their solace is ruined by the constant threat of an enemy blitzkreig. The bikers, like the Germans undermining the morale of the English during World War II, toy with their enemy's nerves.

Their nightly thunder drives away the wild animals, the livestock, the chickens, frightens babies and women who lie awake, listening in fear of the yellow-eyed monster machines.

Their cleated knobby tires rip into the limpid gardens and

tomato patches of hippie communes, suspected of subversive activities.

Because many are merchants and professional men, the trail bikers use their business contacts to get bankers to foreclose mortgages on "family farms."

They persuade their friends in hardware and grocery stores not to extend credit to soldiers suspected of belonging to or aiding the outlawed Army of Ecology (now known as the AOE).

The police are called in to mute the efforts of both groups. Then the National Guard. But they are ineffective. Like the gangland wars in Chicago in the early 1930s, the law enforcers are the biggest threat to both groups of law breakers, and the enemies are forced to unite on the battleground to thwart the meddling of the law.

To live, the ecologists must rely more and more on what they grow, but the trail riders continue to rape their fields of food.

So the outlawed AOE takes to carrying guns and stationing guards at the edges of their campsites day and night.

And as the conflict grows more bitter, the Sierra Club and the Audubon Society and other allied, radically concerned conservation groups pledge even more financial support, exert additional political influence, and send in more troops and arms to reinforce the effectiveness of the AOE.

But then the American Rifle Association, committed to the salvation of personal freedom, mobilizes its men and its artillery.

And all out war begins.

Deer hunters become man hunters and station themselves behind boulders and pick off the soldiers of the AOE as they march by.

Hungry for supplies, more weapons, and ammunition, well trained AOE night fighters slink into nearby towns at night and break and enter and loot the stores.

The Marines are called in.

But both the AOE and the bikers with their supporters are holed up in the hills. Even the Marines cannot drive them out. Many are in fact refusing to turn their guns on fellow Americans. Every day, more Marines are defecting and joining the ranks of those to whom they now pledge allegiance.

The Air Force is called in. Napalm is dropped. Fire bombs are dropped. The soldiers of both sides retreat further and further into the wilderness, pursued by burning trees, scarred, empty land, and platoons of the remaining loyal Marines closely dogging their air assault.

There will be more fire and additional retreat until the Air Force has nothing left to burn or to bomb and the opposing armies have no shelter remaining to hide from authority or from themselves.

And that is when the war will end. The ARA will have no more animals to hunt in this particular section of America. Motorcyclists will have no more quiet, tree-shaded trails to ride. The conservationists and their army will no longer have a forest to protect.

Fantasy? Perhaps. But 25 years ago, who would have predicted riots in the streets because of the Vietnam war—because of any war—or that National Guardsmen would shoot down students on college campuses—or that black Americans would burn their own ghettos? Granted, an all-out war between conservationists and trail bikers is highly unlikely. But continued hostility and unpleasant encounters will surely increase until both sides decide to try to understand each other's position and find a way to compromise somewhere between both.

Bikers claim to be as radical conservationists as the Sierra or Audubon people. But motorcycles, they maintain, provide the only way the family man on a tight budget can reach the back country and have enough time to enjoy it. They feel that the majority of the people pushing for restrictive legislation against motorcycles are a wealthy elite who want to preserve the back country for themselves. Even camping, hunting, and enjoying extended freedom can be granted only to those wealthy enough to buy time to use them.

"Many of the appeals by conservationists—preservationists—really are just appeals that in effect make the out-of-doors their private domain," says Hugh Hauptman, a trail-biking enthusiast from Denver, quoted in The New York Times. "And they are the people who have weeks at a time to go on a back-packing excursion. Most people can't afford a horse."

Trail bikers defend their place in the wilderness by claiming that they are discriminated against while the more deadly enemies of ecology, all terrain vehicles—dune buggies, snowmobiles, four-wheel drive trucks—are allowed to run free and far. But that is like saying that petty thieves should not be punished until the traffic in illegal drugs is stopped. If indeed, the merry men on their two-wheeled machines are raping Sherwood Forest, it doesn't matter who else is doing it and to what extent. All must be stopped.

There are certain responsibilities in using our nation's natural resources, and motorcyclists are just not accepting them. Noise is not just noticeable, it is harmful. Nature cannot contend with man-made thunder. Nor should a back packer who has hiked for half a day in search of tranquility have to put up with a machine whose call echoes in the wilderness and ricochets for miles.

A well-tuned motorcycle will pollute the air 50 percent less than a poorly tuned one. A motorcycle fitted with a good spark arrester will not be a fire hazard. A motorcycle equipped with an inexpensive, easy-to-install silencing device will make little noise.

Yet, motorcyclists are far too large a minority to legislate against. But with conservationists working in conjunction with off-road vehicle enthusiasts, both groups can be legislated for.

Federal and state legislatures must set aside prescribed wilderness areas for all off-road vehicles—abandoned strip mines, for example, or gravel pits, or any one of the 10,000 such holes gnawed from the landscape by hungry corporations, where government reclamation projects have never been and probably never will be initiated. Miles of rocken misery, where no additional damage could possibly be done, not even if tandem trailer trucks frolicked with steam rollers, and Sherman tanks played checkers across the terrain with their shells.

There is hardly a county in America that has not been violated by the remains of progress. These areas would provide ideal conditions for tough, off-road runs.

And those trail riders seeking solace in the back country can follow power line cuts on their bikes, or fire lanes that jag through the wilderness for hundreds of miles. There is hardly a national park, hardly any wilderness remaining, where such lanes have not been blazed by forestry departments or electrical power utilities. For diversity, there are literally thousands of abandoned logging trails and farm roads. County engineers could diagram such areas and make the diagrams available to the public on request.

But motorcyclists who want to dig deeper into the wilderness would just have to walk. And backpackers seeking seclusion would have to avoid those areas set aside for motorcycles.

Many trail riding clubs and enthusiasts have purchased old farms or tracts of undeveloped wilderness, and a few private investors have started motorcycle riding parks where cyclists can cut their own trails, climb hills, camp, race, or relax without interference.

But motorcyclists have always had to go it alone. They have never received the better part of a break in the laws or in public attitudes toward them.

There are public tennis courts, golf courses, marinas, and ice skating rinks. There are playgrounds with bleachers, back stops, bases, goalposts, and $100,000 candles that light up the night for baseball, football, and soccer. Our taxes pay for men to groom horses, cut trails for hikers, pave roads for bicyclists. Public money builds camping sites, public money builds dome-topped stadiums. Public money goes to little league teams, high school wrestling teams, golf teams, rodeo teams, bowling teams, football teams.

These are some of the benefits of living in America, and motorcyclists deserve their share as well. Especially since motorcycling is the most popular participant sport in the nation today. Especially since motorcycling is growing at a rate far greater than any other sport in this land.

In 1970, there were probably two million Americans who rode the woods on motorcycles in the United States. By 1975, there will be more than five million, if motorcycle dirt machine sales are any indication. And by 1980 there will probably be ten million people riding, at least periodically, through the woods on two-wheeled machines.

State and federally operated motorcycle parks would end the conflict between conservationists and trail bikers. A well-operated and well-planned motorcycle park would cancel the problems of law breaking, which in turn eliminates the need for lawmaking. Motorcycle parks could bring families closer together, and provide a place and instructors for novices to learn to ride well, and more experienced bikers to have fun. There would be camping facilities, organization, and order. It is a partial answer and a logical answer to the problems confronting conservationists and trail bikers. And considering the liberties taken for other sports in America, a privilege that motorcyclists deserve.

For years we have been looking for ways to get the kids off the streets. And now we are searching for ways to chase them out of the wilderness. Will we ever learn that the answer lies not in reform schools or punishment, or strict law enforcement, but in providing a reasonable, accessible, and sensible alternative?

If there were no cars, and big tandem trailer trucks did not already knife our diminishing wilderness, then there would be plenty of virgin America for everyone. If the hungry corporations hadn't pocked our mountains with strip mines, raped our deserts with oil derricks, and spat their waste into our purest streams, then there would be no controversy, no cause to worry, no reason to fight. But because of gluttony for economic stature, America has eaten away its natural foundation. Only time and treatment will heal our self-inflicted wounds. The effort wasted on attempts to indiscriminately ban motorcycle trail riding will merely prolong our stagnation.

If ecologists do not include motorcycle trail riders in their plans for the preservation and restoration of our natural resources, then very little will be accomplished. And there is a good chance that very little will be preserved.

Motorcycles deserve a bite of the American pie. Because without motorcycles, 25 years from now, with parking and air pollution multiplying like an incurable fungus, metropolitan life as we know it today could be doomed. Without motorcycles, by the year 2000, the present era of individual private transportation —our freedom and privilege of solitary and independent movement from place to place—will die.

Today, only one twentieth of all Americans ride motorcycles and approximately half of those people ride regularly. But someday we might live in an America of motorcycles, only motorcycles. Someday motorcycles might be the machines of the masses, unlocking the doors of the city for 100 million people, spreading the country out wide. Someday motorcycles might be the only logical means of individual transportation, man's last link to past odysseys of exhilaration. Someday two wheels might own the American road.

Author's Note

Early in the spring of 1971, I contacted Roland Gelatt, then the Managing Editor of the *Saturday Review,* and told him of my plans to explore the United States on my motorcycle. I was hoping he would be interested in commissioning an article about my cross-country experiences. He was and did. So Burt and I left Pittsburgh, not long after, racing the roads that laced America, he taking pictures, I jotting notes, planning how I would write the piece when I returned. I never had any doubts that I could write this story, that it would just flow from my fingers to the keyboard and onto the paper. But it never did. When I got home, I tried a hundred times, maybe more, but I was literally unable to articulate on paper the exhilaration in my heart.

Well, I sent an article to Gelatt anyway, although I knew it didn't quite make it. A writer can tell pretty accurately when he has found the right voice and said the right things, and I could tell I hadn't. All the material was there, but it just didn't sing back to me as my prose often will when I'm writing well. Gelatt returned the article, suggesting ways in which I could improve it, but before I could get myself back into the situation, Norman Cousins, who published *SR,* resigned to start a new magazine, taking Gelatt and most of the other editors with him.

I put the idea to rest in a desk drawer at that point and continued writing and researching the more factual portions of this book. Winter passed in the library and in this office, my motorcycle mostly resting its thunder under the shingles of my old garage. I remained depressed about not being able to recount our odyssey on paper, not even for the book. I was writing well on other subjects, but I just couldn't get the motorcycle out of the garage and over the hill, south into Virginia; I couldn't smell the fresh fertilizer, burning pine, and sizzling bacon; I couldn't hear the music of my machine or the twanging of the back-country people; I couldn't see the dawn swooping orange into Mississippi or the early evening sky fading from Tennessee. I could remember it, but could not recount it. And most of the winter went by.

Late one cold, dry February night I fired my machine and rolled alone out onto the highway. It had been almost a month since I had been riding and for a long while the bike coughed carbon monoxide, choked out condensation, till it finally unlimbered and warmed. I found a straight, fast road and cranked it on, then sat back at 80 mph., cruising in unison with the white line that raced up the highway. The road was as smooth as ivory and I could feel no bumps or ripples, no disturbances, and I could not see my wheels in the darkness, almost as if I was hovering over the road rather than riding on it. I could feel the cold wind rushing around inside my clothes, outside pressing against my face, smoothing my skin. After a while, I could no longer feel the wind, only the cold. Then I couldn't feel the cold. I knew I was cold but I couldn't feel it. I couldn't even feel myself; I had become the machine. I rode that way out of Pittsburgh, passing everything I could see, further away from the city and it's neon, deeper into the dark night.

I'm sure I rode furiously, illogically, stupidly, but I cannot remember. I can't remember if the road was two or three or four lanes, whether it remained straight or started to swirl. I just don't know. I can remember the night, the machine, the needle of my odometer resting at 80. That's all till I arrived in Johnstown, Pennsylvania, and stopped at a tavern called The Inn. I drank two scotches and two beers before I could feel myself coming back, my fingers, my legs, my eyes, coming home. There was a blonde lady beside me at the bar. She had on high white boots and a miniskirt and, in my eyes, the lights of the jukebox and the TV seemed to reflect dully on her nylon-coated knee.

"Quit looking at my legs," she said, laughing, pushing my shoulder, pulling her chair closer to mine. She was not a bad-looking woman, passing forty, but nicely made, slim. She seemed, not dark-complected, but sun-tanned, although I knew it was winter. I asked her if she was from Florida. "Never been there," she said, "although I'm willin' if you are."

I smiled and motioned to the bartender to bring her another beer.

"Where you from?" she said.

"I don't know."

"C'mon, what's your name?"

"I don't know."

"Don't be like that. I'm only trying to be friendly."

"I'm sorry," I said, pushing more money forward toward the bartender. I bought her another drink, then slipped off the stool and went outside. It was colder now that I had once been warmed, but I climbed back on the bike and shivered two hours home.

Of course, I remembered who I was, but still I felt kind of special in that bar. I somehow thought that she should have recognized me—not as me, but as a motorcyclist coming from somewhere far away in the cold. I really did feel special, sort of liberated, not from my responsibilities necessarily, but from my depression. I had broken the bonds of family funk and city drudgery, and I felt free. I was riding back home now, but by choice. Indeed, I was far enough away that I could see other alternatives; I could have stayed longer, but I had had my fill of freedom—it usually doesn't take too much—I was ready to roll home.

The next day the article came in a huge explosion of inspiration, my fingers flying into the keyboard of the typewriter. Like all the very best things we know, it was done joyously and quickly. Yes, it had taken a whole day, but it seemed no more than an hour, not nearly long enough. I sent the story off to Sid Moody at the Associated Press who, in buying it, returned a little note. "A nice paean to the open road," he wrote. "If Whitman had had a Harley, it's what he'd have written." AP moved the article over the wires a month later and the story probably appeared in a couple hundred papers. I was identified in the piece as an assistant professor at the University of Pittsburgh, so it was easy to contact me and I got a lot of feedback. People phoned long distance from all over the country, motorcyclists from Oakland, California, a 72-year-old former biker from a hospital bed in Toledo. Not so much because the article was so good, but more because I was able to communicate, to recreate, to rekindle for them the joy, the sense of exhilaration that comes with riding a two-wheeled machine. Said one man, a forty-year-old father of three children, in a letter from New Wilmington, Pennsylvania:

"Last summer, after a week of riding, going through Texas and seeing sky and land, my head cleared and came together—I realized that everything I saw was mine and no one could take it from me. I understood then that if man can remember that the eyes and brain—the senses—can hold everything he needs to keep his creative core alive, he has almost all he needs to survive and not be bored or lost. I know that this is poorly stated, but I think you know what I mean."

To be sure, I don't necessarily think that writers—or anybody—need long, crazy motorcycle rides before tackling a story or article, or some special challenge. Nor do I claim that man needs a motorcycle to grasp, in his own terms, the meaning and motivation in his life.

But we Americans, especially those in the city, lead a potentially deadly life. We are trapped by skyscrapers and rush-hour traffic; our exhaustion is lulled by the television, our bones and brains are often soothed in martinis and beer. No matter who we are or where we are, the responsibilities we have to our friends, families, and employers are often intolerable. But a motorcycle can change the conduct and quality of our lives because it is indeed a machine that can harness man's spirit. On a motorcycle, riding the road, hugging the wind, man can discover the joy of solitude, the rebirth of independence, the satisfaction of self-respect.

November 26, 1972
Pittsburgh, Pennsylvania

Acknowledgments

The author wishes to express his appreciation for contributions from the following:

Pages 49-50, 53: "The Motorcycle Syndrome," by Armand M. Nicholi, II, M.D. Printed in original form in *The American Journal of Psychiatry,* volume 126, pages 1588-1595, 1970. Copyright © 1970, the American Psychiatric Association.

Page 29: Reprinted by permission from COMMONWEAL. Copyright © February 5, 1954.

Pages 89-90, 91: From "The Forgotten American," by Peter Schrag, HARPER'S MAGAZINE. REPRINTED BY PERMISSION OF CURTIS BROWN, LTD. Copyright © 1969 by The Minneapolis Star and Tribune Company, Inc.

Page 96: Reprinted by permission of CYCLE MAGAZINE. Copyright © December 1971.

Pages 28-29: Copyright © 1953 by The New York Times Company. Reprinted by permission.

Page 39: From "California Takes Steps to Curb Terrorism of Ruffian Cyclists." Copyright © 1965 by The New York Times Company. Reprinted by permission.

Pages 17-18: Copyright © 1965 by The New York Times Company. Reprinted by permission.

Pages 41-42, 52-53: (World, excluding The British Commonwealth, except Canada): From HELL'S ANGELS, by Hunter S. Thompson. Copyright © 1966, 1967 by Hunter S. Thompson. Reprinted by permission of Random House, Inc.
(British Commonwealth, except Canada): From Hunter S. Thompson: HELL'S ANGELS. Copyright © Hunter S. Thompson, 1967. Reprinted by permission of Penguin Books Ltd.

Pages 39-40: From "The Wilder Ones," March 26, 1965. Reprinted by permission from TIME, The Weekly Newsmagazine; Copyright Time Inc.

Pages 118-119: From an article by Harris Edward Park in the May 1967 issue of TODAY'S HEALTH. TODAY'S HEALTH, published by the American Medical Association.

Every effort has been made to trace the owners of copyright material in this book. Should any material have been included inadvertently without the permission of the copyright owners, acknowledgment will be made in any future edition.